THE GREEK HOUSE

THE
GREEK HOUSE

The Story of a Painter's Love Affair

with the Island of Sifnos

CHRISTIAN BRECHNEFF

with Tim Lovejoy

Farrar, Straus and Giroux　New York

Farrar, Straus and Giroux
18 West 18th Street, New York 10011

Printed in the United States of America
First edition, 2013

Grateful acknowledgment is made for permission to reprint the following previously
published material: "The Sail" by Mikhail Lermontov, translated by Alan Myers, from
An Age Ago: A Selection of Nineteenth-Century Russian Poetry, edited by Joseph Brodsky,
translated by Alan Myers. Translation copyright © 1988 by Farrar, Straus and Giroux,
Inc. Reprinted by permission of Farrar, Straus and Giroux, LLC.

Illustration credits: photographs on pages ii, 80, and 142: Michel Zumbrunn;
photographs on pages 220, 274, and 283: E. V. Weissman; photograph on page 6
and all other illustrations: Christian Brechneff

Library of Congress Cataloging-in-Publication Data
Peltenburg-Brechneff, Christian, 1950–
    The Greek house : the story of a painter's love affair with the island of Sifnos /
  Christian Brechneff with Tim Lovejoy. — First edition.
      pages   cm
    ISBN 978-0-374-16671-7 (alk. paper)
    1. Peltenburg-Brechneff, Christian, 1950–   2. Siphnos Island (Greece)—
Description and travel.   I. Title.
ND853.P42 A35 2013
759.9494—dc23
[B]
                                   2012036561

Designed by Jonathan D. Lippincott

www.fsgbooks.com
www.twitter.com/fsgbooks • www.facebook.com/fsgbooks

10 9 8 7 6 5 4 3 2 1

This is a true story, though some names and details have been changed.

To my late parents, Axel and Dita,
and to the people of the island of Sifnos then and now

THE SAIL

A white sail gleams alone out yonder
Amid the ocean's pale-blue haze . . .
What quest has driven him to wander?
Why has he left his native bays?

The waves crest as the fresh wind rises,
The mainmast bending in the breeze . . .
It is not happiness he prizes,
Nor is it happiness he flees!

Beneath, the azure current flowing;
Above, the golden sunlight glows . . .
Perverse, he seeks the storm winds blowing,
As if in storms to find repose!

—Mikhail Lermontov; translated by Alan Myers

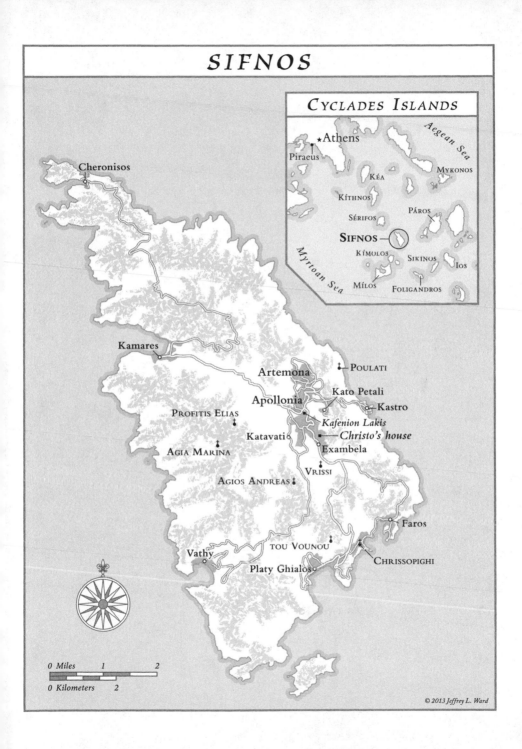

THE GREEK HOUSE

In those days, everybody knew everybody on the island. Or at least they knew who you were. They all knew me. I was six foot four and had blond hair almost to my shoulders, and I stood out. When friends asked how they would find the house if I wasn't in the harbor to meet them—there were no phones on the island then—I would say, rather grandly, "Just ask anyone." And it was true: you could step off the ferry on Sifnos and all you had to say was, *"spiti apo Christo,"* Christo's house, and someone would guide you to my door.

Should you try this quaint exercise today, people would probably just stare at you, shake their heads, and walk away. It's not just that there are so many more people now, especially in high season, but that the tourists, and especially the rich Athenians who swamp Sifnos in the summer months, have somehow changed the spirit, the ethos of the place. In July and August, instead of fishing boats the harbor is full of yachts. Boutiques and tavernas, most of them owned by off-islanders, now line the little main street of the village, while people in brightly colored espadrilles gaze into the shopwindows or wander among crowded *kafenion* tables, for all the world as if this were some kind of mini–St.-Tropez.

In 1972, no one on Sifnos had ever seen an espadrille. There were scarcely any roads. You had to walk everywhere on farmers' rough stone paths and goat trails, and you wore shoes, heavy walking shoes or boots.

Of course, when I first got to Sifnos, I had no idea I would have a house on the island, had no idea I would return there for the next thirty-odd years. I went that first summer to get away, to get out of Switzerland, where I had grown up, and to draw and to paint, but I never imagined I would go back year after year, returning as to a well, to work there every summer. I had no idea that Sifnos would become my source, my inspiration, my Muse.

In Greece one is allowed to talk about Muses—Greece, the Land of the Gods. One can still feel the gods there, or you could then—gods, Muses, Fates, all the deities of ancient Greece that not only filled the sky but walked the earth. It was as if something in the air, something in the purity, the clarity of the place, some combination of mountains and sea and sky invited the creation of those heroic stories and myths, and fed them. Something magical.

You could believe in magic there, from charioteers who drove across the sky to one-eyed monsters living in caves and gods beneath the sea. But Greece had another kind of magic too, not just the magic of enchantment, but a more powerful magic: I believe there are places that have real power, places where the connection between nature and man is absolutely direct, without thought of any kind, places that penetrate you so deeply that they become part of you. Places where you can put your ear to the ground and hear your own heart beating.

Sifnos had that magic for me from the first moment.

1

The night was black, no moon, the sea the darkest ink blue possible, the sky full of stars. The island, much bigger than I expected and even blacker than the sea, rose up over the water like an animal. The two mountains on either side of the little harbor entrance towered above us and seemed threatening. Our ship, impossibly white at night, luminous against all the darkness, slipped quietly between the mountains and over the still water as if on a slick black mirror.

I could make out a few lights along the quay, but the village of Kamares was mostly dark, sleeping. It was almost three in the morning. As we coasted in, the deck still vibrated underfoot, but the ship's motors were stilled and I could hear the sounds of the harbor as it came to life to greet us. As the sea winds died, I could smell for the first time the delicate scent of the island, like a package of spices and herbs suddenly spilled open in the palm of my hand.

The ship dropped anchor out in the middle of the harbor—there was no dock for ferries then—and we weary disembarking passengers had to climb with our luggage down a rope ladder to the waiting fishermen's boats that would take us to shore. Heavy Greek women dressed in black from head to foot; old, old men; boxes and suitcases tied with rope; fridges and stoves; chickens and dogs—anything and everything was handed down the side of the tall ship into waiting caïques. The sea was dead calm, thank God.

My first studio, Platy Ghialos, 1972

Jammed into these little boats, we all stared up at the brightly lit ship, watching this complicated transfer while the passengers who were going on to Mílos stared down over the rail at the near chaos below. When the little boats finally pulled away, we turned as one toward the shore, its single row of one-story white houses and *kafenia* hiding behind the old tamarisk trees that lined the waterfront. Bumping up against the quay, we struggled out of the boats, pushing and shoving and pulling one another and all our things ashore in a messy, noisy scramble. Then, with a deafening hoot and a great clanking of anchor chains, the ship rumbled to life again and we watched as it turned and backed and turned again in a clumsy pirouette and self-importantly sailed away.

The Greeks, islanders mostly, dispersed almost immediately, and in no time only the foreigners, six of us, were left on the darkened quay. We had all found one another within minutes of boarding the ship in Piraeus all those many hours before, and in the way of ship travel we had become instant friends, a little gang, already inseparable. There was Chuck, an American, tiny, elfin, smart as a whip, a touch of Ariel and a handful of Puck, who is to this day my best friend in New York; a young honeymooning couple from what was then Rhodesia, with whom I still keep in touch; and two tall, beautiful girls, sisters, from Australia. We were all in our early twenties, me only twenty-one, still kids, off on an adventure and wide-eyed. Chuck knew Greece and, most important, some Greek—he had been teaching at the American College in Athens—but for the rest of us this was all new, so we clung to each other and to him.

We had no idea where to go. The village had shut down completely. An old woman appeared on the quay who Chuck said was offering us a room to rent—but only one room, and none of us had any money anyway, so we thanked her and said no. Wrapping her sweater around her against the night chill, she vanished like a shadow into a nearby door. Exhausted suddenly, all the adrenaline pumped up by the arrival having drained away, our little band of newfound friends headed off into the night, dragging our things along the quiet dirt street, trying to get away from the houses. Where the village finally ended, we stumbled down to a beach and rolled out our sleeping bags.

"What about a swim?" asked my new friend Chuck. The sea looked inviting, black and silky, and we stripped naked and ran into the water, whooping in shock—it was only May and the water was still cold. "Wow," whispered Chuck in a kind of awe. "Look. Look around you. Do you see it?" The sea was filled with millions of tiny lights, little stars. Phosphorescence, but phosphorescence such as neither of us had ever seen. Every move we made created showers of luminous sparkles, like fireworks in the water. Boys still, off and away on this magical island, we let out hoots of delight into the silent night as our splashing arms and legs created waterfalls of light in the sea.

Afterward, toweled off and cozy in my sleeping bag, exhausted but wide-awake, I stared up at the black mountains rising around me and the amazing sheets of bright, bright stars in the sky. Greek stars. I could hardly believe it. I lay listening to the still night, the lap of water nearby, and the otherwise deafening silence. I felt totally at one with myself—a new feeling for me—and I knew I was going to love this place and I was sure this place was going to love me back and take care of me. Young and romantic as I was, I was sure those two mountains would be like two giant arms holding me tight.

—

Islands are full of romance. Famous artists and writers have fled to them, lived and created on them. Tahiti, Cuba, Capri, Sardinia, Majorca, and Zanzibar, the names ring with mystery and romance. Of course, not everybody actually likes to be on islands, finding them claustrophobic, but the idea of being away, being cut off in some kind of parallel universe, always seemed wonderful to me. I had spent several weeks painting on the island of Cozumel in Mexico the year before, but once I was back in Switzerland, it was Greece that caught my eye and my imagination. Its dozens of islands baking in the sun were within easy reach, yet far enough away at the same time, familiar and yet foreign as well. I imagined the Greek islands as a gateway to the East. And compared with the gray and damp of Basel and Zurich, they sounded like heaven on earth.

It was the Sun, the Sun with a capital *S*, that drew me the most. I was a sun worshipper in the making, and I wanted to see and paint the Greek light, to feel it, experience it, capture it. A friend had described the Greek sun to me as a force. He and a couple of friends were in Greece one summer, and he told me of driving from Athens to Delphi by car, the sun blinding, not just hot and glaring but everywhere, inescapable, almost maddening, so strong that he and one of his traveling companions there in the back had to get down behind the front seat with a coat over them to shield themselves.

Greece was still in the throes of a brutal dictatorship that had begun in 1967 with the seizure of power by a group of right-wing, much-hated Colonels. Given the political situation, I may have hesitated a moment about going there, but not very much. I had been very involved politically the year before, when I was in college in America—the war in Vietnam was something I had come to care about, as had my brother when he was studying there—marching with fellow students at every opportunity. But the Greek Colonels had somehow made little impression on me, nor I think on most Europeans, except perhaps for the French—Paris was full of Greek exiles—and even the French spent more time raging against the United States, as is their wont, and about Vietnam. In any case I was so involved with myself and my art that I didn't worry much about the political pros and cons of going to Greece.

I had just completed basic training in the Swiss army, a literally recurring nightmare, as one had to go every year, year after year, and I was desperate to get back to my painting. I wanted to do work for my master's degree, a three-year course I was to start that fall at the Royal College of Art in London. I was very proud of having been accepted, and I was determined not to fail. On top of that I was scheduled to have my second one-man show in Zurich in

September. I was pretty proud of that too, and had a vision of the gallery filled not just with mountain drawings and paintings from the Engadine, a place I loved to paint, but with new and different work—Greek whites and blues, sea and sky and light flooding the walls.

I needed to find a peaceful island where I could work, an island with no tourists and, above all, no airport. Even back then I was sure that was key. In Switzerland, poring over maps, I hit on the island of Sími in the eastern Aegean. I had never heard of the place, and I admit it may have seemed like closing my eyes and sticking a pin in the map, but in fact I had given it some thought. I had heard about the charms of other islands like Hydra and Mykonos, but I was intimidated by the buzz emanating from them, by their attraction for the rich and famous, and by their homosexual vibrations. Already insecure and confused about my sexuality and knowing how endlessly, hopelessly horny I could be, how susceptible I was, I wanted to avoid a place with too many temptations. Sími, I was sure, was the answer—far away and difficult to get to. Its very isolation, I was sure, would help keep me safe and sane. And out of trouble.

Once I got to Athens, that dream didn't last even a day. In the tiny, dusty student travel office just off Syntagma Square, the center of Athens then as now, I was assured that Sími was indeed lovely but almost impossible to get to. The woman who ran the office sat smoking at her cluttered desk behind a pair of huge dark glasses that must have been hand-me-downs from Melina Mercouri. She listened to my plans for traveling to Sími, my arguments for going there, rubbing her eyes with a mixture of weariness and ennui. When I finally drew breath, she told me in a deep voice with her thrilling accent that I was "grazy to go to Zími." The island, she said, was impossibly remote and backward, there were no regular boats, and if I found passage at all, I would have to change boats at least once. As I didn't speak a word of Greek, I would undoubtedly get hopelessly lost and end up on some altogether different island.

Quite determined, and getting nervous lest my wonderful trip turn into a disaster before it had even begun—I mean, what was I going to do if Sími didn't work?—I kept on arguing. I told her that I had been to many remote places, that I would get to this one, that I knew it would be perfect. Finally she put her hand up to stop the flow of anxious nonsense pouring out of me and said there was another island, an island called Sifnos. That was where I should go. "Fvorr yuu iz perrfect," she said, rolling her English at me. "Iz jusd waat yuu arrre looging forr."

The name Sifnos stopped me in mid-flow. Amazingly, I had heard of it. In my year in America in 1970–71, at St. Olaf College in Minnesota, I had known another foreign student, a Greek girl named Maya Yannoulis. We were never close friends, but with her dark good looks, she had made quite an impression on me. I knew she didn't live on Sifnos, only visited her grandparents there, but I thought, my excitement rising, the very fact that I knew someone connected to Sifnos was like an omen—wasn't it? Maybe it was where I should go. Suddenly I could feel Sifnos calling me. And solving all my problems. Yes, I would go to Sifnos. Everything was going to be all right after all. I booked passage then and there.

—

In the early 1970s, not many boats went to Sifnos either. What they euphemistically referred to as regular ferry service had begun only in 1969, and there were almost no boats in May, as it still was the off-season. I would have to wait for a couple of days in Athens. But I didn't mind. I was ecstatic just to be in Greece, vastly relieved that I had retrieved my trip from disaster, so I wandered the sun-filled streets of Athens until I could get on the boat.

Athens then was a small city, dusty, funky, almost third world, hardly part of Europe at all. A few worn-out Mercedes, Citroëns, or Deux Chevaux and lots of belching, heeling buses were in the streets, but there wasn't any real traffic. The sprawl and toxic pollution of the

1980s and 1990s were still in the future. But even then I immediately preferred the quiet, treelined streets of Kolonaki and its square to the hot glare of Syntagma and downtown Athens. This well-to-do residential part of town rose up the slopes of Lykabettus Hill, with the church of St. George perched on top. Of course I couldn't afford to stay there, nor even downtown, but was happy enough to find a room in Plaka, the old city of Athens, with its huddle of low houses at the foot of the Acropolis.

Finally, on May 19, 1972, I found my way to Piraeus and the boat. Several morning ferries were lined up waiting to depart, and the quay was packed with passengers. My heart sank a little at the sight of the *Kalymnos*, a very old and grubby ferryboat that rolled and slopped from side to side at the dock. In spite of being named for an island in the eastern Aegean, she sailed, very slowly and erratically I was to learn, to the western Cycladic harbors of Kíthnos, Sérifos, Sifnos, Kímolos, and Mílos—to this day the route that most ferries take to Sifnos. From among the crowd waiting to board her I immediately picked out the other foreigners—my friends Chuck, the Rhodesian honeymoon couple, and the Australian sisters—and we fell on one another, strangers in a strange land, exchanging accounts of our adventures so far.

Finally, after an endless wait there in the growing heat—the boat was already several hours late departing—a sailor blocking the gangway stepped aside and the crowd surged forward, pushing and shoving and squeezing. Once on board, leaning over the rail with my new friends, I couldn't help seeing the far bigger ship docked next to us, the *Island of Mykonos*. She loomed over us—newer, sharper, crisper, gleaming white, the very definition of shipshape. Her rail was crowded with people looking down at us in our old rust bucket, and I had a moment's pause, a moment's envy of her splendors, a moment's insecurity about what I was doing. Where in the world was I going? But I soon realized, to my withering disapproval, that the passengers on the *Island of Mykonos* were all tourists, even in those long-ago days, whereas those on the *Kalymnos* were obviously Greeks, mostly island Greeks. And I knew then and there that this was what I had come for, this was the real thing, and I had chosen the right island.

Fifteen hours later, at three in the morning, the *Kalymnos* chugged into the tiny harbor of Kamares.

—

Sound asleep on the beach, we were woken that first morning by the sound of a clanking and sputtering old diesel engine. An ancient prewar bus—the only bus on the island, as we learned later—was making its raucous descent to the harbor, a cloud of dust trailing behind it. Not wanting to miss it, we grabbed our stuff and chased after it through the village, no easy task for me with all my drawing pads and equipment. Of course we needn't have worried; the bus just sat there, panting and shaking and rattling, for a good half hour before it moved again. It had nowhere to go, it appeared, but back up the mountain to the town of Apollonia whence it had come, high in the center of the island.

We piled on board along with a few smiling, nodding islanders, one with a sheepdog, another with what looked like part of an old engine, another, amazingly, with two goats. I recognized him from the *Kalymnos* the night before, lowering his prizes down the side of the ship into a waiting caique. The goats were completely passive in his arms when he loaded them one at a time onto the bus, and they settled down like docile children waiting for the voyage. Greetings were exchanged back and forth—I of course spoke not a word of Greek, but Chuck, sitting next to me, chatted away, and he taught me the basic greetings: *Iassu, tikanis?*

Not only did none of us except Chuck speak any Greek, none of us really knew anything about anything. For the rest of us, arriving here had been a semi-premeditated leap, and we had no idea where we were or where we should go next or what to expect when we got there. We learned from Chuck that Sifnos was famous for its pottery; his then girlfriend, Lisa, who was yet to arrive, was coming for the summer to work with a potter, and Chuck had come ahead to scout out the island. And we knew, from poring over a tiny antiquated guidebook of his, the only one about Sifnos he had been able to find, that the island was supposed to have the longest beach in the Cyclades, Platy Ghialos. We had all decided to go there.

There were no cars on the island, only a couple of battered pickup trucks, six ancient Russian Volga taxis, and this bus, which would take us to Apollonia. And we were very ready to get going, just to get moving. Though it was still early, it was getting very hot baking away in that little tin can of a bus. Finally it leaned to one side as the smiling driver climbed on board. He—his wonderful name, I was to learn, was Fragoulis Psathas—slammed it into gear, and the bus screamed in protest as it lurched forward and started its gasping struggle up the mountain. I was immediately reminded of the little buses I had traveled on in Mexico, where I had gone on a painting trip during my time at school in America. This was not as crowded as a Mexican bus, perhaps—nothing could have been—and there weren't people and livestock riding on the roof, but there was the same motion of heads bobbing and tilting in unison as the bus heeled this way and that, the same battered, dusty body, the same folding door that would not close all the way, the same miserable, worn-out seats, the same strange stains on the floor and the hot sunlight pouring in through the grubby windows. I had loved those buses, and I loved this one.

The road to Apollonia was the only road on Sifnos then. It climbed gently at first, but as we continued, the fields and terraces that sloped up from the harbor gave way to a rougher landscape. We came to a gorge with a rushing river pouring down, pink and red oleander massed along the banks, rocks and boulders strewn everywhere—spills from landslides. The road became incredibly steep, unpaved, a kind of glorified path with nasty hairpin turns, and the bus skidded and spewed gravel at every curve. There were of course no railings, and the land dropped precipitously, sickeningly, away to the valley floor. This harsh, wild landscape went on for quite a while, but as we twisted back and forth, the valley began to open out. The road was still very steep, very rugged, but now there were terraces again, with fields climbing the slopes and orchards of flowering trees—figs, I thought, and olives. It was clear as we climbed that the island was big, high, massive, and unusually fertile, with real rivers rushing down the hills, under and in some places over the road, washing it out. The rains of winter had ended only a few weeks before.

Bouncing on broken springs, we clung to the seat rails in front of us, craning to see out the windows on the left that looked over the valley. Chuck and I, on the wrong side of the bus, eventually stood in the aisle, hanging from the luggage racks, me too tall, crouching down so as to see out. Everywhere there were stone walls, terraces echoing the contours of the mountains, stone paths and stairs winding between them, sheep and goats all over, mules and donkeys grazing everywhere. Clinging to the slopes were strange white towers two or three stories high, with elaborately patterned triangular openings near the top, dozens of smaller triangles set within bigger triangles, like little stone pyramids worked together as in a house of cards, the whole crowned with little turrets and crenellations, like miniature fortified castles. These were the famous dovecotes of the Cyclades, the best and most elaborate examples said to be on Sifnos. And around us, above us, crowning every peak, were monasteries and their churches, white, white against the blue, blue sky, the highest one called Profitis Elias. It seemed that even today, Helios, the charioteer, the sun god of the ancient Greeks, lived on. He had become the prophet Elias (Elijah), and the churches where he was worshipped were built on the points closest to God, symbolizing Elijah's whirlwind assumption to heaven in a chariot drawn by horses of fire.

Still climbing, we finally reached a cluster of whitewashed one-story houses, the outskirts of Apollonia, the capital of Sifnos. The bus wound around one corner, and another, and then, bucking and belching once or twice, ground to a stop in the town's tiny main square, dust pouring into its open windows. All the buildings were freshly whitewashed, as I was to learn they were every spring. Across the square was a small folklore museum set in a little park, where there were wooden benches surrounded by big, shady pines. On another side of the square was a glass-fronted building with an unreadable sign in incomprehensible Greek. "*Tachidromeia*," said Chuck, sounding it out for me: the post office. How will I ever learn even a word of this language? I thought. To the right were a couple of small shops and at the corner a very simple little café, the Kafenion Lakis, its tables and chairs spilling out into the road. This was Stavri, explained the guidebook, the center of the village.

There wasn't much to it, this town center, and as we ventured along a narrow, curving street, we dead-ended almost immediately between two tavernas and a tiny shop selling postcards. There the street opened onto a road that ran along the opposite side of the village, with houses strung to the left and right along a high ridge. In front of us, the land dropped away immediately and dizzyingly down a steep spill of terraces and sharply raked fields to the village of Kato Petali. Next to it was a domed church and a single ancient palm tree. After that, nothing but the sea and the distant islands floating on the horizon. I stood there staring out. I could not believe my luck. This was the landscape I had imagined and hoped for. I looked forward to painting it.

It was perfectly clear that Lakis's was the center of town. Even at this early hour it was full of people coming and going and was obviously Sifnos Central. Starving, we went in for coffee, something to eat, and information about how to get to Platy Ghialos and its famous beach. Lakis himself, the owner and only waiter, came over immediately. An older man with a fierce, strong chin, a prominent nose, and steel-gray hair, he must have been very handsome in his youth and was still good-looking. He took our orders grudgingly and grunted answers to our questions about the island. He had chosen the role of curmudgeon, I was to learn, but there was a mischievous twinkle in those bright blue eyes, and if nothing else, he was

clearly an operator with an eye for the ladies. In no time he was closing in on our two Australian beauties, flirting in a mixture of Greek
and broken English.

All at once I sensed eyes burning into the back of my head, all
our heads. I turned and saw a sharp-faced woman, no longer young,
and, nearby, an ancient crone, both watching Lakis and his every
move. His wife and his mother—the wife behind the counter sourly
preparing the food and pouring the coffee, the old lady squawking,
"*Lakis, pediiimou* . . . ," Lakis, my child, as she sweetly criticized
everything he did. He ignored them both, as we were to learn he
always did, at most responding with a little *tst* of his tongue as he
raised his eyebrows and lifted his chin—the Greek gesture meaning
everything from "no" to "don't be silly" to "bugger off." All his attention was on our blond, blushing, long-legged Australians, and he
poured on the charm, offering them donkey rides to his secret
lemon grove and other no doubt sweet delights. But we had eyes
only for the longest beach in the Cyclades, as did the girls, and it was
clear that he was getting nowhere; the sweet delights would have
to wait.

—

In fact, a dirt road to that faraway beach was under construction, a
mess of gravel and rock and potholes, as it turned out, but passable.
The very young taxi driver, Apostolos, assured us, naturally, that
he was willing to risk the possible flat tires and damage to the car's
suspension to get us there (the suspension, we were to find en route,
was already long gone), but he would need two trips, as six of us
with our backpacks would be too much for his worn-out old Volga
station wagon. That way, of course, he could ask for more money, so,
being a little afraid of being taken advantage of, we dickered a bit
about the price. But it was all quite innocent; soon we agreed on the
two trips, and four of us piled in, ready, raring to go. It had been
decided that Chuck had to be in the first shift, and he sat in front
with his guidebook. I tagged along, using the argument that I could

help too, but in truth I just couldn't wait another moment, and David and Gill, the Rhodesians, sat with me in the back. The Australian girls were to come after. We weren't too worried or guilty about leaving them, since they were no doubt going to get anything and everything they needed from the lecherous Lakis.

Much of the island terrain sat even higher than Apollonia, and I stared out as the road-to-be, this bumpy dirt track, wound along the edge of the village—a perfect puzzle of flat-roofed white cubes fitted together, walls dripping bougainvillea and jasmine, windows and doors facing out over terraced fields to the sea. Climbing higher still, the road followed switchbacks that went up to three huge, semi-ruined stone windmills straddling the crest of the hill. Just past them was a cluster of farmhouses by the side of the road, a church dome or two, and an old palm tree peeping up over the roofs—this was the village of Exambela. And then the road led steeply down toward the southern end of Sifnos.

—

We saw very few houses anywhere, only barns or dovecotes; the farmers mostly lived in the villages. But everywhere were ancient walls and terraces. The slopes and fields were covered in waves of yellow daisies and red poppies, fig and almond trees, and old olive orchards. Here and there the new road cut across paths paved with huge stones that led off to the sides. These paths seemed incredibly old to me, biblical highways climbing across the hills. From time to time the car clattered past a farmer neatly dressed in tweed jacket and cap, switch in hand, sitting sidesaddle or plain sideways on his donkey, off on his way to his distant fields. His dog, loping behind him, tongue lolling out, would cringe as this unfamiliar, noisy, smelly creature, our car, roared by and left them both in a cloud of dust.

As we hurtled on along this mere suspicion of a road, valley after valley fell away on our left to the sea, the slopes covered with oleander, buddleia, and broom. Suddenly a huge vista opened—in one of those surprising views I was to learn one often got on Sifnos, coming almost as a shock, down a deep valley to what looked like a fortified hill town, a perfect cluster of white houses on a rocky headland that reached out into the sea. This, we learned, was Kastro, the old capital of the island. "That's the town where my friend Maya [my friend from college] comes from," I crowed with excitement, twisting around in my seat, craning to see out the back windows down to this perfect town, this perfect composition, a ready-made painting, watching until it disappeared from sight.

After another corner or two, the land dropped away even more steeply, and we all gasped, gaping down at a long, double-vaulted white church with a bell tower above the entrance. It sat lengthwise on what seemed to be a single narrow piece of rock, like a finger sticking straight into the sea. Alarmingly, Apostolos turned right around in his seat, yelling and pointing at the church. "Ch*****p*ghi," he screamed incomprehensibly against the noise of the wind, the rattling car, and the flying gravel. "Chrissopighi. It's a monastery," said Chuck, bracing himself against the dashboard. I had never seen anything so white as that church against the dark cobalt sea.

This dazzling island, the fields of wildflowers, the white churches against the vast blue sea and sky, all bathed in the most amazing clear, blinding sunlight, left us speechless. Of course we were all young and impressionable and struck by what we were seeing, but the magical beauty of this landscape hit me especially hard, like a bulldozer. As a painter, I was stunned, in a kind of trance. I stared out of the car, the sun and the hot wind in my face, and could already visualize my hand, my brush, racing across the pages of my sketchbooks, taking this all down, recording these patterns and shapes, this orgy of color.

—

Rounding a bend in the road, high up still, all at once we saw it below us—Platy Ghialos, a strip of smooth white sand stretching away toward a distant range of hills, with the little island of Kipriani

Platy Ghialos

beyond. As we wound down, we could see that the beach wasn't very long after all, a disappointment, but for a Greek island, usually all rocky coast, it was an amazing sight, and it was totally unspoiled. A dusty lane ran the length of the beach to a newish small hotel called the Xenia, but except for that, there was only one other two-story building on the water side of the road. It was owned by a fisherman's family, and it seemed you could rent rooms there. Otherwise there were only potters' houses with wood- and brush-burning kilns attached. On the inland side, fields of vegetables and olive groves reached to the enclosing hills; there were one or two little farms, but no real houses.

We climbed out of the car and sent Apostolos back for the girls. Possibly overstimulated by so much sun and fresh air, our Rhodesian friends quickly found a room to rent and off they went, back to their honeymooning, Chuck and I joked. When the girls finally arrived, as always the center of excited attention from the men of Sifnos, they were immediately swept off by a good-looking farmer in a beautiful straw hat who promised to show them his fields and gardens—perhaps he too would have lemon groves and sweet delights, like Lakis. Chuck and I decided to camp on the beach until we found the right lodging.

But first, we were starving. The only taverna on the beach, it seemed, had just opened, but its young owners received us as if we were their best and oldest friends. Indeed, I'm not sure I have ever been greeted anywhere with the same warmth and hospitality as we received that day. The food was delicious, fresh, and simple: grilled fish, followed by roast lamb and stuffed tomatoes and aubergine—everything perfect. And miraculously cheap, which was one of the great advantages of Greece, especially the islands, for anyone young like myself. The owners, Vassilis and his brothers Kostas and Iakovos, sat with us. I still spoke not a word of Greek, but as we sat eating this wonderful food and sharing a bottle of wine, or perhaps two, I was sure I would soon be speaking it fluently. And I was sure that Platy Ghialos was where I wanted to stay. I didn't know where I would find a room, but I knew that here was a dazzling beach, delicious, inexpensive food, and warm, friendly neighbors.

Then, not quite believing where I was, I was suddenly thrown into further confusion by the sound of bells approaching, coming closer and closer—Swiss bells? Looking around, I saw that the beach served in fact as a goat path, and hundreds of goats were happily running and bounding along the beach toward home, their bells merrily ringing. Driving them along was an incredibly handsome young shepherd. Like Italians you see in Venice or Florence who look just like a Bellini or Bronzino, the same faces still living there centuries later, this young man had the profile of a figure on a Greek vase, the perfect Greek nose and brow of the ancient world. In truth, unlike in Italy, this is most unusual in Greece, as modern Greeks usually look nothing like their ancient ancestors, having mixed and blended with the Ottomans and Venetians who ruled them over the centuries. A year or two younger than I, perhaps, he had shining black hair and blue, blue eyes. As he came down the beach behind his goats, he seemed to give off sparks. An innocent young man, no doubt, but I am sure he knew exactly what he looked like and happily flirted with everyone, both men and women.

As it happened, I knew something about goats, having herded them as well as cows as a fourteen-year-old in the Ticino, the Italian-speaking part of Switzerland. It was very mountainous there, and I spent six not very happy weeks high up on an alp, milking goats and making cheese. Fairly innocently charmed by Panos, whose name I would soon learn, I was eager to show off my knowledge of these animals, so I spoke to them in goat language, "*Tschaa, tschaa, tschaas, li-mo-tscha,*" I called to them. I may not have spoken Greek, but I spoke Goat. And the goats were suitably impressed. Stopping dead, they stared at me like curious idiots, goggle-eyed, chewing steadily. Panos seemed impressed too, and he invited me to come help him milk the goats that very evening. Not perhaps where my fantasies were leading, but it would have to do.

Pointing up the hill, Panos, with Chuck translating, also told me about a ruin, just above the house of someone called Georgos and his wife, Aphrodite, just there behind us. No one knew whom it belonged to, he said, but it had been empty for a long time, and if I liked it, I could easily set up my studio and live there for free, he was sure. Georgos, it seemed, was a potter, and he and Aphrodite lived in Platy Ghialos in the summers and during the winter months in a house in Exambela, the village we had passed on the way. Five years later, when I bought my house there, they were to be my immediate neighbors.

But on that first day, I had no idea of any of that. I took one look at the old ruin—and it *was* a ruin—but with its long terrace looking straight down the length of this empty white beach to the hills beyond, I knew it was perfect, and I moved in on the spot, thanking my lucky stars for being something of a flirt myself and for having learned to speak Goat.

Chrissopighi

—

A letter to my parents:

Platy Ghialos, May 22, 1972

Dearest Axel and Dita,

I am in paradise here and I have never been happier. I found my own house. Imagine. It is just up from the beach on a cliff overlooking all of Platy Ghialos and the Cycladic island world.

Views into the infinite, the movement of the sea, the endless horizon. All of this with the help of a local shepherd who is impressed with my goat-milking talents from my days in the Ticino. And it is free! A ruin that no one has used for years apparently. The sister-in-law of the local taverna owner has given me a slightly worn mattress (perfectly clean, I hope) and I am installed. One large room with a fireplace for cooking, which I fear I'll never use, a table for my painting, some shelves and an open door to the bedroom. It remains cool and wind protected and all seems ideal.

The world of color here is incredible. I have already started drawing and painting and work all the time. Lots of light studies in the morning and evening. There is a joyous atmosphere here, an interplay of work and simple pleasures, all nourished by the Aegean sun. I work and then lie in the sun on my rock doing nothing, thinking of nothing, keeping my mind empty. Being still and silent—me silent! It is very healing. My new work is fresh and clean, I think. I hope. I am trying to paint, to find the light.

Love, C

Those first days were magical. Sifnos seemed to be everything I had imagined it might be. There was endless sea and sky, and this strange, charged atmosphere. There was sun such as I had never known, an actual force, wind that came from every direction at once and not only cleared but emptied your head, clean, dry air without any of the gloom or murk or fog of Europe, and moonlight so bright and sharp it made you want to howl with all the island dogs. I loved the mountains, the Swiss Alps above all, but this was something else again.

Being there, after Switzerland, was like day and night. I had just finished my first stint in the army, an annual misery for all Swiss men. Some men loved it, of course: for them it was an annual visit to a summer camp for grown-ups, a world of men away from home, away from wives or mothers, a world of men giving orders, men following orders, a bit of physical fitness, a bit of playing with guns, good macho fun. I had loved summer camp and the Boy Scouts, but I hated this. For me, it was mind-bendingly boring, an exercise in having other people kill your time for you by teaching you things you didn't want to know or running you ragged through the mountains to keep you in shape in case the Chinese invaded, an overriding Swiss fantasy at the time.

For me it was also an uncomfortable exercise to be surrounded by so many men, men whom once in a while I was attracted to, of course, but with whom for the most part I had no connection whatsoever. And who had no connection with me and, I am sure, found me even more alien than I found them. Half Russian, thus not truly Swiss, very tall and slim and blond, and a painter, for God's sake. I was not part of their world. At one point in those first years—you had to go every year—I was made acutely aware of my alienness. I found myself attached to a medical corps where the officer in charge of the physical examinations of new recruits—a sneering, superior sort—ordered me to assist him. He gave me the unenviable job, no matter how gay I might have thought I was, of sitting in front of the naked recruits and sticking two fingers up in their scrotum while they coughed—testing for hernias. There were hundreds of recruits; the parade went on and on, students, farm boys, bankers, all of them smirking down at me. This little cruelty seemed to amuse the officer, and the other officers too. Obviously they all sensed something, maybe that I was gay, or that there was simply something about me, too arty, too different from them, and they pounced.

How did they know, I wondered, or how did they guess? At that point I had only the haziest notion that my attraction to men really meant anything, that I might not grow out of it but might actually grow into it.

—

As the summer days passed, the magic of Sifnos settled over me as lightly and gently as some fine golden powder, as light as the fairy dust blown by Tinker Bell into the faces of the Darling children to get them up and flying on their way to Neverland. My days there were peaceful and I hoped they would never end. Each morning I woke to the smell of the fire in my neighbor Aphrodite's kitchen—a fire of brush and homemade charcoal—to the crowing of cocks and the clatter of hens, and to the slightly melancholic tones of bells as the goats were driven along the beach to their fields.

The dry heat never seemed oppressive; in truth, the warmth of the sun and the fire one sensed behind it always excited me. The landscape, with olive and fruit trees growing in profusion, with the sea always nearby, seemed the perfect place to live and work. The days were long, and one could accomplish an enormous amount. Pictures poured out of me, piling up on the table or pinned to the flaking walls of my ruin.

And if I wasn't painting, I was reading—reading as I had never read before. I had brought stacks of books with me that summer, Russian mostly, Tolstoy and Turgenev, Chekhov and Goncharov, all books I had—to my embarrassment, as the son of a Russian émigré—never read. Being so busily anxious and distracted and ambitious, I had never given myself the time to concentrate on books as I might have liked. Now I contentedly found myself reading and reading and reading for the first time in my life.

It was bliss. The only problem was that I was alone much of the time and very lonely. Chuck had moved back to town with Lisa when she arrived, the Rhodesians as well, and anyway they and the Australian girls were soon to leave the island. Very few people made it all the way to Platy Ghialos, beach or no beach, and everything you needed was in Apollonia—the post office, the pharmacy, the bank, food, and most of the tavernas on Sifnos.

Fortunately, I was getting enough work done that I usually felt I had plenty of time to hike all the way up to Apollonia whenever I wanted to, and a hike it was, more than two hours each way. But there was no other way to get there; the road was not finished and would not be for another year or more. Happily, I discovered that I loved to walk on Sifnos. My route led through the same richly fertile farmland we had passed on the way to Platy Ghialos that first day in the taxi, but the walking route was more direct. I took paths that the islanders had used for centuries, up into the hills, across donkey paths and goat trails, skirting terraces and climbing huge stone stairs that led up and over the high back of the island.

The view was vast and changed constantly. From very high up I could see, and came to know, the surrounding islands, Mílos, Kímolos, Páros, Foligandros, and Sikinos, all of them floating in the distance, sometimes faint in the midday haze, other times so close and clear you felt you could reach out and touch them. Everywhere there were flowers and flowering shrubs. I knew the names of only a few of them—anemone, delphinium, wild cyclamen, monkshood, and broom—but there seemed to be thousands of them of all kinds. By early June the rain had stopped, and the fields and flowers began to dry up, but the olive trees retained their silvery gray-green color, and the dark pines and cedars stood sharp against the golds and yellows of the dry fields.

As I walked, I was bombarded by waves of smells and sounds. Sage was the dominant scent, but there were any number of other hot, dusty herbal smells, along with the deafening sounds of crickets and cicadas. If I needed a rest, it seemed there was always a little white church or an empty monastery with a spring-fed well nearby, an old bucket close beside it, and a tree to sit under to cool off in the dry, dry air. I often ran into farmers on their donkeys, almost always in old buttoned-up tweed jackets, their sun-browned, bony wrists and rough hands poking out of the sleeves, and caps or straw hats on their heads against the sun. They would offer me figs or tomatoes or whatever they had in their pockets. Eventually they all got to know me and, I think, thought well of me for walking the island; walking made me somehow closer to them, made me feel I belonged to their world a little.

Reaching the summit, I would start down toward Apollonia, its houses stretching out in front of me along the spinelike ridge that ran down the narrow middle of the island, the land dropping steeply on either side to the sea. From up above, one could see the long flight of marble steps that curved down into and through the village to the square in the center of town, and then another flight of steps that climbed up again, winding and twisting through Ano Petali to the handsome village of Artemona sitting even higher up across the way. The lines of paths and steps, my route through the three adjoining villages, were like arteries in a living organism.

They were my great inspiration, those walks. I took my black sketchbook with me wherever I went, and I did endless sepia and black ink drawings of the island. I was recording everything, gathering it in, soaking it all up to make pictures of the mountains and monasteries, the terraces of windblown trees. Even the marble stairs with their whole range of pale, elegant colors turned up in my work—tender whites, grays, silvery mauves with gold threads through them—the steps actual paintings in their own right.

—

In Apollonia, my first stop was always Lakis's, where I would sit and reconnect with the world and with my more worldly, sociable self. Lakis's was the magnetic center of the island. All information passed through this little *kafenion*—about the erratic comings and goings of the always terrible ferryboats, the newest arrivals and the latest departures, the perilous state of fishing, or the crop damage caused by too little rain—all the gossip in the island villages about marriages, pregnancies with or without marriages, illnesses, and deaths.

It was where you saw your friends, made new friends. Over endless cups of Turkish coffee—this was before the Cyprus crisis, and Greeks still called it Turkish coffee—we chatted and swapped stories while the island fishermen, calling *"Psariaaa! Psariaaa!,"* sold their catch in the square, and the bread man shouting *"Psomi! Psomi!,"* outscreaming them, stood nearby with his beautiful white mule loaded with different kinds of bread. All the vegetables and fruits one might need were laid out in old baskets under the pines, the farmers showing their produce while their donkeys stood dozing nearby in the shade, tails switching lazily at the flies.

After resting awhile I would run my errands. There was the post office next door, where telegrams were sent and received and phone calls were made—there were no private phones on Sifnos yet. Thomas, with his small grocery shop, ran the licensed National Bank of Greece office, and all minor money transactions were handled there. The butcher next door was called Christo, and very soon, so was I.

Christian is not really a Greek name, and I was quickly rechristened Christo. *"Iassu, Christo,"* I would hear as I walked down the street, entered Lakis's, or visited the island shops. *"Iassu, Christo, iassu. Tikanis?"* I heard wherever I went. I loved it. It was a new identity, a new skin. It was like being part of the language itself. And it was like being somebody on the island, a kind of personage, it seemed to me. I began to introduce myself as Christo to islanders and foreigners alike. People like Chuck who had known me as Christian still called me that, but everyone new called me Christo. In time, Christo the butcher would affectionately call me Christaki or, fonder yet, Christaki *mou.* I loved it.

There were very few shops in Apollonia then, very little real business as such. The islanders were quite innocent about money, and much of the local economy was barter, the islanders trading their crops and wares and animals. The only good general store, Katerina's, was farther along, up in Ano Petali, up the steep steps that led to Artemona. The shop was dark and cluttered, foodstuffs and canned goods packed to the ceiling, and you could find almost anything there, or Katerina could. Whatever you asked for, she would give it a moment's thought and then go to one top-heavy pile of goods or another, find what you wanted, and write out the price of each purchase in a neat schoolgirl hand on the back of an old envelope. Her sons helped in the shop, and if you needed a fresh chicken or rabbit, they would kill it for you right there, neatly wrap it up, and hand it to you.

Katerina's husband's father had been a collaborator during the Italian occupation of Sifnos during the Second World War, and many Sifniots would not go near his daughter-in-law's store. They had suffered greatly in those years, and life had been very hard for them, the occupiers claiming all the livestock they could and plundering everything that was movable. Many people came close to starving. Some young married people in the war years were never able to have children, and they blamed it on the malnutrition of the time.

Decades later, the war years still cast a shadow on the island. In Artemona, a rather grand village with much larger, patrician houses and noble nineteenth-century neoclassical villas, stood a handsome white stucco house with high windows and a tiled hip roof that sat far back from the gates behind an avenue of pines. It seemed like a house with a secret, and indeed, the islanders still whispered when they told you that it had been the Italian headquarters during the war. Though meticulously cared for still, it always appeared empty, the gates and shutters closed, not a sign of life, not a sound other than the wind in the pines. It seemed set apart, cut off, at a remove, quarantined, people not even looking at it as they went past, as if avoiding not only memories but contamination.

Returning from shopping at Katerina's, one had to pass Lakis's again, and there was no way not to sit down and have an ouzo and a delicious *meze*. Ouzo, an anise-flavored drink like the French absinthe or the arrack of Turkey and the Middle East, is clear when drunk straight, milky and sweet when mixed with water. Its high is closer to being stoned than being drunk. And *mezethes* are little snacks, which Lakis's wife grudgingly prepared under her mother-in-law's watchful eye. In spite of his grim-faced wife and his ancient mother watching his every move like two hawks or two old buzzards, or perhaps because of it, Lakis was always up for mischief. He played the grouchy Greek to strangers, but he was actually a playful devil, not above giving pretty, young tourists a pinch. I always had the feeling he did this just to torment his wife, all this flirting around. She and I never actually warmed to each other much, but Lakis and I became great friends; I even got him to part with one of his precious *kafenion* tables to use as a bar in the house I was one day to buy. This was considered a great sign of affection, but he made sure that his wife and his mother were never to know; it was our secret.

—

Like the line from *Casablanca*: everybody came to Lakis's. For our little gang, which grew and shrank with the arrival and departure of the island boats, that was where the evening began. After a few drinks, though, we would have to deal with the problem of where to have dinner. You couldn't stay at Lakis's; there was no real food. But the choice between the only two tavernas in town was fraught with dire consequences: we knew that either we were going to infuriate *Kyria* Sofia at her eponymous (from the Greek, thank you) restaurant, or we were going to make the widow Kaliope very unhappy at her little taverna.

These two ladies ran the only two tavernas in town, both of them on the main street, right across from each other. If you decided to eat at Kaliope's, probably the better restaurant, old, chubby Sofia, sitting there with her always silent husband in front of her door, cutting beans or shucking peas, would glare fixedly at you from under her tightly wound head scarf—she was pretty much bald—and try to ruin your dinner as punishment for your betrayal. On the other hand, though Kaliope remained in her kitchen and was rarely seen, she always knew who was in her restaurant and who wasn't, and she always remembered.

Probably never having smiled much to begin with, Kaliope appeared to have decided never to smile again after her husband's death. Her son-in-law, Lukas, waited on tables, and his three little boys tried to help, though they mostly created havoc, running between the tables out under the trees and generally treating the place as a playground. In spite of the recent death and Kaliope's unsmiling face, it seemed a happy family. And it was delicious food: her *revithia keftedes*—tiny, highly seasoned fried chickpea balls—were the best on the island, and she knew it.

Lukas was a charmer. He had a magnificent mustache, and his smile was huge, beaming, radiant, and full of sex appeal. Good-looking, strong as a rock, yet playful too, he had a kind of inner glow, as I found many islanders did. It was a warm blush, a bloom, not on the skin but behind it, coming through it. That his smile and his charm made me want to eat at Kaliope's every night was a fact I was unlikely to broadcast to my newfound friends. I mean, at that point in my life I wasn't quite ready to say, "Let's go to Kaliope's, the waiter's cute." Like most Greeks, Lukas smoked constantly and was among the first islanders to succumb to what eventually seemed like a plague of lung cancer.

Sofia's, besides having no Lukas, was less charming anyway: a few teeny tables jammed together tightly on the "sidewalk"—where, in the years to come, cars went whizzing right over your toes—and inside, a high-ceilinged, bare, dreary room lit with harsh neon lights. The food was good, though, and local Greeks ate there, but it was rarely full. Sofia and her husband made up for it, business-wise, by renting rooms upstairs in the equally eponymous, rather grandly named Hotel Sofia, and they were considered rich. Their son, Francesco, of whom I became very fond, was the chef. He was also the local information center for the island's few real estate transactions. Sifniots, as I was to learn, were very shy about telling anyone if they were selling houses or land. It was all a great secret, yet the minute a conversation turned to real estate, everyone, in hilarious opera buffa style, would begin whispering excitedly behind their hands.

One of the curiosities of Greek island life was that Sofia, Kaliope, and Lakis's wife—indeed, all the women on Sifnos—owned their own houses. When a daughter married, she usually received a house of her own. Either she had one bought for her by her father, if he could afford it, or, in a rather brutal system, she would receive her parents' own house on her wedding day, forcing them out into a smaller dwelling, a barn, or even a shed to make way for the next generation. This protected the women from wandering spouses, either runaway husbands or hardworking ones. For generations, men all over the Greek islands had been leaving to work on ships or in Athens, often for years at a time, or they emigrated, most often to America, and the women were protected by owning the houses they lived in. Thus Greece, or the islands at least, for all the men's macho bluff, was actually a kind of matriarchy in disguise. This arrangement, I thought, lent a certain ominous weight to the glaring looks of Lakis's wife and old Sofia.

After dinner we always went to Vassilis's, another *kafenion*; his *chocolatinos*, washed down with some brandy, made a grand dessert. By this time, quite a lot of alcohol would have been consumed, and if I decided to walk home instead of staying with Chuck and Lisa, the hike over the mountain paths, never easy, was downright perilous. But I never gave it a thought. I never needed a flashlight, for the often dazzlingly bright moon made it easy to see the route and gave a sharpness to the night. And even without the moon, the darkness was never so black that I couldn't find the path. Like a version of "day for night" in old films, it seemed like a kind of false, backlit darkness, and you could always see.

For me, the island night was full of sensuality and mystery. The shape of Sifnos and the neighboring islands floating off in the dark sea, the flowing terraces and walls, and the strange black forms of the trees—all the mysterious images from those nighttime hikes soon found their way into my paintings. The night-inspired images were not only darker but more abstract than the ones I gathered during my daytime walks. The mountains were there, and the monasteries and churches, but the mountains were swirls of dark paint and the churches often dark red against an even darker sky.

I loved those night walks, tearing along over the rocky paths and steps. The exercise, the wind, and the moonlight combined to clear my head of booze and, more important, of the frustration over not having made love to anyone or even having had sex with anyone. I imagined what Chuck and Lisa were doing, and what I assumed everyone but me was doing, and sometimes would get nearly crazy with desire. But by the time I got home, I was sober and exhausted and fell into bed, images of the island at night running through my mind.

—

July 1972

Dearest Axel and Dita,

I am writing this letter sitting on my little stone wall overlooking the sea, and feeling pretty much at one with myself. I paint about five hours a day, walk and sketch a bit, read Russian literature, swim and eat fresh food. Not a bad life. Sometimes I go up to Apollonia to see friends. There I get to eat fruit and vegetables which are rare here at the beach. But much of the time I just stay here in Platy Ghialos. The owners of the taverna are very kind to me. Sometimes in the evening musicians arrive and play folk songs, and the men all dance. There is a Cretan girl who works at the hotel down the beach. She is the only woman dancing and of course rather popular. She has her own Cretan steps, different from the local dances. She dances with the youngest brother of the taverna owners, who must have the bluest eyes I have ever seen, forget-me-not blue eyes. The piercing eyes combined with the black hair and the olive skin and the rosy cheeks is pretty impressive. I imagine those two are having an affair, though of course no one knows for sure.

Sex is very much taboo here even though I am told the Sifniots get quite busy sexually in the wintertime. All these little farm huts, thimones they are called, second homes for the farmers when they are working faraway fields, have little bedrooms—obviously easy places to meet. One can't help noticing that all Sifniots look a bit alike. There is a Sifnos look for sure. I am forever seeing people I think I know, and it is someone else entirely. I suppose any island is sure to have serious in-breeding, probably incest too. When I asked Christo, the owner of the butcher shop, if he was related to so-and-so, he just grinned at me through his big mustache—how do they grow those?—and said "No, no. Or at least I don't think so." Then with a wink, "But of course it could be." Wink wink. "No. Maybe. Ha ha ha."

Tonight I am asked to a church festival nearby. "Christo," as everyone now calls me, is a minor celebrity here. I am probably the tallest person on the island, certainly the blondest, and I do stick out. Of course I don't mind that. I need to find a book about the Orthodox Church, though, to know more what it is all about, what is going on during these ceremonies. There is something about these churches with their golden screens, and the priests with their tall hats and long beards, that seems curiously familiar to me, almost like some kind of unformed genetic memory. I wish, Axel, you had talked more about Russia, Petersburg, the Orthodox Church. I wish we had made you talk more about it; I know you put it all behind you but I know so little.

Anyway, I am well and healthy. I sleep wonderfully well. My dreams are very sexual, as I imagine you can tell from this letter, and I am writing them down. The island has serious sexual vibrations. Part of its charge for me. It is not sweet or pretty here, like France or Italy. Never "lovely," but somehow stripped down, primitive, primal, raw.

My skin is darker than sepia ink, and my hair has turned Naples yellow from the sun and sea.

Love, Christo

My mother, Dita, was a psychotherapist, a very serious one, with much of her work, aside from seeing her patients, devoted to endless research and papers done for the Jungian Society in Switzerland. I am aware that most young men do not discuss their dreams with their mothers, certainly not their sexual dreams. But I actually read most of her papers, and at home we talked a lot about dreams and all those Jungianisms such as the *anima*. And she enjoyed it when I talked with her about my dreams.

I suppose I was trying to please my father too, telling him about the Russian books I was reading, though I don't think he really cared. He had read them all when he was young and could quote from them freely, but after his unhappy youth, he had left all things

Platy Ghialos, with "my ruin" perched above

Russian behind him. Oh, there were a few old Russian prints and drawings, a few rare books, and some of the silver and smaller objects my grandmother and stepgrandfather had managed to get out of the Soviet Union when they fled in 1937. These were objects of fascination and near veneration for me, coming from a past I had never known, but for my father it was over. He even let his Brechneff name go, choosing to be known by his Dutch stepfather's name. He called himself Dr. Peltenburg, and we were all Peltenburgs when I was young. My biggest regret was that he never taught me or my brother a word of Russian. He spoke Russian only to his adored mother for as long as she was alive.

—

I suppose my mother's interest in Jung was part of the reason why my brother, Michael, and I both ended up in the Rudolf Steiner School in Basel. As a Jungian, she was naturally well disposed to

Steiner's theories about education. Neither Michael nor I did well in the regular schools; primary school, for me, was bad enough, but when I went on to the *Humanistisches Gymnasium*, I completely fell apart. My brother, two years older, had already been transferred from the *Gymnasium* to the Steiner School and had done so well that I was soon enrolled as well.

There, my life began to turn around. I did better in all my studies and began to enjoy myself at school and with friends. But there was a downside. Going to the Steiner School, I lost my best friend, Martin, who it was clear had been told by his parents to drop me. In Basel, certainly then and probably now as well, one simply went to the *Gymnasium*; anything else was deemed to be for the lower classes or idiots, and no proper Swiss went to the fancy international schools such as Le Rosey or Zuoz unless they couldn't make it in the regular schools. Once I went to Steiner, Martin's extremely grand family felt that I was no longer a suitable friend for their very golden child. For me the inexplicable loss of my best friend was incredibly painful, and for years, whenever I had anxiety dreams about not passing the baccalaureate, or about a gallery opening in Basel, or indeed about anything connected with Basel, he was always present in them. Many years later, after we had reconnected and he became once again one of my closest friends, I told him about this, and he put his arms around me and hugged me tight and said, "Now you will never dream about all that again." And I never did.

After a few years, though, I had to go back to the *Gymnasium* in order to get my baccalaureate. This time I was sent to the *Realgymnasium*, and besides hating every moment of it, I once again went through the experience of being dropped by my best friend. Only this time it was worse, one of those classic unhappy experiences that young boys with homosexual tendencies—or actual homosexuals in the making—go through. At the *Gymnasium* I had become friends with David, a strikingly handsome dark-haired, green-eyed boy on whom I developed a huge innocent crush. We were best friends for a time, incredibly close, inseparable even, but then quite suddenly his very wealthy Jewish parents forbade him to see me anymore. I think, indeed I am sure, that his parents were afraid that I was homosexual—one wasn't "gay" back then—and if Martin's parents had thought I was unsuitable for their son, David's parents considered me a catastrophe. And he dropped me. Worse, he turned on me and became my enemy, mocking me to my face and making fun of me to the other students. I was shattered. I couldn't understand how my beautiful friend could be so cruel. I still can't. And I often think I have spent half my life chasing down that handsome dark-haired boy in every man I meet.

In part because of Martin and David, and as a reaction to all the unhappiness of those horrible school years, when I was about seventeen, I started to paint. I had never before thought of painting; perhaps I had imagined myself a kind of wunderkind fashion designer, a baby Yves Saint Laurent rocketing to fame at an early age, but never a painter. But once I started, I discovered that painting totally absorbed me. I would paint every night at the kitchen table, watercolors—the images all archaic and primeval and, well, Jungian: huge eyes, ladders to the sky, snakes, flying witches, entire villages in trees, and, my favorites, a series of pictures of a small white plane flying above Europe, the Dan-Air plane I had taken in 1967 when I went to Scotland alone to learn English, my first flight and my first real adventure abroad.

In 1969, when I was nineteen, I had a one-man show at a gallery in Zurich. In the papers I was described as *der malende Gymnasiast*, the high school artist, and I loved every minute of it, becoming a little bit famous. It was largely because of this show that I was able to get a scholarship to study for a year in America, once again copying my brother, who had already spent a year there in college. The glitch was that I still had my baccalaureate to get through; my American college would withdraw the scholarship if I didn't pass. But by some miracle I passed, thus proving to Martin, who passed the exams the same year, and, most especially, to his parents that I wasn't a little Russian idiot with immigrant parents who had to go to the hopeless Steiner School, but that I was as good as their golden boy.

—

The Xenia Hotel, at the far end of the beach, had been built in the 1960s, before the Colonels, in the then plausible hope of attracting tourists. During the Junta years, though, almost no one came—to Greece or to Sifnos. It was quite a simple place, really, a chunk of plain government-guesthouse architecture, but in those days it seemed very posh and expensive to me, and I never went there. Close by it, however, was a wonderful hidden rock where the swimming was heavenly, the temperature by June wonderfully, softly warm, and the sea perfectly clear and clean. I never liked going into the water from the sand, so I would go to this rock to swim and sunbathe and read. And soon it became pretty much my rock.

My friends and I never met and rarely even saw any guests from the hotel, whom we thought of as "fancy people." They usually kept close to the hotel grounds, swimming from the hotel beach and eating their meals in the dining room or on the terrace. One evening, though, I was at my little taverna on the beach when a young American couple from the hotel, newlyweds from the looks of them, arrived all dressed up for dinner. That tiny restaurant was a pretty simple affair—chairs and tables out on the beach, an umbrella pitched tipsily to one side, a scraggly tamarisk tree growing in the sand. Just then Panos and his two hundred goats, their bells tinkling, passed by in a huge cloud of dust.

Paying no attention, indeed barely taking his eyes from his new little blond wife, the man turned and ordered, "Two martinis, straight up, very dry." "One olive," he added, turning back to his wife. I snorted a mouthful of retsina through my nose. Aside from the absurdity of ordering a martini there on Sifnos, I was amused by the idea of "one olive" in Greece, the land of olives. The waiter of course had no idea what the man was talking about, so I—a beginner there myself and the only other guest—tried to help them as best I could. But it was useless. They would have to settle for retsina; there was nothing else to drink.

I never saw them again.

Not many people ventured to Sifnos back then, certainly almost no real tourists. There were very few ferries, the *Kalymnos* being the only one that season and the next, and absolutely no cruise ships. For years the rather poky Xenia and a small hotel in Artemona were the only hotels on the island besides the Hotel Sofia and, beyond that, some rooms to let in private houses. Aside from having no dock in the harbor and no cars to get people around, no buses, and no roads, Sifnos also lacked most of the conventional Greek island attractions. True, there was the supposed longest beach in the Cyclades and many beautiful sights, but no great classical ruins like those on Delos, no huge monasteries like St. John's on Patmos, no dramatic volcanic craters like Santorini's. Nor was there any Mykonos-like nightlife— no clubs or even bars other than a few *kafenia* like Lakis's.

For most people, I suppose it was too quiet, Sifnos. But people who came and stayed loved the scale and wildness of the island, as I did, its isolation and simplicity. They were hikers or solitary artist types like myself who came to draw or sketch or be alone. More than anything, though, I think they loved Sifnos because of the islanders. It was the Sifniots themselves who charmed you; they seemed so genuinely warm, so cheerful and gracious, their lives so rich and full. The people and the life they lived there, with its seemingly timeless, unchanging rhythms and habits, had a quality of the ancient and eternal alive and well in the here and now. Over time I was to learn that it was a fragile thread that connected them to the past, to their earlier selves, a weakened artery already under attack and compromised by the twentieth century, but for now, blood was pumping through it.

One tended to meet most of the people who happened onto the island; there were really so few of them. There was, for example, a young English couple working on the first maps of the island paths— maps showing everything from the ancient stone "roads" to the narrow, winding, crisscrossing goat trails. They had been coming to Sifnos for some time and were regulars at Kaliope's. They knew every inch of the island, and walking everywhere with them, I got to know just about every path as well. To this day I believe walking is the best way to experience Sifnos.

Most of the visitors I met that summer were young, wandering backpackers, traveling on the cheap, spending the summer drifting from island to island in the sun. Some of them caught my eye, I must confess, girls and boys who became objects of a fantasy romance, but during those first years I was still very young, and even with the girls I tended to be circumspect. Many of them became part of our gang for a while, friends but nothing more. No matter how much I fantasized about sex with this one or that, I wasn't about to start having any wild romances in my ruin. I was a novice on the island, a guest, and I had no desire to rock any boats.

One group of young people I got to know quite well: four college students, three of them—Lewis, Richard, and David—Americans, the fourth, Reinaldo, from South America. They were my age or a year or two younger. They had met at school in Paris and were traveling together through Europe. I had very fond memories of my year at St. Olaf College and liked Americans anyway, and we rapidly became friends. And all four of them fell under the spell of the island and stayed for several weeks, one of them going so far as to buy a piece of land high up above the beach in Platy Ghialos. I was quite impressed by this, by someone so young buying land there, but I have no idea whatever came of it, as when he left that summer, I never saw him again. Possibly because their visit had a slightly dicey conclusion.

They all stayed with me in my ruin most of the time, sleeping bags scattered everywhere. I was being particularly hospitable because one of them, Lewis, caught my fancy and I developed an enormous crush on him. But it was a fantasy, I am afraid, indeed worse than a fantasy, a total misapprehension on my part. About everything. Too timid to make my feelings known, too worried about what they might think of me if I made some kind of advance, I was also apparently too naïve—and too self-involved—to realize that Lewis himself was having an affair with one of the other boys.

One night when I was up in the village late and decided to stay with Chuck and Lisa, one of the four of them—Richard, I think—was bitten by a scorpion; in considerable pain and total panic, he ran from the beach all the way up to Apollonia to find me, someone, anyone, to get him to a doctor. By the time we got him to the tiny island clinic, his arm was hugely swollen and the doctor couldn't do much except give him something to stop the swelling and some tranquilizers, which the poor fellow poured down his throat. We were all nearly hysterical by then, and I gulped a handful of them myself. He was told that if he should ever be bitten again, to soak the wound in his own urine, but he assured the doctor that that was not likely to happen, as he was "going to get the fuck off this fucking island." He and the would-be landowner, I think it was, left on the first boat the next morning.

I stayed on in my wonderful ruin, but in truth, I never really slept there peacefully again. From then on, I was sure my rough stone walls were alive with scorpions and spiders, and as I drifted off to sleep, I would start bolt upright, sure that every tickle or itch on my body was something crawling up my leg or across my face.

A doctor's child, I was fascinated by all the island remedies and folk medicines. For example, another remedy for scorpion bite involved catching a scorpion, putting him alive in a pot of oil, and letting him slowly die there while the oil soaked up the poison. And if you'd been bitten, you just rubbed this now magic potion on the bite and it would cure you and ease the pain as well. It seemed a rather complicated remedy, I thought, and I wasn't about to go rushing about catching scorpions, but most Sifniots had jars of that oil in their houses just in case. And probably still do.

Panicky as I was about scorpions, I was and am even more terrified of snakes. Sifnos is full of very poisonous snakes, vipers living in the stone walls and terraces all over the island. Walking everywhere as I did, I was always coming across them, lying in the sun on the hot island stones, suddenly lifting their sinister heads to glare at me, or slithering away into the brush. When the island farmers encountered them, they killed them and spread the dead creatures across the paths as a warning to other people on foot or as a talisman against them, I was never sure which. Whenever I saw one of these corpses, I usually screamed in fear, not realizing the creature was dead. I even started carrying a knife to cut open a bite so as, I imagined, to suck out the venom, an extremely unlikely scenario.

Later, in the years when my parents started coming to Sifnos, my father, who loved to carve wood, made me a magnificent walking stick from wood he found deep in the valley behind Platy Ghialos. It was very long and beautifully worked, with a wonderful flourish at the top, a bent piece of wood with its sharp end fitted into and through a hole in the main shaft, making a looped handle. He added a metal tip at the foot, a sharp point against snakes or other possible attackers, and I never hiked anywhere without it, endlessly tap-tap-tapping in front of me like a blind man, striking every wall and dangerous-looking rock pile to warn the snakes that I was coming.

Besides protecting me, I fancied it gave me a biblical look as I walked with it all over the island. I was proud of this beautiful stick, and the island men were very admiring too, and a little envious. I lost it several times, and it was always found and returned to me. The whole island knew that stick belonged to Christo, and I have it to this day.

—

When I was young, I both worshipped and feared my father. He knew how to carve wood and build campfires and fry eggs outdoors on a flat stone over an open fire—a boy's dream father figure. But he was also autocratic and controlling in a patriarchal way. He never permitted my mother to learn to drive. And when she thought of changing her Protestant faith and becoming a Catholic, he forbade her to become anything other than Russian Orthodox. I dreamed about him a lot, and in my dreams we had fights, actual physical fights.

As I grew older, I began to realize how sweet he was—almost like an overgrown boy, pottering around their place in the country, a place more Russian than Swiss, a kind of run-down dacha with a huge tile stove that heated the whole house, a woodshop in the shed out back, a rushing river that roared almost through the house, and shaggy, unpruned bushes covered with berries growing up through the overgrown lawn.

Looking back, I see that he was quite wonderful to me, as was my mother. But distant, as I suppose most parents were then. Especially in Switzerland, where it was so formal and strict. People hardly used first names; my mother was *Frau Doktor* to everyone. And no one talked about sex. I mean, there they were, he a doctor and she a psychotherapist, and I was just as uninformed as any child my age when it came to sex. They told me nothing, nothing at all. I remember poring through my father's medical books trying to find a diagram of the human body, male or female, with sex organs. I only learned about women and sex while hitchhiking in Italy in my teens from a group of Italian boys who had a pornographic magazine with them that was so terrifying to me, so crude, so bloody and violent, showing an actual deflowering, that I couldn't get the images out of my head for ages.

And it seemed I liked boys. As I grew older, I knew I liked girls too, but didn't know what to do with them, how to be with them, how to treat them, anything, and in my late teens it seemed easier to satisfy my seemingly endless need for sex by letting men who followed me in the streets pick me up. And soon I was picking them up in turn. Strangely, I was quite pleased with this hasty, improvised, no-strings-attached solution to my problem. I don't think I imagined it would go on forever, after all; it was just pleasurable and convenient, I thought, a handy outlet.

But I suppose my ignorance wasn't really much greater than most children of that time, nor all that dire or all that deforming. Some of it was innocent, like anyone's childhood experiences. I have an early memory of me at age ten or eleven, walking back from the *Gymnasium* in Basel as I did every day and passing, at the corner of the Rennweg and Lindenweg, a crowd of Italian laborers digging up the street—not an unusual sight in Switzerland, where much of the work was done by Italians or Swiss-Italians from the Ticino, the poorest part of the country. There were ten or fifteen of them, most of them big, burly men with curly hair and hairy chests. As I walked by, one of them who was leaning on his shovel, taking a break, suddenly reached out, put a hand into what I discovered to my horror was my wide-open fly, grabbed my little-boy cock, pulled it out of my pants, gave it a couple of good sharp yanks, and said, laughing, in his very Italian Swiss-German, to never go around with my fly open or I would get into all kinds of trouble. Some of the other men laughed too. He turned away, back to work. I was so startled I stood stock-still for what seemed like several moments and then hurried away home.

I was, however, so turned on by this event that for weeks—long after the workmen had finished and moved on—I would pass by that corner, lingering a bit, hoping against hope that this terrifying, marvelous encounter would be repeated.

—

I was often lonely and melancholic that summer on Sifnos, and the next ones as well. It was not just physical loneliness, longing for companionship or sex, though that was constant with me. Nor even that I spent so much time on my own in the little ruin above the beach. What overwhelmed me was my awareness of this sexual confusion and frustration, and of having no one to talk to about it.

Back then, few young men or women admitted to being homosexual. It was all pretty secretive and lonely, and I had no gay friends, or none that I knew of. I had had plenty of sex with men, but I had no examples of homosexuals or how homosexuals might live in the world. Oh, there were a few people in Basel, homosexuals one knew about and people talked about, most often sneered about, but I didn't know anybody who was openly gay. I felt totally alone with my confused feelings, longings, and fantasies.

I learned about a couple on the island, Serge and Roger, two men from Australia who had been living on Sifnos for some time, buying houses, fixing them up, and then selling them. They were a bit older than I, both physically quite attractive, and I was dying to get to know them. But they isolated themselves and never made any kind of overture to me. We saw one another only at large parties, and even then they seemed to avoid me. I would often walk by their house in the evening, hoping to run into them, hoping they would see me and ask me in, but they never did. I would just stand there, waiting for something to happen, but they never paid any attention to me. Maybe they thought I was a kind of stalker, hanging around out there, peering into their garden, perhaps a bit of a sexual predator, but either way, they continued to ignore me.

Curiously, their presence there on the island only made me feel even more isolated and alone as a gay person, and I felt this even when I moved later on to the village where they lived. If they would not talk to me about being gay, who would?

—

I met Onno at Lakis's, of course. He was a Dutch architect living in the village of Artemona while he built a house near Poulati, one of the most beautiful churches on the island. He had been coming to Sifnos for several years and knew the island well. Very attractive despite a childhood accident that left half his face paralyzed, he had dark hair and dazzling blue eyes, a particular weakness of mine, as the reader may have noticed. I was very young for my age and very naïve. He was older, openly gay, and very experienced. He had a lover who often came to visit from Holland, and a life that was all pretty much over my head, but here maybe was somebody I could talk to. And we did talk and got to know each other well.

He was attracted to me, and I must have been a terrible little flirt. One day a year or two later, a serious "what do I do now" moment arrived when we returned to his, by then, completed house after swimming and lying naked all afternoon on the rocks below Poulati. All at once I found myself being seriously kissed, and naturally, I was about to kiss back, when I realized the situation could end up being very complicated, and I pulled away.

If I had allowed Eros to take over that afternoon, a lot might have been very different, not only for Onno and me—we remained fast friends—but about my life on Sifnos. It was very clear to me that if I were going to "fool around" with this man, who had a house on Sifnos and came there all the time, I had better mean it; otherwise, hands off. I did not want to be the sort of person who was playing around, sleeping my way around the island as some people did. I followed that instinct for thirty years and more, and though at times it was torture, it served me well. Eventually I had affairs on the island, with men and women, but I never went to bed with someone who was a regular repeat visitor or who had property there. Well, once, a few years later with Joanna, a South African—you will hear about her soon enough—but that was it. And I never touched an islander, ever.

It wasn't just that any such encounter had the potential for high drama—two people on an island and everything blowing up in their faces. It was about my relationship with Sifnos itself and with the islanders, or what I thought I wanted that relationship to be. I was not there on holiday, passing through on a visit. I knew from the start that I wanted to come back, to stay on Sifnos and work there, and I wasn't about to muddy my life with emotional traumas and hurt feelings with people I could not escape. I also wanted to provoke as little gossip as possible. A raving artist type I might be, and sex starved I certainly was, but I have always had a strange streak of conventionality about sex, and what I am afraid I must call my "reputation" on the island was very important to me from the very first day I walked into Lakis's *kafenion*. I respected the islanders and their systems and codes, and I craved their approval. The newly minted Christo was not about to put his foot wrong.

This isn't to say that I wasn't horny and frustrated a great deal of the time. I was still a seriously oversexed twenty-one-year-old, and I spent much of my time fantasizing about everyone I came across. I was sure everyone was having sex, everyone I knew, everyone I saw. Be they gorgeous backpackers, beautiful, tanned European boys and girls, or martini-craving American honeymooners, they were all having sex. And the islanders, the beautiful shepherd Panos, the handsome fishermen in the harbor, the wild-looking farmers I met on my hikes, I was sure they were having sex too.

Fortunately, I could express much of this frustration and yearning in my painting. Many of my paintings that summer were filled with strange, menacing birds in whirling dark skies. Phallic cypresses, hills like breasts, hips, and buttocks. But I think I sensed intuitively right from the start that life on Sifnos would actually save me from this sexual turmoil. I knew somehow that I was too young and unformed for the real world, the Great World, sexually or artistically, that here on this faraway island I could mark my boundaries and live within them. Here I would have time to grow into myself; I could grow, I thought, at my own speed and not have my little boat swamped before I had even begun my voyage.

—

Panos. Panos with his goats there on the beach. He was so handsome, so playful. I often visited him that first summer and helped him milk his goats. I spoke no Greek, and he no English, but we joked together, laughing and winking, and made lewd signals at each other over the goats' backs. I had myself fairly well under control around him, but he must have sensed something. Did he really think I liked milking goats? Did I? Does anyone? But my relationship with him remained totally platonic, then and always.

There was a strange moment, though, a year or two later. I was lying naked on what had become my favorite rock in those early days, all the way at the end of the beach. As with the rock at Chrissopighi that a few years later became "my rock," everyone in Platy

Ghialos knew this was where I went to swim. I was lying there reading when suddenly Panos appeared. Out of the blue, literally. Or I thought it was Panos. No, I was sure it was Panos. He went to the next rock, and ignoring my presence, acting as if he were alone, this most beautiful young man took off all his clothes, lay back, and proceeded to masturbate there under the blinding sun, with the sea pounding against the rocks below, almost shaking them and us, the spray shooting up. By the time I realized what was happening in front of my sun-blinded, lonely eyes, he was gone.

It never happened again. Did it happen at all, this . . . gift? He never mentioned it, never gave himself away with a wink or a sign or a special smile. Nor did I dare do any such thing.

Sometimes I doubt it was truly he in that blazing sun.

No, I know. It was Panos.

—

Day by day that summer in Platy Ghialos my friendships with the locals grew and deepened. By midsummer I had been accepted, and was treated as a kind of prized guest. Platy Ghialos was a tiny, remote community lost on a remote island, a handful of people really, struggling to eke out a living from the little valley that rose up behind them or from the sea that stretched endlessly in front of them. The fact that I stayed there in my ruin, living among them in this sleepy, faraway place, was almost a source of pride for them, as if by being there, I did them honor, and they responded to my gesture in kind, welcoming me into their world.

I think my favorite among the locals was Iulie, a fisherman who, it appeared, was equally fond of me. He had a charming grin under his heavy mustache and was always in the best of moods, bursting out laughing whenever he saw me. Totally uneducated and perhaps a bit simple—hence his noisy affection for me—like many islanders, he had never left Sifnos. For him even a trip to the harbor of Kamares was a rare occurrence.

Iulie, together with his brothers Stelios and Stamatis, had a small fishing boat, and every night, unless the winds were too strong, they would set out in their caïque. In the mornings when they returned, I would find them in their brightly painted boat anchored just below my terrace. They would sit there in their sleeveless home-knit sweaters and caps, barefoot, trousers rolled to their knees—on the island, only young boys wore shorts, never grown men—singing to themselves while they cleaned out their nets. I was often up with them, up with the sun, working on light studies of the water and sky, and I loved watching the three of them, singing and happy, the rising sun creeping up behind them over the Aegean. During lobster season they would sell me a lobster for a hundred drachmas, about three dollars, and I would bring it to the taverna to be cooked for me later in the day. Did anything ever taste so good as those lobsters?

Over the years, when I would run into Iulie down in Platy Ghialos, he would scream "Chriiistoo!!" and slap my back, clap my hands between his, and laugh hysterically. Then, winking and leering, he would ask if I were finally married. "*Oxi*," no, I would reply, shaking my head. And I would ask the same of him. "*Oxi, oxi!*" he would answer, screaming with laughter, and we would hug again, two bachelor brothers.

His brother Stelios never married either, nor their sister; both had had polio as children and had bad limps. But their brother Stamatis married a girl called Maria, who was from Exambela. As with Georgos and Aphrodite, who moved back and forth between Exambela and the beach, there were longtime connections between many of the families from these two villages. Maria—with her huge brown eyes, a very low brow, and the alarming hints of the mustache one saw on many young island women—was no beauty, but she was an excellent wife. I knew she had a little crush on me, and whenever she saw me, her eyes would flutter and her smile would freeze.

She and Stamatis were the first to build a house on the inland, mountain side of the road behind the beach, and Maria was especially proud of her garden there. Most people on Sifnos had no gardens, as freshwater was—and is—scarce and far too precious. Yet plants such as red, yellow, or white bougainvillea grew with abandon everywhere, dazzling blue plumbago climbed the walls of houses, and the path to every door was lined with lavender, all seeming to live without any water other than winter rains, the lavender even thriving in hot, dry weather. People kept more delicate plants and flowers in pots, jars, and old tins that could be frugally watered. Pots filled with balls of Greek basil or old cans with huge vines of heavily scented jasmine stood outside most village doors.

There was no running water anywhere on the island, and the only freshwater was what was collected in cisterns from the flat whitewashed roofs during the winter rains. You would see the women recycling water from the kitchen sink and from their washing, even bathing water, carefully doling it out among thirsty plants. But at the beach, curiously, there were actual wells everywhere, and Maria's garden was a local showplace. She would flutter her eyes at me and smile and proudly point out her latest triumph, a magnificent tomato plant or a tall blue vitex.

Right below me, of course, were Georgos and Aphrodite. That summer and over the years, especially when we became neighbors in Exambela, we were to become firm friends. One late afternoon in July the weather suddenly turned, as it can in Greece. In what seemed like only a moment the endless blue sky vanished, a cloak of gray cloud was thrown over the island, and the wind began to howl. When the wind comes to the Cyclades, it is usually preceded by an uncanny stillness, so profound that if you are asleep at night, it is the absolute silence itself that wakes you. And quickly, while you are still trying to figure out what you thought you heard—in fact total nothingness—the wind slams into your house like a fist, banging windows and shutters and doors. And then it may blow for days and days and days. At sea, it can be terrifying; the beautiful Aegean, stretching away so calmly and serenely to the horizon, can in a moment become the wild and treacherous sea one knows from Greek myths.

That day in Platy Ghialos, the sea turned a deep blue-black, the waves crested with foam, while the sky grew darker and darker and the wind howled down from the hills. It was everywhere, coming from every direction. And then, suddenly, rain came pounding down as well. With no electricity, no radio, none of us had had any warning; certainly I had absolutely no idea what was happening. I stumbled out of bed from a nap, stark naked, and raced around in the now almost pitch-dark, trying to protect my drawings and my supplies and especially my still-to-be-used, very expensive handmade watercolor paper.

Over the roar of the pouring rain and the crashing thunder and lightning, I heard Aphrodite frantically screaming, "Christo! Christooooo!" Assuming she was in trouble, I ran out into the storm to look for her. In a huge flash of lightning, I saw her below, and she yelled and waved up at me to come down from my ruin and stay with them in their house. I yelled back, *Ola endaxi! Efxaristo!*, everything's fine, thank you! In truth, I felt safer between my own four, albeit shaky walls, where I could keep an eye on my two months' work. Only when a second flash of lightning came did I realize that if I could see her, she could see me, buck naked outside my ruin on the terrace wall, and I fled inside. Then, in a matter of minutes, almost as suddenly as it began, the storm was over.

Such a storm was almost unheard of in the summer, and later on when this remarkable event came up in conversation, Aphrodite would turn all giggly, vastly amused, it seemed, by the memory of the near typhoon and Christo naked in the dazzling flashes of lightning. Her hand over her mouth, she would lean over and whisper to her friends among the village women, in their black skirts and aprons, their thick stockings and clunky shoes, all of them giggling, whooping, and slapping their fat thighs, and giving me sly looks.

Of course everybody was overjoyed by the storm. No one had been hurt, and to have your cisterns filled in the middle of the summer was a gift from the gods.

Another favorite of mine, old Iannis, had also been a fisherman.

He owned the only two-story house on the beach, right there in the middle, the upstairs rooms for tourists. He had two very good-looking sons who, when their father retired, took over the boat, fishing at night and selling their catch during the day from big hand-made baskets in the square in Apollonia, making the tremendous daily journey with a slow-moving donkey, as it was more lucrative than selling the fish in Platy Ghialos. Both sons were getting married and starting families, and the house was full of life and laughter.

Iannis had a wonderful face, and I did a couple of portraits of him. Interestingly, he became a painter himself and built a tiny studio to work in. He painted his world of churches, boats, terraces, vegetable gardens, donkeys and chickens, women in black and men in wonderful straw hats, and always the mountains and the sea. He painted in oil, carefully hoarding his paints and using worn-out brushes; in the years to come, I always gave him whatever I didn't need or hadn't used when I left in the autumn. I visited him almost every day and grew fond of him and of his paintings. His naïf and very colorful work had tremendous charm, and he also had an extraordinary sense of composition. His pictures were the real thing—nothing kitschy about them. To this day, I regret never having bought one of them; by the time I had a little extra money and could afford it, he was dead, and his family had given his pictures away or destroyed them.

Next door to my friend Iannis was Stavros, a farmer. Very handsome, and always turned out in a wonderful straw hat, it was he who had carted off the beautiful Australian girls and made himself their guide for the few days they stayed at Platy Ghialos before they retreated to the greater comfort of a room in Apollonia. A lifelong skirt chaser, he was already proudly and happily married to Evangelitsa, a sixteen-year-old girl. She was underage, but they had the parents' consent and, far more important, the permission of the church. Though still almost a child, she was already luscious, zaftig— her name meant "good news"—and Stavros walked around with a little smile and a knowing wink: the cat that ate the cream. Indeed, they produced many handsome children over the years.

Iannis, a fisherman

Stavros was to become quite rich, for he caught the rising tide of tourism on Sifnos right at the very beginning and rented out rooms in his house on the beach for years. He had not inherited the property, but had had the imagination to buy land on the waterfront when it was cheap, and he made good money when the tourists started coming. Still, he went on farming all his life on his land in Platy Ghialos and his fields up by Exambela. He was to play a large role in my Sifnos life, being the one who took me to Exambela, where his parents and his sister lived, and showing me the house I was to buy.

Quite a few of the people living on the beach were potters, and I enjoyed visiting them in their workshops. These simple huts right by the sea had only rudimentary equipment, usually just a potter's wheel and a glazing oven. One potter, more up-to-date than the others, used oil to heat his kiln, but most of them still used brushwood. The clay came from the hills behind the beach. When it dried, it varied from light to dark ocher and, when fired, turned a dark reddish brown. They glazed some of the pots and bowls dark green or deep blue with a hint of mauve, and sometimes they traced simple patterns and designs in white on them. These were not objets d'art but useful mugs, plates, bowls, and pitchers, and I bought them when I could. Once I had a house, I filled my kitchen with their pots and dishes.

Sifnos pottery was famous; between the First and Second World Wars, there were said to have been at least five hundred potters on the island. But by the 1970s there were only ten workshops left, pottery appeared to be a dying art, and the potters were pessimistic about the future. But with the coming of tourism in the following years, the craft of pottery had a rebirth of sorts. True, only a few potters still make the old objects whose shapes and colors have evolved over centuries or the more complex pots that their ancestors made for celebrations, settling instead for decorative stuff that is easy to take home in a suitcase, but they are still there, still working.

At the far end of the beach was another couple, total outsiders really, and the butt of many jokes in Platy Ghialos. A colonel, not one of *the* Colonels, but a colonel nonetheless, had a house there by the road-to-be as you came down to the beach. It was new and quite large, surrounded by a high wall. The colonel himself was rarely in residence, but he parked his ostensible wife there, where she lived mostly alone above the beach. All the women in Platy Ghialos joked about her having a past in Piraeus, and indeed she looked very like Bouboulina, the old prostitute played by Lila Kedrova in *Zorba the Greek*, but that was probably just jealousy. Whatever, she was a jolly, friendly soul and always gave a broad, perhaps too-friendly smile and sighed maybe a bit too deeply when we passed each other during her daily constitutional on the beach. Few people spoke to either of them, but in the evening she often sat, in one of her too-short skirts, in the tiny *kafenion* at the end of the beach, laughing with the fishermen.

As the weeks passed and during the years ahead, I was flattered to be treated more and more as a member of this little community. People took to shyly inviting me to their village and church events and their festivals, and into their homes. I was invited to join them in evenings at the taverna with the barber from Apollonia who played the *lauto*, a lutelike island instrument, and the farmer from Katavati who played the violin and sang with an incredibly anguished, haunting voice. Unlike on other, less isolated Cycladic islands, whose music often came from neighboring islands or even the mainland, the songs of Sifnos were primarily composed by local poets and musicians, fathers over the centuries teaching their sons the words and music. New songs were often improvised as they sang, slipping in their favorite saints or even local stories and figures as they went along. The music could seem a bit monotonous, more Arabic and Eastern than European, a part of the Ottoman heritage, but there were rhythms and long melodic lines that were very Greek.

Mostly it was the men who sang, as it was the men who danced, alone or together, in circles, slowly at first and then picking up speed until (as we have all heard about) plates started flying, even chairs. Vast amounts of retsina were consumed during these evenings. This wine, which has been made in Greece for centuries, gets its name, and its special taste, from the pine sap (mythically the Tears of the Wood Nymph) that was used to seal the amphorae and barrels in which the wine was kept and shipped. Each farmer was very proud of "his" retsina, and one had to be careful not to offend any of them by favoring one over another.

Retsina is an acquired taste, doesn't travel well, and is best with local food. It took me a while to get used to it, but I got the knack soon enough, I'm afraid. It was light, and you could drink quite a bit before the buzz turned to a kick. Watching my neighbors during those evenings, I could imagine them during the long, damp, cold winters, singing and dancing like this, late into the night.

—

Not everything I witnessed was happy. During the summer I made friends with a young couple who had a house on the beach in Platy Ghialos and a larger house in Exambela. The husband was Angelos, another of the taverna owner's brothers, and his wife, Nicoletta, was pregnant with their second child. I almost ruined things one morning when, without asking her, I innocently borrowed her red plastic bucket to do some laundry. She was not at home, but still . . .

"*Panagia mouuuuu. Panagia mouuuuu,*" she howled when she returned to find her red bucket missing. She ran up and down the beach, searching everywhere, screaming all the time. I could hear the ruckus up on my terrace, where I was rinsing out my boxer shorts, but I had no idea what it was all about. By the time I figured it out and came down, bucket in hand, half the women on the beach had joined her in her search, and now they all pointed at me, calling out that the bucket had been found. I felt terrible. Men are not supposed to do laundry to begin with—Greek society, like the Arab, is riddled with dos and don'ts about what men and women can and cannot do—and obviously you are also not supposed to borrow things without asking. I returned her precious pail with all the smiles and excuses I could muster, but I don't think she ever really forgave me.

That screaming was nothing compared with what we heard only a few weeks later when, for some reason, her husband went to Kamares to meet the ferryboat. In spite of having had a lot of retsina at lunch, Angelos took his old motorcycle, without a helmet of course, bumped up over the paths and the steps to Apollonia, tore down the steep, twisting road toward the harbor at Kamares, and, missing a curve, sailed off the edge and dropped more than a hundred feet to the rocky valley floor below. He somehow survived the fall and was flown by helicopter to Athens. But to the islanders this was a sure sign of death: once you left on the helicopter, it was thought, you only returned dead, if at all. And indeed the poor young man died in Athens the same day.

I found out about this when I heard the fearful shrieks, the strange, almost ecstatic grieving and keening, not only of the new widow but of her women neighbors in Platy Ghialos. They were all there with her, all in black, hands over their faces, heads thrown back—much as you see mourning women in pictures or news footage from Palestine or Baghdad or elsewhere in the Middle East, their mouths open, literally howling. Being Swiss, I had never heard or seen anything like it, and the hairs stood straight up on the back of my neck.

At the funeral, the first of many I attended in the church of Agios Nikolaos in Exambela, the very pregnant widow in the front was still weeping uncontrollably, moaning, groaning, beating her knees with her fists, and clawing at her bare arms in an extravagant display of grief. Two of her neighbors came to sit with her and restrained her, holding her arms down at her sides. This was a venting of raw, open emotion such as I had never seen, and I soon found myself crying along with many of the other mourners. All these men and women crammed inside the church, weeping and keening, the strange, smoky candlelit atmosphere, the somber, bearded, chanting *pappas*, as they called the priests, and the sobbing widow were fixed in my mind's eye, and the cries of grief rang in my ears for long after.

The widow gave birth to a boy a few months later, but she was never again seen in anything but black.

This was my first initiation into the cycle of life as the people of Sifnos lived it. Even though this death was unusual—an accident, and such a young victim to boot—in the end it was simply a death, and for them births and deaths, baptisms, weddings, and funerals were doorways of life one had to pass through. The accompanying ceremonies were layered with traditional, often theatrical rituals, with candles burning, incense swinging, and the mourning or celebrating actors in these dramas crying in grief or dancing in joy. But once the obligatory rituals were completed, life went on as usual. Following this dramatic funeral service in the church in Exambela, the mourners sat together at a reception, drinking, gossiping, laughing, talking crops and business, and arranging marriages.

They had lived this way always.

Sifnos, and indeed all of Greece, was then and basically still is Greek Orthodox. The church is the greatest landowner in the country and hugely powerful politically. Orthodox means "right belief," and pretty much all Greeks believe that the Greek Orthodox Church, in whose embrace they are born, baptized, married, and buried, is indeed "right." On Sifnos, almost everyone wears a crucifix and celebrates his name day, and it is a Sifniot dream to build a chapel in honor of the saint you are named for. More than three hundred of these little chapels are dotted around the island.

Sifnos had been Orthodox since early Christian times, taking its cues from Constantinople, capital of the Eastern Roman Empire, and this allegiance continued even during the centuries when Sifnos was ruled by Roman Catholic Venice. The conquering Ottomans who came next, ruling their vast Islamic empire from what was now called Istanbul, interestingly made no move to interfere with local religious practices, choosing instead to manage the Greeks through the Orthodox Church. Thus the curious fact that most of the many large churches and monasteries on Sifnos were built during the more than three centuries of Turkish occupation, during which the church thrived. And when the Turks were finally expelled in 1830, the Orthodox Church was the only real power left standing.

—

Even the Greek monarchy that succeeded the Ottomans was never a challenge to the power of the church, perhaps because it wasn't very Greek. King Otto, the first modern Greek king, was a Bavarian installed on the new throne in 1832 by the British. He was deposed in 1862, but the line of kings who replaced him didn't have any Greek blood either. In fact they called themselves kings of the Hellenes, not of Greece, and they were actually Danish, with a little German and Belgian thrown in—part of the doubtless *hochgeboren* but incredibly confusing Schleswig-Holstein-Sonderburg-Glücksburg family, among whose dubious products is Prince Philip of Great Britain. Their hold on power from the start was iffy at best, and they never managed to create a court or an aristocracy of Greeks with a stake in their hold on power. The monarchy was abolished in 1924, re-established in 1935, and finally snuffed out for good in 1974. And once again, through all these years, it was the Orthodox Church that remained the one and only Greek absolute.

The church is long on ritual and ceremony, and the church calendar is cluttered with many festivals honoring different saints and biblical days. Most of these are taken very seriously and celebrated religiously, so to speak, and among the most popular, at least on Sifnos, are the *panaghias*. There are several of these each year, rotating around the various, often hard-to-reach island churches and monasteries, some on mountaintops or remote promontories. Most are in the evening, and they are as much social as religious events—with crowds of cheerful islanders not only chanting and praying, but cooking, eating, and drinking, feasting long into the night in the refectories or outside in the whitewashed forecourts of the churches.

The first *panaghia* I attended was in midsummer of that first year, and it was held at the church of Agia Marina. I learned about it the day before at Lakis's. Chuck and I were told that it would be at an unusual hour, very early in the morning, and that it was a good three hours' walk or more, so we would have to leave at the crack of dawn. I decided to stay in Apollonia with Chuck and Lisa. Lisa decided to skip it, but Chuck and I were determined to go, and well before sunrise, alarms clanging, we dragged ourselves awake and struggled into our clothes.

It was a glorious morning, the light before sunrise clear and pink-gold. The sea was calm, and there was a gentle breeze. We didn't need directions, as we could already see a steady stream of pilgrims hiking up the valley of Profitis Elias and along the mountain ridge toward the tiny chapel of Agia Marina, a white dot in the far distance, hanging on a cliff high above the sea. Chuck and I were pretty much out of breath early on, scrabbling slowly up the steps and along the rocky paths, sweating in the warm air while the old farmers in their home-woven woolen undershirts and buttoned jackets zipped by us, whistling away, smiling, tipping their caps, showing no signs of fatigue. They had been hiking up and down these steps and paths all their lives, but we were still humbled by the show of fitness, in awe of those strong legs and lungs.

At the chapel we were served icy water from the well and offered a glass of retsina or an ouzo by the *panigiras*, the host of the festival that year. This person was either from a rich Athenian family with connections or family on Sifnos or, just as often, a Sifniot who had saved all year for the honor. It was he who carried the icon of Saint Marina, the central object of the festival, up to the church to be blessed. The host of the following year's *panaghia*, already chosen, would have the privilege of lovingly carrying it back to his house, where the holy image would, it was hoped, bring him luck and blessings in the New Year.

Resting, catching our breath against the wall of the forecourt, we could see the island stretching away dizzyingly far below us, and we watched as more and more pilgrims came along the path we had just struggled up. Everyone wore their best clothes, the men striding along together, the ladies trailing behind, some of the older people riding mules or donkeys, all very jolly and festive, like figures in a Brueghel painting. This centuries-old procession wending its way to the church seemed to be coming not just from distant villages but out of the past, an ancient, biblical past, weaving and threading its way into the present.

Once the *pappas* in their flowing black robes and tall, cylindrical black hats arrived on their mules, it all became a bit more serious. Dipping their heads, they passed through the low door into the small white chapel and slipped into their grander chasubles, and the pilgrims began to squeeze through the door after them. Being the only foreigners, Chuck and I were trying to be as inconspicuous as possible, but everyone, apparently pleased that we were there, nudged us forward into the chapel, smiling and nodding.

Toward the end of the long ceremony—very moving in its

solemnity, even though incomprehensible to us—the priests blessed and cut the holy bread into small pieces for everyone to receive. It was delicious bread, but there was more to come: we could smell lamb grilling and potatoes frying in the old kitchens adjacent to the chapel, and soon the crowd started to move across the forecourt to the refectory, everyone pushing ahead to be the first to share the table with the priests and the host. Even at a religious festival, it seemed that Greeks were wont to push and shove, as if someone had just yelled "Fire!" in a theater. Being adjudged honored guests, Chuck and I were escorted to the front of the line.

The refectory was not large, and clearly the pilgrims would have to be fed in shifts; the long, narrow table down the center of the room seated only about thirty people. At the head sat the senior priest, the host proudly to his right, and we, feeling terribly important by now, were touched to be treated so generously. Chickpea soup and bread were already on the table along with glasses of retsina, little plates of lemon slices, and olives. The priest blessed the meal, and almost instantly the soup bowls were emptied and replaced by plates of the lamb and potatoes we had smelled cooking on the open fires outside. Everyone was starving and ate quickly, Chuck and I among the best of them; with no breakfast, having climbed all that way, we were faint with hunger.

As I ate, I stared at the head priest, transfixed. I was to see this sight again and again on the island, and it never failed to astonish me: he and the other priests, along with the farmers, had removed their hats for the meal, and across the foreheads of all of them was a sharp line where the hats had been; the lower half of their faces, even the priests', was dark and weathered from the sun while the top half—their foreheads—was startlingly white, milky, eerily smooth, almost translucent, somehow naked. One could imagine that the skin below their collars and above their rolled sleeves was like that— smooth, pale, young. Boyish and innocent. Oops, I thought, too sexy for now, and blushing slightly, I looked away, returning my gaze to my plate and my meal.

Suddenly everyone in the room began rapping their forks and spoons on their plates, making a terrific racket, lifting their glasses as they loudly toasted and thanked the *panigiras*, the host and donor of the feast, calling out, "*Eviva tou panigira!*"—good health to the *panigiras*! Bang, came down the glasses on the table. Then everyone went on loudly and merrily toasting and thanking the cook: "*Eviva tou magira!*" Bang, went the glasses again. And then toasting the waiters: "*Eviva ton servitoron!*" And bang, went the glasses one more time. Looking around me in this plain whitewashed, sunbathed room high above the Aegean, looking at those weathered, smiling faces, a bit of retsina in me to be sure, I suddenly found myself tearing up. Maybe I was just young and sentimental, or maybe I was feeling nostalgia for something unknown but somehow remembered subconsciously from my lost Russian Orthodox heritage, but the golden screens and clouds of incense, the bearded priests slipping in and out of the chapel doors by the altar had seemed more connected to me than the austere Protestant services in the vast, beautiful but always icy *Münster*, Basel's cathedral.

More important, though, looking around, I felt not only affection for these people but a near yearning to enter this community I had discovered, a desire to be in some way part of this place I had stumbled upon. A homeless émigré's child banging on the high, closed doors of the city of Basel—always closed, it had seemed to me—I suddenly felt that maybe this was a home, a place of my own that I could come to and feel that I belonged. Then I noticed a farmer I knew slightly from hiking across the island, a man with a weathered, kindly face, watching me from across the table. As our eyes met, he nodded at me and smiled shyly, raising his glass in welcome, as if he knew what I was thinking and understood it.

I was woken from this reverie by a nudge from Chuck, who pointed to the people crowded outside the door, the next shift waiting for their meal, and all of us at the table got up and poured out into the sunlight. The musicians had started to play, and people gathered in the courtyard to sing and dance. But the day was now becoming hot, and instinctively Chuck and I, by some kind of silent mental telepathy, started together on the long walk back down to Apollonia. We walked, almost unseeing, in a kind of trance, neither of us speaking, unwilling to break the spell of that morning.

—

One of the charms of these *panaghias* was that over the years, they led me to places I might never have gone on my own, beautiful spots that were too far off or too high up to think of struggling to alone or without a specific reason. Sifnos was about seventy-four square miles; there were big stretches of high land, mountains, and valleys where you could not see the sea, where you had no idea you were on an island. Trekking off to these celebrations was one way I learned to know the island's paths and byways, its more remote beauty spots. Over the years, I got to be sort of an expert among foreigners on Sifnos, guiding friends and guests on walks to far-flung villages and monasteries.

Vathy, for example, was a harbor town directly across the southern tip of the island from Platy Ghialos, a beautiful, sleepy place on a closed, protected bay, with a double-domed church almost in the water and the tiny village, only a few houses and potters' sheds, stretching away to either side. Most people went there by boat from Kamares, a long ride, but once you knew the way, you could hike there across the island—a magnificent walk following farmers' paths, up and over the top of the island, then through a cut, a rough, wild gorge, and down to the picturesque harbor below. Vathy had only one little taverna, right on the water. You couldn't order, couldn't choose, you had to eat whatever it was they had that day, but the food was delicious and you always got a warm welcome.

Artemona, aside from having a couple of the best restaurants on the island, was another favorite place of mine to visit and draw, with its grand villas, with their columned porches and walled gardens, and its several big old rambling farmhouses. In the heart of this handsome town was a large open square with a few houses and the main bakery of the island at one end, some houses and a taverna called Mangana on one side, a big open field on the other, and the church of Agios Konstantinos at the far end. At dinner, one sat facing the field and the church in the fading light while skinny-legged boys in shorts played *cache-cache*, hiding behind the parked cars or wagons in the square, or football in the field beyond.

The church itself was a unique piece of architecture. Its rather conventionally handsome west front, with two vaults and a bell tower between them, faced the square, but around the sides and to the back, massive slablike walls leaned and heeled and slanted this way and that, like a bunker designed by Le Corbusier. And on the north side of the church an exterior staircase spilled down the raked wall, every step a different size and shape, dipping and tilting and twisting crazily, the whole a piece of sculpture, really, cockeyed and absolutely perfect. And murder to draw.

Vathy

And there were any number of places closer at hand, nearer to Platy Ghialos, to explore or take people who came to visit. There was Faros, then still a charming fishing village with a harbor full of brightly painted boats and the nearby ruins of the sixth-century B.C. gold and silver mines that had been the basis of the island's wealth in ancient times. Or Exambela, a farmers' village reached by narrow stone paths and steep steps. There were no streets, no cars, only farm donkeys tied up by the doors waiting to be ridden to the fields. Almost across the road was the high, fortresslike monastery of Vrissi, its rather grand courtyard a wonderful place to draw—if you were prepared to dodge the advances of the rather smelly monk who lived there alone at that time. He was even more desperate and horny than I, it seemed, and as you stood staring at the altar screen, he was apt to slip up behind you and give you a painful pinch.

Another monastery I loved to draw was tou Vounou, which sat high above the sea overlooking Platy Ghialos and the beach. It had a large flagged terrace shaded by huge pines and a bright red entrance gate set deep in a high white wall. Inside were two courtyards of monks' cells, one large, one small, on either side of a large, square, domed church; smaller domes, miniatures of the central dome, were arranged at the corners. It all looked a little crooked, almost hand-made, somewhere between a sand castle and a leaning, tippy cartoon cake. It is one of the charms of Greek island architecture that nothing is quite straight or symmetrical, but the shapes dip and weave and curve and fold into themselves or into neighboring buildings.

The interior of the church itself was a high white vaulted space, the dome rising above the nave, the altar screens covered with icons framed in gold. The entrance was through the smaller courtyard and a vaulted sort of porch that was a miracle of arches within arches, doors large and small, and even tiny flights of stairs mysteriously going every which way. Here the old lady who took care of the monastery kept her masses of plants, all in pots, some of them vines that climbed up on strings lovingly strung from arch to arch.

Along the opposite side of the courtyard was a row of monks'

Faros

cells—one could rent one to stay in—and a small apartment with a kitchen and dining room where this same lady served dinner to the people staying there. She and her husband actually lived in Exambela, but she was at the monastery every day and sometimes stayed the night if she felt she needed to keep her eye on the guests. Many were young and naturally "misbehaved," sharing cells and beds. Her husband was often there with her. I assume she was paid for caring for the church, but mostly I suspect it was an honor to have the keys, to be in charge of the monastery, opening and closing it morning and night, hiring people to clean and whitewash it.

The walls of her suite were covered with photographs of islanders dating back to the nineteenth century, farmers and fisherman, their festivals and weddings, decades' worth of the life of the island. The people in the photographs all had what I thought of as the "Sifnos look," and they all looked just like the islanders I knew.

Among the most interesting images were pictures of King Paul and Queen Frederica's first—and maybe only—visit to the island after the Second World War, the two of them in uniform riding up to Apollonia on donkeys. The islanders line the path dressed in their best clothes, obviously excited, beaming at their handsome king and queen, exhibiting none of the ambivalence that many Greeks came to feel about them—especially Frederica, with her German past (which included a stint as a Hitler Youth)—an ambivalence that was to grow and poison the early hopes for their son, Constantine, when he became king.

The most astonishing monastery, then as now, was Chrissopighi, which we'd seen on our very first drive, a long white double-vaulted church on a narrow rocky point that stuck straight out into the sea. The point had split in an earthquake and was broken in the middle, the monastery courtyard being as it were on the mainland and the church on a little island, the two connected by a slim walled bridge arching over the cut below. Legend has it that the rock was split by the Virgin in order to save the lives—and of course the virginity— of three island women who were fleeing pirates. Another legend says that the church was founded when an icon, discovered floating in the sea by sailors who brought it on board their ship, magically turned toward this rocky promontory and the church was con- structed to house the holy icon on the spot.

Arriving, you enter a courtyard with a well and a huge tamarisk tree, a few rooms to let, old monks' cells to one side, and a kitchen and large refectory to the other. From there you walk across the bridge to a terrace in front of the sky-blue church door, which is set in a finely carved marble molding with an arch above that rises to the bell tower. Inside, the double-vaulted space is plain, except for a gilded screen of icons in front of the altar, punctured by three doors, the middle one open to the altar. The windows, with painted blue frames, open directly onto the sea, and hanging from the ceiling is a miraculous model ship, quite large, but in fact a simple caïque, a gift from someone whose prayers have been answered by the Virgin.

Outside, beyond the church, out in the wind, is a handsome marble baptismal font dug into the rock, with a little blue iron fence around it. Beyond that are shelves and sheets of rock where people come to swim. Over the years, those rocks became my favorite spot for swimming and sunbathing, one rock in particular, "my rock," where I went every day to read and swim after lunch in the taverna on the beach.

Throughout my first years there, the kitchen and the few rooms, and the rocks below, were ruled over with an iron fist by a very large, portly lady named *Kyria* Kathe. She, like the mistress of the monastery at tou Vounou, lived in Exambela during much of the winter, but in summer she was at Chrissopighi, watching over the visitors. She doled out the little rooms and made sure that no one had a guest in his room and no one on the rocks went swimming naked. Or she tried to. I confess I often swam in the nude from my rock, but it was very sheltered and off by itself, and few people ever stumbled across it. Or else, as is often the case, they incomprehensibly preferred to swim and sunbathe where everyone else swam.

She also cooked meals in the old kitchen for anyone lucky enough to stay there. She was a wonderful cook; her french fries in her own olive oil were the best I ever tasted. We are not talking Cordon Bleu cuisine; Sifnos cooking, like most Greek cooking, is very simple— fresh vegetables, stuffed tomatoes and peppers, fried potatoes, meatballs, grilled lamb chops or stewed lamb, fish, and cheese. I don't think Greek dishes, any more than retsina or ouzo, travel particularly well, but eaten there in that climate, that air, in those rooms, the windows open to the crashing sea, the food was fresh and simple and totally wonderful.

In later years, when I had bought my house in Exambela, Kathe and I were close neighbors and became friends. Forced out of the big house when her daughter married, as was the custom, she and her husband lived in a rough little house that had been a stable. It was the last building in the village, literally at the end of the road and at the top of a narrow path leading to fields and terraces that

Monastery of Chrissopighi

dropped down to the walled village of Kastro and the sea. It was a splendid spot, but unimaginably windy. Many barns and outbuildings faced the sea, but no Sifniot in his right mind wanted to live in such a spot. All Greek island houses and villages face inland, away from the rattling, whistling, unpredictable Greek winds. Today rich Athenians and foreigners often build spectacular houses with splendid sea views, but they spend half their time trapped inside, their sealed windows and shutters rattling in the August *meltemi*.

Kyria Kathe was no longer portly or stout but so immensely fat that she could barely walk. She used two canes and moved very slowly, but she remained cheerful and happy, perhaps because of her husband, Iannis. He was a very sweet old man, smiling down from his mule, his greatest, proudest, most beloved possession. The two of them, he and the mule, and of course Kathe beside him slept only a wall apart in the tiny stable they shared. At night Iannis could hear his mule eat or drink or sneeze or cough or fart, and the mule could hear them too, no doubt, all the same personal sounds. Through a mixture of love and respect and coddling, that mule lived to be more than twenty-four years old.

The little house had virtually no windows and no plumbing, no running water at all, but Kathe always managed to set a most welcoming table with delicious food. To help her earn extra money, I would invite myself to her house for dinner with friends or with my parents, paying her for her hospitality. And it was always a delightful evening.

She, like many of the villagers, loved my parents, Axel and Dita. Because my father was a doctor, and a Swiss doctor at that, he was particularly revered on the island. Sifniots hated going to the doctor, and some farmers never set foot in a doctor's office in their entire lives. The older generation still practiced folk medicine, herbs and teas and even cupping treatments, something that in Europe went out with bleeding. I had seen it in *Zorba the Greek*: hot glasses applied to the body—actually to that same poor Bouboulina—to make a partial vacuum, puckering the skin. It looked like agony. And nonsense. Others believed in miracles, of course, offering promises and prayers to their favorite saints. The walls of many of the island churches were covered with silver amulets that showed images of legs and knees, eyes and ears, any and every body part, as tokens given for cures accomplished by the saint of this or that church. But a foreign doctor was something special, something different, a real treat, and wherever he went, Axel was bombarded with questions about the islanders' health problems.

No matter what they believed in, modern medicine or near-voodoo island cures, all Sifniots loved talking about their health, and they assumed that as the son of a doctor, I automatically knew about medicine too. Whenever I met someone on a path, after the formal greetings the first thing they would tell me was where and how badly it hurt, whatever it was. *"Iassu, Georgos. Tikanis?"* How are you? I would ask, not wanting to know. "My back hurts. And my legs too. *Panagia mou.*" That's terrible, I would say. And, pointing at his crotch, he would say, "And here there is nothing. Hahaha."

—

The other major walking destination was to the village of Kastro, which sat on a hill thrust into the sea far below Kathe's house. From there, Kastro was a perfect little hill town, surrounded by a fourteenth-century wall built to protect it from pirates and other enemies. Some islanders suggested that the citizens of Kastro had actually been pirates themselves, but in fact Kastro, crowned by its little ruined acropolis (now rebuilt), had been the capital of Sifnos from antiquity until the nineteenth century. Indeed, it was said to be the oldest continually inhabited town in Greece. In 1832, after the Greek war of independence from the Turks, the capital was transferred to Apollonia, and Kastro began a decline from which it has never recovered—a decline parallel to that of the whole island. In ancient times, Sifnos had been wealthy, for it had more freshwater than most islands. It became rich from agriculture, and it had lucrative gold and silver mines. Under the Turks it continued to thrive; in 1836 the population was eight thousand people, of whom five thousand were year-round residents. By the time I got there, though, there were fewer than two thousand year-round on the island, and a mere one hundred souls living in Kastro.

Legend has it that the island's decline had in fact already begun in ancient times, when the Sifniots tried to trick Apollo—always a big mistake, as we know, trying to fool the gods. Every year the Sifniots were supposed to bring a golden egg as a tithe to be deposited in their splendid treasury at Delphi, but one year, thinking no one would ever know the difference, they decided to bring only a gilded egg, not a solid gold one; it was their treasury, after all, and no one ever checked anyway. But it was a very bad move: "Such was the wrath of Apollo," as these things are classically put, that he caused the mines on Sifnos to be flooded and destroyed by the sea, and then, rather than protecting it from its enemies, he let the island be attacked and plundered by the Samians.

From my very first days on Sifnos I had been determined to go to Kastro. I wanted to see it for myself, and I wanted to see if I could find my friend Maya Yannoulis's grandparents, or perhaps Maya herself. But getting there was not easy. There were plans for an eventual small road down from Apollonia, but meanwhile, the existing path was barely passable, and one of the old Volga taxis struggled and skidded up and down only during emergencies.

My first visit was with my Rhodesian friends, who were as avid about hiking as I was. We chose what looked to be, and was, the most beautiful route, a donkey track that led steeply down from the monastery of Vrissi, near Exambela, past a couple of windswept little farms, goat huts, and dovecotes to the valley floor, where there was a miraculous stream that poured water even during the driest months. The stream, lined with masses of oleander that bloomed profusely, was home to a myriad of croaking frogs, alarming numbers of snakes, and thousands and thousands of butterflies. They were everywhere, yellow and white clouds of them dancing over the bushes above our heads.

This became my favorite route to Kastro, walking down through what I came to call the Butterfly Valley. I would often sit there drawing views of the town rising up in the cleft of the high, terraced hills on either side of the valley, or of the flawless little white church below the walls, or of the pair of domed churches that sat perfectly together, catty-corner, one slightly higher than the other, within the high walls of the village cemetery. These little, perfectly square domed churches dotted Sifnos—some in small villages; others, like these, built along farmers' paths. They were lovingly tended, whitewashed annually, and cleaned regularly by farmer' wives or village women. They were the very meaning of homely—very small, very simple, with stone floors, a few caned chairs, and the simplest altars, but they always had fresh flowers and smelled of wax and soap.

That first time, after hopping and slipping over the wet stones in the stream, we emerged from a virtual wall of oleander to find ourselves at a small bay called Seralia. The name probably came from Seraglio, as Kastro was once called, no doubt an all too vivid reminder of the island's Ottoman past, since the name had long ago been changed. During the Venetian and Turkish periods, Seralia was a busy port, a safe harbor in bad weather. Now it had only a cluster of deserted little houses, and when we arrived there that day, we found one lonely fisherman working on his nets. Startled to see us stumble out of the bushes, but full of smiles, he offered us some water and then guided us up the steep path toward the town that towered over us.

Full of anticipation, we climbed the marble steps and entered the village through one of three massive iron gates set in huge arches, or loggias, a hint of the village's grand Venetian past. A tiny stone-paved street that twisted away in either direction following the outer walls was lined with white houses, each with an outside staircase to the upper floor. In some cases these projected into or across the street to form low, arched bridges to the next street up, making the town a veritable warren of houses and tunnels. This was not quite what we had expected—such a narrow and rather claustrophobic street— and we could immediately see that most of the medieval buildings rising up toward the center were in ruins. The whole town had a slightly abandoned air, with a strange, empty, hollow quiet to it.

"Where can we get something to eat?" I asked the heavyset lady who ran the tiny general store tucked in the village wall by the gate. We were starving after our long walk. Without looking up from her newspaper, Sotiria, as we were to learn she was called, lifted her chin and clicked her tongue, *tst*, in that classic uncompromising Greek negative I was coming to know, sometimes finding it hilarious and sometimes, as in this case, not so very amusing at all. There was no food to be had in Kastro, she baldly lied. Of course she might cook for us, she added, and quoted an outrageous sum. She also had rooms to rent, it seemed, but at vast expense. She had nice postcards too, but unless I bought stamps as well, I couldn't have them. And when it turned out she was asking double the normal price for the stamps, we fled her store.

A bad beginning, but along the street we soon found what we

learned was the only taverna in the village, with a terrace clinging to the walls and a lovely view up the valley we had just descended. We got a welcoming smile from Maria, the cook and owner, and her husband. He was from Artemona but had married into a Kastro family. The Kastro blood seemed to have come out mainly in their daughter, who was as grumpy as the shopkeeper by the gate, slamming my plate piled with food down on the table and shuffling back to the kitchen in her broken-down slippers. Looking back, I realize that it must have been a Sunday, as they were serving the traditional Sunday *revithia,* a chickpea soup. Even here at Maria's everything was several more drachmas than anywhere else on Sifnos, but the terrace view was spectacular and the food delicious. As we sat there in the sun, Kastro was beginning to seem more charming.

I asked Maria if she knew the Yannoulis family. Yes, she said, but they were most likely not there. They rarely came to the island. But she told us about Margaritha and Fotis, caretakers of the Yannoulis house, and after lunch we were directed to their home nearby. Margaritha, it turned out, was the most beautiful Sifniot woman I had ever seen. Sifnos girls, usually quite short, are often very pretty between the ages of twelve and seventeen, but then they start to lose their looks. Married by twenty or so, they tend to get heavy and, dressing as they all do in drab blacks and grays, long dresses covered with baggy sweaters, they often seem to have just let themselves go.

Margaritha was big from the waist down, but her face was that of an Italian Madonna, and I could sense the Venetian blood flowing through her veins. She glowed with smiles and warmth, and one could not help loving her. Fotis was good-looking, rather fine featured, and friendly. He drove the only car in town, the battered old Volga used for emergencies, which sat outside the walls below. They had a little boy and a girl, whom I was to watch grow up over the years, and the whole family, especially here in slightly spooky, unwelcoming Kastro, appeared totally charming.

My friends and I were supposed friends of the Yannoulises, or anyway of Maya's, and so they welcomed us into their house, offering us delicious coffee and fresh milk from the pride and joy of the house, their first refrigerator. Electricity had just been installed in Kastro, it seemed. Given the heat of the long Greek summers, I wondered how people lived without these machines, but most did. Some of the tavernas had kerosene refrigerators, but many villagers didn't even have that.

"Ah, Maya," they smiled, thinking of her, as I stumbled over my questions. They had known Maya since she was a little baby, and they loved her. Sadly, they said, she came very rarely to Sifnos, but they would certainly let me know if she was coming. Maya's grandmother lived in Athens most of the time—in some splendor, I suspected—and the house here was empty. I didn't dare ask them to show it to us, and it was many years before I saw it, a beautiful place, high up in the village, with panoramic views of the sea from every window.

As we were about to leave, Margaritha suddenly turned my cup upside down and, intensely studying the remnants of the coffee on the saucer, started to tell me my future, a common practice on the island. I had never been keen on knowing the future, and of course this time I could barely understand anything she said, but I was startled when she began talking about my being in love with a girl called Pamela: this was actually the name of a girl I had very seriously dated at St. Olaf College. How did she come up with that name there in Kastro? I wondered. I listened more closely, but unfortunately, or rather fortunately, the rest of what she had to say seemed pretty generic. "There are many problems." Of course. "You will have two children." Really? "You will have a long life." Despite this potted nonsense, I couldn't get over her hitting on the name Pamela, and I thought I would come back sometime and hear more. Besides, I loved her voice and I enjoyed watching her face; I could have watched her for hours, the light pouring in on her.

Afterward, strolling through the village and, as we climbed up toward Apollonia, stopping and looking back in the afternoon light, I fell a little in love with the beauty of the place, the fantasy of this tiny fortified town, a kind of miniature Mont Saint-Michel built out into the sea. I imagined coming back to Sifnos the following summer and staying in Kastro, renting rooms in the town and painting there. Nothing seemed more idyllic.

—

I already knew I would come back to Sifnos. I just knew it. In truth, it had not all been easy and wonderful that summer. In spite of friends like Chuck and my neighbors in Platy Ghialos, it had been a lonely and sometimes frustrating time for me. There were days when I hardly spoke to anyone. To be sure, my Greek was mostly mispronounced words and sign language, but it was also true that much of the time I had no one to talk to. God knows I had had no sex, hardly even a flirtation, something almost unimaginable for me. The whole place was emotionally and sexually charged, I felt, but I had been more alone there than I had probably ever been.

Still, I knew that being there mattered to me, that it was important. Most of the time I had been at peace with myself, maybe for the first time. I knew that somehow Sifnos—the island, the nature, and the people—had repaired me. The army, my career, problems with my family, my sense of being an outsider, every kind of tension and anxiety, personal and professional, seemed less important. Here, for the first time, I felt in harmony with my surroundings. My tumultuous dreams had calmed and my work had gotten stronger and stronger, I was especially convinced of that—the most important thing, really. I was sure I had good, new, very different work for my show in Zurich in September, and I was ready to face the challenge of moving to London and starting at the Royal College of Art, a huge leap.

I had come to Sifnos by pure chance, but I knew I had found something, something of my own. It felt like my own invention, this place, and for young Christo, a whole new start, a whole new me. And I knew it was not just a passing fancy, a notion I would forget by mid-February in some amazing studio in amazing

London, an idea I would let go of the moment someone suggested something else, someplace new. No. I knew I would come back. Sifnos was already a kind of home. Some instinct had brought me there, and that same instinct—protecting me and giving me time to grow and develop in safety—was going to bring me back.

2

That winter passed quickly. My exhibition in Zurich was a success, and my new work from Greece was well received. With my earnings and an award I won, I made enough money to support myself in London—not nearly as difficult in the 1970s as now, but still something for a twenty-two-year-old student, I thought.

It was tremendously exciting being there—the school itself, the city, a real city full of museums, theaters, and music, fabulous music. Basel of course had great art and music, but it was small and parochial, nothing like London. This was the real thing, a huge, world-class capital city. I worked and worked at school. I started making new friends, and most exciting of all, I began an affair with an American, a museum curator—my first affair with a man. Everything was a new adventure, and I felt incredibly alive and in the midst of my life. But it was also stressful, competitive, and anxiety making. In the case of my big love affair, it was also heartbreaking: the great romance fell apart almost as soon as it began.

And of course it rained and it rained and it rained, or so it seemed to me. I found myself looking forward to the isolation, the calm, the peace of Sifnos, to say nothing of the warm sun.

Arriving in Athens this time, I felt I was an old hand, I knew my way around. The streets, the sounds, the smells, the heat, all seemed familiar, and the sun was heavenly after the long London winter.

Georgos, my neighbor

I even had an adventure or two: I discovered the National Garden, which stretches from Syntagma Square to the Columns of Zeus, and a new Athens was revealed—an Athens full of boys, good-looking boys, available boys. Indeed, Athens came to be a minor playground for me during the next thirty-odd years. If I lived a bit like a monk on Sifnos, I did nothing of the kind in Athens.

I was so happy to be back in Greece that I was not even put off by one of those wild and unpleasant incidents one can have there. Arriving in Piraeus in a cab with all my luggage, I got into a huge screaming match with my taxi driver, who was displeased, it seemed, with his tip. Fortunately, fights with Greeks tend to be more bark than bite, a lot of yelling and macho puffery. But yell he did. I understood hardly anything of what he said, but I screamed right back at him in English, German, French, Italian, any language I could lay my hands on.

Then, as everyone waiting for the boat stood watching, he took the drachma notes I had given him and with a great deal of ceremony held them up in front of my face and tore them again and again into smaller and smaller pieces that he scornfully let fall through waggling fingers to the ground. Turning on his heel, he stepped into his taxi, ground the gears, and started to drive off—with, I suddenly realized, all my luggage and drawing cases and expensive paper and paints piled in the backseat and locked in the trunk. In a movement somewhere between James Bond and a long-legged Charlie Chaplin, I leaped onto the hood of the car and clung for dear life as he swerved right and left, trying to dislodge me. Fortunately, a policeman appeared and got the driver to stop and helped me get all my stuff out of the car. Still hurling insults, the driver drove off in a cloud of dust.

Boarding the old *Kalymnos*, I breathed a sigh as the ship shuddered and started to pull away from the dock. This would come to be one of the moments in the yearly trip to Sifnos that I looked forward to: the ship slipping away from the dock, from Piraeus, from Athens, from the world. In that brief moment I would be flooded with a sense of freedom and relief that I was indeed going, going, gone, to somewhere no one could get me. A few of the Greek passengers stayed on deck or in the smoke-filled lounge—I had forgotten how much they smoked—but most of them were down below, shut in their stuffy little cabins. I stayed on deck pacing about impatiently as the *Kalymnos* crawled from island to island, each one appearing in the far distance as a speck on the horizon, then slowly coming nearer. We would pull into Kíthnos or Sérifos, and with a lot of turning and backing and yelling and blowing of horns, the ship would grind to a stop in the harbor and we would all lean over the rail and watch the passengers get off, climbing down over the sides, and watch new ones get on. Then, with more turning and backing, we would sail on, an endless journey.

Finally Sifnos loomed up in front of us, and I was there. The ship sailed into the now familiar harbor of Kamares, a little smaller perhaps than I remembered, and the well-known smells of farmland, wildflowers, dusty plants, and woodsmoke drifted across the water. I breathed it in, soaked it all up in a kind of happy daze.

"*Christo! Iasssssuuuuu, Christo!*" I heard from one of the caïques below. "*Christo. Tikanis?*" It was Kostas, a fisherman I knew slightly, smiling, calling, and waving up at me as I looked over the rail.

"*Iassu Christo!*" came another voice.

I was home.

—

Kastro, May 1973

Dear Parents,

I am installed in Kastro and my work is going well. Still intoxicated from the incense, chanting, and retsina at the Ascension Day Festival at Chrissopighi, an amazing sight, perfect weather, a mob of people (a few more foreigners this year) in front of that wonderful little church.

I am sitting in front of my rooms in Kastro, the village dark and silent around me. The moon is full and the play of silver on the sea is creating slivers, shivers, splendors of light. The near mountains are Chinese ink black, but as your eyes get accustomed to the darkness, you can make out little houses and even terraces.

All the nervous stress from my London college year has vanished. The Greek light has taken over and I am full of concentration. Already eight pictures are hanging on my once virginal white walls, all sandy golden colors, all full of light, heat, and sun. The perfect Kastro skyline from Poulati along the shore or from the path that comes down from Artemona is wonderful to draw and I have done a series of ink sketches. The terraces, I imagine, give it an Asian feeling. There is also a connection to Mexico, the drawings from San Cristóbal especially which I imagine also have something Asian about them. But the light is totally different.

Thanks to some of the light studies I did over the winter and the discipline of school and studio work at the Royal College, I see Sifnos with a fresh eye, I think, and am doing the most powerful Greek pictures so far. I am painting the white light of the midday sky, white white white with lots of color underneath. At the other extreme, the darkness of the night here is full of tension and drama, and I am trying to capture that too. I hope this eruption of work continues; I shall have a great series by the fall when I go back to London.

Am reading all the time too. "The History of Art Criticism" by Venturi for my Ferdinand Hodler thesis. And for myself I am reading Durrell, "The Alexandria Quartet," "Justine" right now, and lapping it up. Especially being here in Greece, so close to Alexandria and all the Greek connections.

"Comment vous defendez-vous contre la solitude?"

"Je suis devenu la solitude moi-meme."

I am alone most of the time but I feel strong and content here. My dreams are less crazy and anxious. And everything that comes flying at me I throw back with paint at paper and canvas.

Your hermit son,
Christo

Well, I was twenty-two.

And a little full of my painter self on his island in Greece.

Lawrence Durrell was a hero to me. I idolized him, even felt a kinship with him, with his childhood on Corfu, his love for Greece, and his Alexandrian novels. For me, he was the embodiment of a connection to the East, to Alexandria, Istanbul, and Beirut, which I

Astro, Sifnos, 21.7.73

Liebe Eltern,

Ja nun bin ich also wieder auf meinem Sifnos und lerne wieder dass Zeit und Dach zum Glück nicht überall eine Rolle spielen. — Alles war wiedereinmal voll missgeschicke, als ob es diese Stadt mit mir nicht so recht will, dann bin ich dann meinem "Gschpüri" nahe gegangen und alles kam doch bestens heraus. Ich wollte nämlich noch nach Patmos meine Freunde besuchen und das Schiff sollte am nächsten Tag fahren, Ich telegraphierte und alles schien bestens... Dann zwei Stunden später heisst es das Schiff fährt heute nicht erst wieder morgen nach Patmos. So habe ich dann mein Patmos Boot auch verpasst und erst am Freitag ging das nächste. — So entschloss ich mich bald to drop Patmos go to Sounion for a day + ½ und das Schiff am Freitag nach Sifnos zu nehmen. Nochmals Telegramm und aus Athen heraus nach dem Strand (bei diesem Scheiss Telegramm meinen Parkerkulli

Letter to my parents

felt was an essential element of Greece. And my sympathy with him remained part of my youthful self-image for some time. I did have a major slap-down the following winter in London at a very elegant dinner party where, much to my delight, I found myself seated next to a grand Alexandrian-Greek lady, a Madame Zervoudaki, the mother of my host. In my memory she was wearing a tiara, and if she wasn't, she certainly carried herself as if she were. Perfect, I thought, and after a bit of small talk I threw out what I fondly imagined to be an excellent conversational card, a glittering bauble for this glamorous dinner partner: my love for Durrell and especially for his novel *Justine*. With a sniff, in her heavy Greek-French accent full of rolling r's, she snapped, *"Monsieur Durrell ne faisait jamais parti de la société alexandrine. Il ne savait rien de la société alexandrine. Et ses livres ne sont que des fantasies et des mensonges."* With that, she turned away to her dinner partner on the other side.

And that, as they say, was the end of that.

—

The rooms Fotis helped me find in Kastro were high up in the village. I settled in tentatively at first, but then found my rhythm and began painting, turning out pictures. But almost immediately I knew the town was not quite what I had expected, or wanted. Part of the problem was its physical nature. Some of the grander houses were kept up—and filled, people said, with Venetian treasures—but the town had definitely seen better days, and very soon the narrow, twisting, covered streets, the houses fitted tightly together in that amazing Cycladic way, began to feel suffocating.

And the people themselves were different from any other people on Sifnos. Unlike the sunny islanders I knew, many of them seemed unfriendly and greedy. Kastro was a world unto itself, and a slightly creepy one at that. Over the years, its isolation had created a lot of near-incestuous marriages and affairs, it seemed, and to walk the main street of the village was at times a little like going down a hospital corridor with moaning or, worse, silent invalids lying on their beds, their blank eyes staring out at you through doors left open to the street for fresh air. I found it spooky and depressing, and after a while I began escaping to Apollonia whenever I could, literally running away up the steps to the village high above us and the tables up at Lakis's.

I also often went to Poulati, one of the most beautiful spots on the island and an easy walk along a path built into the cliff above the sea to the north of town. The rather large church and monastery there were tucked against a steep hill that rose up behind it, or rather in front of it, since the entrance court and monks' cells faced inland, to the west, and to Artemona. The vaulted nave of the church stretched east toward the crashing sea below, and an astonishing cerulean-blue dome ringed with bright red tiles floated above it.

A beautiful steep path of marble steps led down from Artemona—which sat high up behind a row of windmills on the crest of the hill—to Poulati. The steps were kept up by a fund left by a wealthy old lady from Artemona; when she was alive, she swam from the rocks and the little beach below the church every day, marching down from her grand house and then climbing back up, a major workout, as I soon found out. Indeed, in later years I would always try to plan my visits to Poulati by starting from Artemona, at the top, and walking down to Poulati, then returning to Kastro along the level trail by the sea. I would tell myself there was no point in getting all hot and sweaty again after swimming, but in reality, the climb back up to Artemona was enough to kill anyone.

Also, there was another climb between the church and the little beach, with its sweet-water spring and grove of bamboo. Tall rocks, like cliffs to nowhere, rose above the beach on the north side, protecting it from the harsh winds. And the lower rocks, scattered at the edge of the water where one sunbathed and swam, were set quite far apart, making it unusually private and wonderful for nude bathing. I would draw, looking back at Kastro from the church or from the rocks themselves, and then strip down, swim, and lie dreamily in the sun, any and all sounds buried by the crashing surf below.

The water there was delicious—warm and clear—but it could be quite rough, and you had to be careful not to be slammed against the rocks when climbing out. One day, swimming happily, blissfully alone, I was suddenly startled by a long, dark shape swimming toward me. My first thought was "shark," and I swam screaming and kicking frantically back to shore. It seemed to take forever, like a bad dream where you swim and swim but cannot escape. But nothing grabbed at my feet, and I was finally able to pull myself, panting and gasping, onto the rocks. Looking back at last, I found a charming face smiling at me, laughing at me: a big seal was floating and bobbing on the waves. I couldn't believe my eyes. No one on Sifnos had ever said anything about seals. I had seen dolphins, and years later I even swam with them once with my visiting nephews off the rocks at Chrissopighi. But this was totally unexpected, and I couldn't wait to get to Lakis's and tell everyone my news.

"I saw a seal! I saw a seal!" I hooted and bragged as I strode in that evening, but no one would believe me. Lakis himself was particularly scornful, telling me I had had too much sun, there were no seals in the Aegean. Finally an old fisherman in the corner said that yes, there actually was a solitary seal out there off the north end of the island. Fishermen had been trying to catch him for years. They hated him because he destroyed their nets and ate all the fish and then came up and floated nearby, grinning at them, taunting them. But he always got away. "You see, you see," I crowed, telling my story again and again to whoever would listen. Of course I carefully omitted my initial terror, my panicked screaming flight from the beast. And as the evening progressed and the retsina kicked in, the seal grew larger and larger, and pretty soon I was swimming with it, playing with it.

Quite a few years later, a small road was built to Poulati, which took away the privacy and exclusivity of its tiny beach, and too many people started going there. It also became known as the place where a slightly crazy island boy would expose himself to screaming ladies and startled men. He was hugely well endowed and would display his member with considerable pride. Even though he was often reported, no one had the heart to arrest him.

I saw him only once in all the years I swam there. He was from Exambela, and I knew him when I had my house there; indeed, I watched him grow up. Once, he tried to climb into my bedroom at night, scaring me half to death, and as gently and politely as possible I turned him away. I talked to him, though, quizzed him about what he thought he was doing climbing into a man's bedroom, and he said he didn't really care what he fucked as long as he fucked. I knew that feeling well enough, I thought. Totally oversexed all the time myself, I could only feel sorry for this boy, this outcast, whom everyone looked on as a half-wit and pervert. Certainly no Sifniot couple was ever going to let their daughter marry him. He still comes to the harbor, meeting ferries regularly, hoping I imagine for someone to step off the boat and love him. Or maybe just for someone to fuck.

Most of the time I was pretty much alone in Kastro. My original friends from the year before, Chuck and the others, were all gone, and though people were always coming and going on the island, most of them didn't spend much time in Kastro. And I didn't seem to make any friends there. A well-known Greek painter lived quite near me—he had his studio in an old school, and I often watched him through the window as he worked—but I was too shy to introduce myself.

My friend Onno, the architect, was nearby, though, only a short walk from Kastro. As I said, he was building a house just above and behind the church at Poulati, back in a little valley above the beach, with a tiny old chapel nearby. From his house-to-be, you could just see the blue dome of the church above the trees. It was an enormous job, building that house, as everything had to be brought down from Apollonia or across the path from Kastro by mule. Though I had no idea of buying a house, as I watched Onno's house go up, a fantasy house of my own must surely have gone through my mind.

The people I saw most often that summer were Onno's half sister

Kastro

Mechtilt and her husband, Jan Meyer, who arrived on the island with their two little boys, Julian and Igor. They were a spectacular-looking couple, tall and blond both of them. Jan was particularly handsome. The boys were beautiful too, and people stopped in their tracks to stare at them. They were both painters, Jan quite famous in Paris, and besides being secretly attracted to him, I was quite envious of him as well. His work seemed very strong, gleaming abstract plains of color laid on with a palette knife, much of it influenced by Nicolas de Staël, with whom he had at one time shared a studio in Antibes, some years before de Staël killed himself by jumping from his eleventh-floor terrace there.

The de Staël connection was impressive to me, since de Staël was a particular hero of mine, for his art and for his Russian heritage, and I was always asking about him—and about Antibes too, where my Russian great-grandparents had had a house that had been built as Henri IV's hunting lodge, called La Bastide du Roi. It was an enormous property, several hundred acres that ran from the outskirts of the hill town of Biot to the sea east of Antibes. They had wintered there for years before the start of the First World War and were there in 1917, when the Russian Revolution began; they stayed on, assuming that the war would end and the tsar would be restored to the throne, and that they, like characters from Chekhov, would one day go back to Moscow.

But when their business, the Dux factories that had produced airplanes for the Russian air force, was confiscated, and when, worse yet, the British, in some kind of Perfidious Albion deal, started closing all private émigré accounts in London and giving the money to the Soviet government, it all began to appear more and more hopeless. My grandfather Georges Brechneff killed himself in Nice. In truth, part of the money problem may have been a family tendency to gamble: my great-grandmother was famous for running up enormous gambling debts year after year, and my grandfather may have had debts of his own. To survive, the family started selling the land in Antibes bit by bit, and some years later the house itself was bought by Mme. Lanvin, founder of the fashion house, as a wedding gift for her daughter, the Comtesse de Polignac. My great-grandparents ended up living out their years raising chickens and rabbits in one of the cottages on what was left of the property—quite a comedown.

My father, who had spent much of his childhood at the Bastide, would never go back there and never talked about it. I never saw so much as a photograph of it. I wasn't even sure if it really existed, and I am sure people I mentioned it to often thought I was making it up—La Bastide du Roi indeed! But Antibes was a magic name for me, and I always wanted to hear more about it.

Mechtilt and I became inseparable, the two of us together all the time, talking, talking, talking. Also a painter, albeit less successful than Jan, she was a remarkable woman, with long blond hair, the bluest eyes, and a glorious body. She knew it too, and was a major flirt with a serious past. I was smitten, but intimidated. She was older than I, married, and very sophisticated. I knew I was way out of my depth and wouldn't have had the guts to make any romantic or sexual advances, but somehow Jan got it into his head to become very jealous of me, and he made life rather difficult for all of us. The absurd part was that I was assuredly more interested in going to bed with him than with her. The situation became impossible, but just when I had decided I should leave the island because of all this tension I appeared to be causing, a telegram came telling Jan that his father had died, and he left on the next ferry. Mechtilt stayed behind with the boys, and peace returned.

A year later, when I was back in Platy Ghialos, everything had changed. Jan was on Sifnos and I found out that he and Mechtilt had separated. I was, of course, intrigued by his being single and upset, at the same time as I was beglamoured by them as a couple and loved them both as friends. I also felt sorry for the little boys. Jan was well over his jealousy by then, eager to be friends, it seemed, and attentive to me and my work. When he visited me, he saw the walls covered with pictures I had made that summer. Studying them, discussing them with me, he made it clear that he thought them too controlled, too tight, not free and abstract enough.

Young as I was, I already knew that the best pictures are the ones that surprise you, but it was very hard for me to let go. Still unformed, eager for a career, anxious about my sexuality, worried about what people thought of me, and far too interested in—what? vindication, I suppose—proving myself to my friends and family, I knew he was probably right. I did tend to control my pictures. Fearing that I was a needy, shapeless boy stumbling around in life, I was desperate to create, in my work at least, a vessel that held water and didn't leak and spill all over the place. And I had a sneaking suspicion that even when I "let myself go," there was possibly something contrived about it, a kind of performance as a young, free, dangerous artist. I wasn't sure I had really tapped into me, into my self, and as he spoke, I wondered whether I ever would, in the same way that I worried whether I would ever sort out my sexuality or whether I would become someone about whom people said, "Isn't he sort of AC/DC?"—a wet, flippy-floppy state of mind and soul and being in which I had absolutely no interest.

As he left, Jan said, "Christian, if you stop looking in the mirror, someday you'll be a good painter."

Certainly I know now, and even then I had the idea that he was not just talking about my vanity. He was talking about my self-consciousness and my efforts at self-control, about my somehow painting a self-portrait, a self-image for the world rather than what I truly meant and felt and saw. Indeed, a teacher at the Royal College had said something similar when he noted that my best pictures were the drawings I did outdoors—quickly, directly, from life, work that was immediate, just eye and hand, without all the thinking and posing and posturing.

Over the years, I have come closer to working like that, but painting in the studio, I still often find myself with the whole picture worked out, literally preconceived, and I know it is too self-conscious, in the real sense of its being about me and my self-image. And it might have been only in work I did later still, in pastel and on the spot, that I approached an instinctive connection of eye and hand and feeling that wasn't compromised by my mind.

It wasn't easy for me. It isn't ever easy, making art. Many painters resort to drugs and liquor to free them up. Francis Bacon and others painted when drunk (though in his case it may have been part of his personal myth making, and very self-conscious indeed), and the sad result is that the history of art is littered with Basquiats who died of their excesses when much too young. In this respect I've always been disciplined. Too disciplined? I don't know. In spite of one of my favorite lyrics in the world being Leonard Cohen's "Like a bird on a wire / Like a drunk in a midnight choir / I have tried in my way to be free," I have never lost sight of what I was doing and what I wanted. And I certainly was never even slightly self-destructive. I've had to be sober to work and maybe to survive—a grandfather who killed himself can make you cautious about these things. But Jan's little tutorial struck home, especially his parting words. Our time that day was intense, personal, intimate, and when he was gone, I collapsed, exhausted—and changed, I was sure. Very moved by his generosity with me and even more smitten than before.

After that summer I never saw him again. Mechtilt and the boys continued to come to Sifnos, and I watched them grow up. It was very hard, later, to learn that Jan died an alcoholic, largely alone, his career having withered away.

—

Platy Ghialos, September 1973

Dearest Parents,

Coming back to Platy Ghialos now at the end of the summer feels like coming to a different island. I did do a lot of work in Kastro, but I was so lonely there, locked away in a tower with these gloomy, often downright hostile people. Finally I got in a fight, one of those Greek blow-ups, with my landlord this time, about who was supposed to supply the toilet paper. Totally stupid, I know, but I got in a huge huff and packed my bags and left. But thank goodness I didn't decide to just stubbornly stick it out and stay there. The moment I arrived back here, everyone was calling, "Christo, Christo." Everyone was happy to see me and welcomed me back. The taverna owners showered me with food and drink and all the potters and farmers invited me by.

I am renting a room from a potter right on the beach. It has one door and one window overlooking the sea, one big bed and a hot plate and a water basin. The swimming is wonderful: I just step out of my room onto the beach and into the water. The landlord's family could not be nicer and bring me sweets, and the grapes that are just coming into season. Further down the beach, at the end of the bay, I can see Georgos's pottery shop and the little cluster of houses that make up the fishermen's village where I lived last year. As

I write, a farmer is walking by on the beach, his donkey loaded with baskets full of pears, and I buy a kilo.

Heaven.

The only thing: they all worry that I live alone and not with a koritsi, a girlfriend. And I try to explain how being here is work for me, not a holiday.

I had slowed down work-wise toward the end there in Kastro, but I hope to throw myself into more paintings before I leave. I did finish a white-on-white painting, my room and the view out through the door to the sea, trying to re-create the white light of day there. [I sold that picture to a friend in Zurich who has since died. I never wanted to sell it, and I now sadly have no idea where it is.]

A few friends are coming tomorrow to celebrate my birthday. Quite a lot of people I know have already left the island. There was a big goodbye party a few days ago in Kamares. The Kalymnos of course managed to be 8 and ½ hours late, finally pulling away at 3.30 a.m. Everyone was totally plastered—waiting for the ferry, what was there to do but drink. Like many departures here it was all quite dramatic, people with heavy backpacks falling noisily, hilariously drunk off the little fishing boats and sinking immediately below the surface. Rumor has it there was quite a bit of action in one of the lifeboats. I crashed on the beach, like the first day I arrived here.

But a few friends will still make the trip tomorrow. It's easy to get here now. The road to Apollonia is finished and a little blue bus struggles back and forth, driven by Iannis with his young smiling cousin Apostolos collecting tickets. The bus gives me more flexibility. And less exercise. No doubt more tourists will come to Platy Ghialos now and though I am happy the locals will make more money, it will change the place. The same for the whole island I guess—they have started building a mole in Kamares, a real dock, so that bigger ships can land with cars and trucks, and of course that will change everything.

I suspect that September is the best month; the tourists have vanished and we have the place to ourselves. The Greeks are busy counting their money from the summer, and even more busy with their grapes and the wine-making season. Last night at the taverna, they danced and sang late into the night and we all got pretty drunk.

I shall reserve the same room next year.

You should come here and take over the room next year when I leave. There's an idea.

Sending you sun and sea.

Christo

23 years old! It is insane!

Twenty-three. I thought I was terribly grown-up, of course, but I was still very young, and young for my age. My life seemed sophisticated to me, living in London, going to the Royal College of Art. The school had such an enormous reputation, and so, in a way, did the students there. And I loved it. Many of the staff were famous—William Scott, David Hockney, Jack Tworkov—and a few of them, like Robert Buhler, I loved. There were some classes and lectures, but mostly it was tutorials, professors coming to your studio and talking about your work, much as Jan had on that summer afternoon. It was a system I loved, and I was good at taking criticism.

But not so good at taking it from my fellow students, whom I loved less. They were so earnest, so serious, so critical—and so competitive. (So, of course, was I.) There were nervous breakdowns and even a few suicide attempts with these high-strung, intense young people out on their creative limbs arguing about Art and trying to make Great Art and, they hoped, to get rich and famous too.

I thought my housing was pretty sophisticated. I had rooms, as the British say, in Evelyn Gardens in South Kensington, where I gave little dinners, strange little quiche-and-salad affairs, with some quite grown-up guests. Half the time I would be running downstairs to the phone, trying to reach my American curator—my lover, as I thought of him—who was dumping me or maybe had dumped me or maybe had taken me back; it went round and round. I would beg and argue on the phone, overexcited and overly emotional, ecstatic one moment, in despair the next.

I was twenty-three.

He was thousands of miles away, in New York, but except for needing and wanting to be in love so badly, I didn't exactly need him there in London. Sex was everywhere. In the early 1970s the city was alive with it—at parties, at clubs, in bars, in the park. Though I had my streak of conventionality and imagined that one day I would go home to Switzerland and marry "well"—indeed, marry up, if possible—that was in the distant future. For the moment, I was very young, and handsome, it appeared—catnip, I was learning, for many kinds of men and women—and in truth the novelty of *that* overexcited me even more than just being in love. I was spinning.

None of this was quite so glamorous or decadent as it sounds. I was such a kid.

Walking home from a party one night, I realized that I was being followed—seriously cruised—by a young man. Rather uncharacteristically, I ignored him at first, hardly glancing back at him, but he kept following me, on and on, even into an alley beyond a small mews that was my quickest route home. Tired, cranky, maybe even a little scared in that dark alley, I finally wheeled on him. "Who the hell are you? What do you want?" A bit nervous, he shyly said his name and told me he was an actor in the West End. He was in fact charming and, on closer inspection, quite good-looking. I thought, Who wouldn't want to go to bed with a West End actor? And what could be more sophisticated than a West End star as a boyfriend. So I did, we did.

It was only afterward that I learned he was not quite the young Larry Olivier I might have been dreaming of, but was playing Eeyore in *Winnie-the-Pooh*.

"It's not much of a tail," says Eeyore, "but I'm sort of attached to it."

—

From my diary, August 26, 1974:

Arrived yesterday in Athens. At the airport, amazingly, no photographs of Colonel Papadopoulos staring down at you from the walls, no passengers, no tourists either, the terminal empty except for a few Greek baggage handlers lounging around on the dead-still conveyor belts and Nothing To Declare counters, smoking endlessly and talking quietly among themselves. Everything subdued. Everybody numb. The Greeks are in shock, their world at a standstill, or at least pausing for breath.

The Junta has fallen, the hated Colonels are gone, and Karamanlis is back in power.

Greece overnight has transformed itself from a pariah state, a military dictatorship famous for arresting and torturing people, into a republic. Although the immediate cause of the Junta's collapse was an ill-fated adventure in Cyprus, a crisis which is still bubbling away—war with Turkey is a real possibility—it was the student uprisings and the Colonels' ferocious response that shredded forever the myth that the Colonels were progressive revolutionaries. They are thugs pure and simple. And, amazingly, they have collapsed like a house of cards.

The streets are hot and dusty, almost empty. Most people seem to be staying in their homes, not quite hiding but . . . Nobody knows what will happen next. Will the Colonels regroup and come back? Will the king, whom the Colonels exiled, return? Do the Greeks want him to return? Not much. He had seemed so much better than Paul and the hated Frederica, young, handsome, an Olympic gold medalist, no less, but he was totally compromised by his complicity in the Colonels' rise to power. And then only seemed pathetic when he tried a coup against them from the North, from Thessaloníki—a flat-out catastrophe.

Athens is waiting for the page to be turned for good. No Ottomans, no Germans, no Italians, no Kings, no Colonels. What was called the Cradle of Democracy actually finally is one. And I guess nobody can quite believe it.

—

It was an amazing time—with the Colonels' collapse, their trials and imprisonment, all unthinkable a year before, and King Constantine, no doubt dreaming of a warm welcome home from his exile in Rome, being voted out by the end of the year, this time for good. I was not a big diary keeper, but at the time, even I was aware that I was living history and should put down what was going on and what I saw.

From the airport I took the bus to Piraeus. There were a few ferries in the harbor, but none of the usual cruise ships, no yachts, no pleasure boats. Instead, the harbor was full of warships, dozens of huge, hulking gray things bristling with guns pointing in every direction, hovering incongruously out there on the perfect, glittering blue-green sea. I found a sleazy hotel-slash-hostel, booked a bed in a room I knew I would probably have to share—it had three other beds—and, exhausted, dragged myself out for dinner at a nearby taverna. There was hardly anyone in the tiny restaurant, no one talking. Everyone was reading the papers, just reading and smoking and drinking, reading every article, every word.

I was happy that the Colonels were gone, but I was politically naïve. I knew hardly anything about Cyprus other than that the crisis had come from a flare-up of the longtime hatred between the Greeks and the Turks there. I didn't realize that Cyprus, even more than the collapse of the Junta, was the reason there were no tourists in Athens, since the situation could blow up into a war at any moment. I couldn't get a handle on it, didn't really understand it. All I cared about was my art and Sifnos and going back there no matter what. I was tired from my trip, and after some calamari and wine I headed back to the hostel and bed.

Then suddenly, in the street, a handsome young sailor right out of a Yannis Tsarouchis painting came up to me. Tsarouchis was famous for his wonderfully sexy pictures of half-naked sailors in Piraeus and was, even back then, a favorite of mine among Greek artists. Standing in front of me, hands on his slim, perfect hips, he said, "Hallo." Big smile. "You like sex with boys?" What? "Yes. *Ne.*" Yes, I replied eagerly, suddenly wide-awake. But it was over before it even began: he had nowhere to go, and I thought there would be someone else in my horrible dormitory room in the hostel, and I didn't have enough money to take a nicer room.

I watched him walk away, so desirable in his tight white uniform, watched him until he turned a corner and disappeared.

I went up to my room only to find two sailors asleep in their beds there. Curiouser and curiouser. I collapsed onto mine, had a moment fantasizing about sailors, and then fell sound asleep. Only to be woken in the middle of the night by the two of them having sex! And not very quiet sex. I nearly went crazy. What to do? Watch them? Join them? Tell them to shut up? Finally it was over, and they slept like babies. I was awake all night.

Piraeus had its charms, it seemed, but sexy as my evening both was and was not, I knew I had to spend a little money next time and, as they say, get a room.

—

The *Kalymnos*, the old tub, sailed the next day at nine in the morning, almost on time. No fresh paint since the year before. I guessed a political explosion was as good an excuse as any for zero maintenance, but it made me wonder how much longer she would be making this trip, especially now that there was the new mole and dock in the Kamares harbor. The *Kalymnos* had no big gates or off-ramps to load and unload cars. Perhaps her owners were just saving money, knowing that (I hoped) her days were numbered.

At the boat too, there weren't any tourists, but there was the usual hustle and bustle of island Greeks going aboard, weathered old farmers, fishermen, a few Athenians who summered on islands, several popes in black. Finally, surprise, surprise, an old pickup truck was hoisted on board and secured on deck for the voyage, the ship's horns and whistles blew, and we began to move.

The ship was old and dirty and smelly, but for me it was heaven there on the deck as she wove through the warships packing the harbor. After looking at the rather intimidating firepower on view, the islanders as usual made their way down to their cabins. They dreaded the open air at sea and would sleep the whole way, portholes and doors shut tight, blankets over their heads. Exhausted from the sleepless night before, I found an empty bench in the shade, where I could stretch out and sleep.

In spite of, or maybe because of the brand-new mole, an ugly pile of concrete and stone sticking straight out into the harbor, the arrival seemed more chaotic than usual. No longer having to wait to go over and down the ship's side to the caïques, the passengers getting off drove those ahead of them forward like cattle—old men, women, children, it didn't matter who, toward the tiny exit doors and the gangway. I was fairly pushy myself, eager to get off the stinking tub, hoping to find Apostolos, the cabdriver, to help get me and my luggage to Platy Ghialos.

"*Iassu, Christo. Iassu,*" people greeted me as they pushed by to meet their friends and family on the crowded dock. "*Iassu, iassu,*" they called out, shaking hands, slapping me on the back as they struggled with their mysterious boxes and clumsy sacks. Then, for a moment, we all stopped and stood gaping as the pickup truck was lowered over the side. When I turned back, Apostolos suddenly appeared and helped me take my mound of luggage and supplies to his old taxi. I climbed in—and all the strangeness of Athens and discomfort of the journey was completely forgotten.

I had come straight from Cornwall, where I had been painting, and the contrast was a shock. In Cornwall there was nothing but green—heavy, lush, almost wet green. And I hated green. A painter's privilege: it is murderously hard to paint. But midsummer Sifnos was already dry. Bouncing over the still-new dirt road, the warm air blowing in my face, I stared out at the dusty golden fields, the silver-leafed olive trees, everything drowning in light mauves and silver, gold, and rose tones in the early-evening light, soft and weightless—can light have weight?—like the pale, shiny color inside the chambers of a nautilus shell. As we came over the ridge at the top of the island, the sun setting behind us, the sunlit islands sparkled and glittered like gold and turquoise jewels against the already dark sea and sky. In my room in Platy Ghialos, where I went after more hellos, I lay in my fresh bed thinking about this other world of mine—it was my third year—and stared around me at the white, white walls, imagining all the pictures I would cover them with.

The next day, I started working right away, slipping back into my island routine, painting in the morning, reading, hiking, and sketching, visiting friends in the afternoon and evening. I was struck by how untouched Sifnos was, how unfazed the islanders seemed by this Big Moment in Greek History. In Athens, everyone had appeared poleaxed, knocked sideways by the change, but riveted, engaged, closely following events as they fell out. On Sifnos one hardly felt that anything had happened. They knew all about it—Cyprus, the Colonels, the king—but for them the news was a message in a bottle about a cataclysm in an alternate universe.

Isolated and deeply traditional, basically royalist at heart—back then almost every house on the island still had a picture of the king on the wall—the Sifniots had always been at several removes physically from the Greek present. And of course there were no televisions or telephones, no newspapers unless they were weeks old, and only recently had electricity or radios appeared. They didn't know about the changes sweeping through Athens, the exiles returning from Paris, the trials of the Colonels, or films like Costa-Gavras's *Z*, a movie about the Junta that had enthralled and appalled the world and was now finally being shown in Athens, years after it had been made. Sifnos was a world unto itself, nearly as far away as a village in the depths of the Amazon jungle. The people at Lakis's talked not of politics or the new Greek world, but about crops, local business, local gossip.

Mind you, there was nothing tragic or melancholic about them. This was not the forgotten, cast-off village of Fellini's *Amarcord*, whose provincial citizens yearn for the world of Rome or Milan, all the villagers sailing out in their fishing boats to meet a huge new ocean liner only to have it sail by, aglitter with lights, towering above them, the Great World nearly swamping them as it sweeps past, leaving them in its wake.

Monastery of tou Vounou

Sifnos was not lost or forgotten or even provincial; it was a small island of the past, a living tradition captured like a creature in amber. Now there was a mole and a road, and I had seen a pickup truck being unloaded from the ship—the arrival of the wheel—but for the time being, it seemed that nothing had changed.

—

That first week, I hiked up to Agios Simeon, a four-hour walk from Artemona, for a *panaghia*. As I approached, the sky suddenly turned violent—dark, dark blue-mauve, the whiteness of the monastery walls splashed with pink from the setting sun. I got an ouzo and mingled with the largely Artemona crowd, most of them local farmers but also summer people or people with Athenian connections. Even they talked almost exclusively about local things, crops, a neighbor's death, a child's illness, an inheritance, the land. On Sifnos it was always all about the land.

The church service was long, but eventually the chanting ended and the traditional feast began, followed by songs on the *lauto* or violin, singing and dancing under the full moon. By midnight, with the priest's permission, I crept back into the lovely church, only one or two candles lit now, and lay down in my sleeping bag to try to sleep there. At three, I was woken up: the church was full again, with the priests celebrating Mass before pilgrims who were now slightly drunk. The smell of incense, the celebrations and music, the warmth of the islanders filled me with happiness. Finally everyone filed out, and I watched them as, still singing, they slowly went down the mountain to their villages in the moonlight. I went back in and slept.

I woke at sunrise, the sky turning golden red as the sun came up between distant Naxos and Páros, and I started down the mountain. By eleven-thirty, tired but exhilarated, I was having figs, bread, and coffee in my farmer-neighbor Stavros's house.

How could one not be grateful that such a world existed, complete and intact.

—

Looking back now, I know I was witnessing a watershed, a turning point, the beginning of Greece's reentry into modern Europe and the modern world. Since the end of the Second World War, or at least the Greek Civil War, Greece had been assumed to be part of the new postwar Europe, a distant, slightly backward part perhaps, but still guaranteed a seat at the European table. With the takeover by the Colonels in 1967, Greece had been cast out, left standing "over there," dead economically and politically. But now Greece was about to be brought back into the fold.

For a time, in truth, Greece seemed to continue to stand still. For the next few years it remained a near–third world country, poky and backward. But the change had begun, certainly in Athens, and eventually it would be everywhere, on the islands, even places as remote as Sifnos. And the change was irresistible. Mechtilt, remarkably prescient, wrote me a postcard that summer: "Enjoy to the depth of your soul and body the island. It won't last forever."

It was tourism that started the change. What began as a trickle of mostly young tourists on the mainland and the bigger islands turned into a wave. The older and richer tourists generally came on cruise ships and stayed on cruise ships, but the young ones fanned out across the Aegean and its islands. Greece was famously sunny and warm. And cheap. Backpackers from northern Europe and America started pouring off the boats, sometimes renting rooms but just as often crashing on the beaches and in the caves dotting the island shores.

Sifnos stayed relatively apart from all this and has till this day, mostly because it has no airport. But even Sifnos began to change, however slowly. The new mole and new dock in Kamares brought the world to Sifnos. From now on, bigger and bigger boats were going to dock, opening their bows and sterns and letting cars and trucks laden with all kinds of goods onto the island. The little caïques sadly went out of business, and soon the sons and grandsons of fishermen became bartenders and hotel clerks.

In the early 1970s you felt you could count these young tourists on the fingers of two hands. But soon there were more and more of them—boys and girls traveling together, swimming nude together off the rocks and beaches below the churches, sleeping together, having tons of sex together, and taking drugs together, I am sure.

And almost immediately this had an impact. The islanders were innately hospitable, and they wanted the money that came with tourism, even low-grade, backpacker tourism like this. But they were often scandalized by the behavior of these young people. On an island where traditionally, teenage boys and girls never so much as touched one another, all these kids swimming nude and having sex all over the place deeply shocked them.

I was at times, in spite of myself, part of this culture clash, the islanders being so very conservative and me often being turned on by one beautiful, slim, tanned young tourist or the other. On the beach one day I met a petite dancer from Boston who moved in with me for a time. Meagan, who had an incredible body and occasionally posed for me, was on her way to India on the cheap, and aside from our mutual attraction, she did not seem unhappy to share a cozy room on the beach with me for a time.

Early on in our fleeting relationship, she told me, rather brazenly, I thought—this kind of talk was new to Swiss me too, not just to old-fashioned Greeks—that she had picked up crabs from bed linens in a cheap Piraeus hotel. Hmm, I thought, a likely story (though the same thing was to happen to me a few years later, getting crabs from the bedding in the Delphini Hotel, cross my heart). When she got to Sifnos—a week or so before we met—desperate to get rid of the horrible itching, biting things, she found her way to the island's only pharmacy, no easy task, as it was hidden away in a private house on a side street. Sifniots were not yet used to modern medicine, and they slipped off to the pharmacist furtively, as if visiting a drug dealer.

Since she hardly knew a word of Greek and certainly not the word for crabs, she just walked into the shop holding a tiny wriggling crab between her fingers while pointing at her crotch. As if a rocket had been fired and was streaming toward the front stoop where his young children were innocently playing, the horrified pharmacist began yelling at them, grabbing and shoving them to the back of the shop, where he slammed the door on them and his baffled, panicked wife. Hurriedly, he got Meagan the necessary medicine and unceremoniously threw her out.

A few days after telling me this, unbeknownst to me, Meagan made the decision that we really should be using condoms, so she took herself off again, back to the same, the only pharmacy to buy them. *"Panaghia mou, panaghia mou,"* the unhappy man howled at the sight of her, wanting to throw this obvious whore out of his shop. But tiny Meagan was not to be dissuaded, and she showed him in vivid sign language what it was she wanted and then insisted on "extra-large" condoms (I blush), much to the amusement of some village ladies in the shop, who collapsed in hysterics. She got her condoms but never dared go there again for fear of being stoned to death.

—

Years later I came to refer to the hill that rose behind and above Chrissopighi as the Gold Coast, since so many grand houses and villas were being built there, where once had been none. The first, indeed the first "villa" to be built on Sifnos since at least the 1920s, was started at the beginning of the seventies, while the Junta was still in power. It was owned by a wealthy American family whom the island rumor mill had as friends of the Colonels, probably for no other reason than that they were Americans, and Americans, back then, were all assumed to be in cahoots with the Junta.

The older grand houses, in patrician Artemona especially, seemed part of the organic design of the villages. This large new house sat alone astride the top of the hill, a tan, Spanish-looking three-story stucco structure with lots of windows, arches, and French doors. The island people disliked its size, especially its height, towering as it did above what was considered the most beautiful church on Sifnos, and I certainly didn't disagree. When I first had a chance to tour the house, all I could manage to say was that it had beautiful views, which indeed it did, amazing views. But now, some thirty years later, the cypresses and pines and olive trees the owners lovingly planted on that windswept hill have grown enough to better integrate the house with the landscape.

In fact, I was to become fond of the owners, for they loved their house and loved Sifnos—and they are still there. I met them at a wedding in the church at Chrissopighi, the wedding of Aleco and Helen Philon. In years to come, Chrissopighi was to become probably the most famous wedding site in Greece, and people booked the little church years in advance, but this was the first big wedding there, most likely the most extraordinary event anyone had ever seen on the island, and people talked about it for years.

I knew Aleco and Helen slightly from London. He was a diplomat, son of (I love this) Philon A. Philon, Greek ambassador to the United States just after the war. Aleco was soon to be an ambassador himself, and Helen was an art dealer from a shipping family with roots on Sifnos. I scarcely knew them, but when they arrived on the island and learned I was there, they were kind enough to invite me to the wedding.

The invitation to such a major event rather dramatically changed my position on Sifnos. "You must be rich if you know these people," the owner of my little room on the beach said, smiling hopefully. "Oh, no." I tried to explain. "These are people who have bought my pictures in London, and I was only invited because they knew I was here." But no one really believed me. And all at once Christo was not just a poor young artist, but a well-connected somebody. This was an odd feeling and a mixed blessing, I thought, my gaining a little glamour and glory but losing anonymity and control over the way my Christo persona was seen.

I was ambivalent, and not just about the islanders imagining I was some little princeling. I knew I was cruising rather closer to the sun than usual, and excited and flattered as I was (I would have loved it unquestioningly in London or Zurich), I was uncomfortable about it on Sifnos. Sifnos was my secret place, my retreat from the world, and suddenly here were all these people who were about to arrive—some of whom I knew—from London, New York, even Switzerland. I think it was the Swiss who made me the most anxious. I mean, in a way I was delighted to have them see me there, swanning around at this wedding, but they were the last people I wanted anywhere near my sanctuary, stomping around on my newly found and barely secured turf.

But on the wedding day there I was, sipping champagne in the little churchyard of Chrissopighi, with the *von* Thises and *de* Thats, with elegantly dressed Greek shipowners, diplomats, art dealers, and jet-setters, while around us, in the bay and off the rocky point, dozens of flag-decked yachts rolled and bobbed on the unusually rough sea. Clouds and heavy winds had been building all morning, and the arrival of the bridal party was pretty dramatic. Looking up, we watched the bride in her salmon-pink Zandra Rhodes dress and all the other ladies in their Saint Laurents, Diors, and God knows what other haute couture dresses as they came down the steep marble steps—there was no paved road, remember, no road at all—tottering on their high, high heels while holding on to their dresses and their broad-brimmed hats, trying to keep them from billowing and flapping away in the wind.

They were amazing, these creatures, fabulous, like long-legged exotic birds, a vision from a Fellini film, I thought. I was dazzled; we all were. But what did the islanders think of this spectacle? Indeed, what did they think of a salmon-pink wedding dress? Of course Helen had been married before, even had a son, who was there, so she would not wear white. But there was no such thing, really, as divorce on the island, and salmon pink? On Sifnos?

Suddenly the sky filled with dark, threatening clouds, making all the dresses seem even more vivid and astonishing. Yipes. Would it rain? "Happy is the bride it rains upon," said one of the dark, handsome young Greeks standing near me, laughing, quoting what seemed a pretty dubious proverb. But then, just as suddenly, the sky cleared, and as the sun poured down again, the bridal party entered the courtyard and we all turned and followed them into the church.

I hung back a bit while all these beautifully dressed people, in their big hats and brightly colored clothes, packed into the tiny church. In front of the golden altar screens were a whole slew of priests in their fine robes, a few metropolitans and patriarchs among them, I was sure, brought in from Athens for the ceremony. I looked around at the incongruous crowd—literally jet-setters, I thought—marrying off two of their own in this little white peasant church with its little blue fishing-boat model hanging from the ceiling, the old blue casement windows rattling in the wind, the rough sea crashing on the rocks just outside.

I had been to weddings on Sifnos before, but never one like this. The location notwithstanding, the ceremony was very high church, long and complex. There were two parts to it, a Service of Betrothal and a Sacrament of Marriage, and as if that weren't enough ritual to keep us occupied for quite a while, each part, every single step, had to be repeated three times, apparently symbolizing the Holy Trinity.

The wedding began when candles were handed to Aleco and Helen. The priest took and blessed their rings, placing them on the third finger of their right hands. The *koumbaro*, the best man, swapped the rings back and forth between them three times. Then the priest placed crowns on their heads, joined by white ribbons, and the *koumbaro* switched them back and forth three times. With the reading of the Gospel—the passage about the marriage at Cana, when Christ turned water into wine—Aleco and Helen were given wine, each drinking from the cup three times. The priest then led the bride and groom around the altar, you guessed it, three times, the ever-busy *koumbaro* following along, holding their crowns in place. Finally, the priest blessed the couple, separating their joined hands with a Bible to remind them that only God could break this union.

This seemingly interminable ceremony was strangely moving,

and at the end there was hardly a dry eye in the church. I'm a weeper at weddings to this day, and I found myself quietly tearing up too.

The wedding party made its way out of the church onto the terrace, the rest of us streamed out after them, and everyone stood around chatting and laughing and air kissing anyone they hadn't already air kissed. Soon, though, smartly uniformed crew members began handing some of the luckier guests into the elegant launches that would take them to their yachts, in which they would sail around to the other side of the island to the reception in Kamares, where Helen's brother-in-law, Costa Carras, had a house. The rest of us climbed up the steep hill, no mean feat, especially for the dressed-up ladies, and then piled, gasping, into the little island buses waiting there to take us to the party.

And what a party! I didn't even know such a world existed on Sifnos. Uniformed servants passed elegant hors d'oeuvres and poured champagne, and a feast was spread out on the tables—huge platters of lobster prepared by Nikos, a local fisherman I knew, who stood proudly behind his table, beaming, and gave me a big, conspiratorial wink. There was music and dancing, the most fun to watch being the *syrtos*, an elegant but quite athletic dance in which the dancers hold on to each other by handkerchiefs, which they wave back and forth over their heads; they follow a leader, who sets the complex pattern of steps, with the line crossing and recrossing, and also sets the pace, which becomes steadily faster and faster, wilder and wilder. I felt sorry for poor Helen: she had removed her shoes but was being danced to death in all the excitement, and she looked exhausted. Indeed, after the meal was served, she and Aleco disappeared into a room upstairs.

There were any number of beauties there, men and women, dark, sexy, and charming, as young, wealthy Greeks can be. At dinner I fell under the spell of a Greek woman named Hara, a handsome creature dressed in pale apple green with a huge silver belt. She puffed Gitanes throughout the meal in the Greek manner of those days, and she had a deep smoker's voice and a marvelous accent.

She was a journalist from Athens, very politically involved—and captivating. Sensual, full of mystery, she had a deep sadness in her eyes, I thought, in my youthful romantic way. Alas, she was there with a girlfriend and had little interest in me; she vanished with her lover after lunch the next day, leaving on the ferry back to Athens.

Suddenly, rather startlingly and confusingly for me, the bride and groom appeared on the balcony above, shaking out their "sheets" covered with red stains and hanging them over the balcony rail. I had heard of this Mediterranean tradition but had never witnessed it; it was impossible to imagine such a thing at the weddings of off-spring of the gnomes of Zurich. It was obviously a joke, a kind of sophisticated prank, a modern take on an ancient Mediterranean custom. Everyone laughed and applauded. I understood the joke, but, perhaps having no true relationship with the earthy tradition behind it, I wasn't sure whether I thought it funny or strange or even possibly offensive. I knew it was meant as a witty comment on their culture, but I couldn't help wondering what it seemed like to a fisherman such as Nikos or any of the islanders working there that day.

Not everyone left the island right away, and the next day, I hiked up to Profitis Elias, the highest mountain on the island, with two of the guests who had stayed, two very attractive men. After a delicious picnic of leftovers, we watched the sun going down, dropping suddenly, almost violently, a red splashdown over the Cycladic world that was spread in front of us. And then I spent a restless night in my sleeping bag, tossing and turning there between them, as usual in an agony of dim-witted indecision. Were they gay? Or just one of them? What to do, what to do? Who had meant to do what to whom? Who was the one too many? Should one have sex or even make love in a church courtyard? I was later to learn that they were both gay, and one of them in particular was interested in me, but timid and baffled, I spent another one of my restless, sleepless nights.

Early in the morning we ran down the mountain path, snakes and vipers slithering ahead of us, scattering in fear.

The night had been confusing, but the whole thing was confusing—my worlds, my lives colliding here for the first time. I wouldn't have missed the wedding for anything, but I had no idea where to put it, this experience, where to fit it into my life there.

—

September 1974

Dear Parents,

I have no sense of time here at all. It flows, it flies, it drags, it stops and flows again. If I didn't have my new pictures creeping across my white walls day by day, marking time, I would have no way to measure the days and weeks. I work here every morning, then in the afternoon walk all over the island, wandering everywhere, stopping here and there to draw. I sit in a grove of olive trees, drawing them, rows of them, their branches dancing in the wind. I sit in front of one of them, mimicking with my pen all those oddly human shapes, trunks and roots like ancient arms and legs, and those strange sexy holes, cavities, orifices, really, where the roots grow into and over one another.

Reading a lot of Anaïs Nin, her journals. Thanks for suggesting them, Dita. Not wanting them to end, no matter how repetitive and self-involved she is—feel right at home with that. Love her. And I worship Henry Miller who I am also reading, "The Colossus of Maroussi." Takes me to the heart of this place, this world of earth and sky and light that is becoming my mother and my muse.

Speaking of Greek light, he says:

". . . Light acquires a transcendental quality: it is not the light of the Mediterranean alone, it is something more. Something unfathomable, something holy. Here the light penetrates directly to the soul, opens the doors and windows of the heart, makes everything clear without being known."

How can I paint that? Capture that. That holy light. It is a holy light, that light, everywhere, penetrating. Wisdom without a lot of intellecting, without sitting parsing, dissecting, analyzing everything.

But how to paint it?

Indeed my paintings are becoming more figurative, more specifically this landscape as it is, abstracted yes but, more figurative than even before. The mountains, the churches, the olive trees, even the fields of bright flowers, the red poppies especially are creeping into my work.

My landlords here are so kind to me, asking me to supper last night, fresh fish from their day's catch. They, like everyone, treat me a little differently since the wedding. Or maybe it just seems that way, me being so self-conscious. Two days ago I was invited for lunch at one of the grand Artemona houses through wedding-party acquaintances. My first time in one of those villas. Very impressive, high ceilings, square rooms with tall windows, large columned porches and terraces looking out over island farmland and the sea—dreamy. MAIDS in uniform serving a kind of French-y lunch, no smelly mizithra, no lamb, no stuffed tomatoes; vichyssoise to start with, then langoustes, and take it from there. Linen napkins, beautiful glasses, crystal. Guests in dark glasses talking right and left in French and English, smoking smoking madly. Sort of strange for Sifnos.

We should all be here someday together.

Your Christo

—

During those years, my world on the island was growing. By now I knew everyone in Platy Ghialos and I had begun to know people in some of the other villages. Obviously one got to know all the shopkeepers and restaurant owners and taxi drivers, and I had at least a nodding acquaintance with the regulars at Lakis's. But I was beginning to know other Greeks who had houses there and also the *xenoi*, foreigners, who owned or rented houses. Truth to tell, any off-islander qualified as a *xenos*; an Athenian, even someone from nearby Mílos, was a foreigner, and I wasn't so sure that deep in the heart of a farmer from Exambela, someone from Artemona or Kastro wasn't a *xenos* too.

Returning every year, I was bound to get to know people, if only from running into them in restaurants or at the beaches. And perhaps because of the wedding, I was no longer just some kid who kept popping up every summer. I had somehow grown up for them, become a person they recognized. Some of the people I met were quite grand, such as my linen-napkin acquaintances in Artemona, whose friendship was a direct fallout from the wedding. And some were quite famous painters, writers, poets, and musicians. I wished I knew many of them better, but I often felt my Greek was simply not good enough. I was learning it slowly, and although eventually I got a tutor and became relatively fluent, at least to other *xenoi*, the island Greek I spoke often embarrassed me and made me shy with educated Greeks.

Evangelos Profilengos, a well-known poet, lived in a wonderful big, shabby old house on the edge of Exambela. The famous artist Panayiotis Tetsis was virtually a next-door neighbor in Kastro, but I had been too shy to talk to him. And Argyris Kounadis, a composer married to a German, had a house in Exambela and a charming son and daughter who often visited. And there was also a well-known art critic, Mr. Xidi, whose name means vinegar in Greek, a perfect match, given his criticism and his acidic personality.

Naturally, it was easier as a foreigner to get to know other foreigners. Among them was Paul Mitarachi, a Greek-American architect who lived in Boston with his American wife and young son. (There was quite a group of Greek-Americans from Boston on Sifnos for some reason.) He came from a well-known Chios family but had been born in Alexandria. His late father, a painter, had exiled himself to Paris during the time of the Colonels, and his French mother had been born in Romania but now lived much of the time on Sifnos. This wonderfully polyglot family made us Swiss-Russian Brechneffs look like pikers when it came to multiculturalism, and I envied Paul's ability to glory in not belonging. This was part of the romance for me of Durrell and his Alexandrian world, of course—a city of Egyptians, Greeks, Italians, Jews, and more, all mixing together, the absolute antithesis of the tight, closed world of Basel, and a world that is sadly gone forever.

Then there was an American family I came to know well—Steve and Brenda Star, he a professor at Harvard and then MIT, she a sculptor, the two of them returning regularly with their two amazingly bookish young boys, Alexander and Anthony. Neither boy went anywhere on Sifnos without a book in his hand, and not, I assure you, a child's book, but Dickens, George Eliot, or Fitzgerald. For the Stars, as for so many of us, Sifnos was a magnet drawing them back year after year until Steve died, way too young. The Stars rented the Psacharopoulos house, a big square Artemona villa set on a high terrace with a breathtaking view of the island down to Kastro and the sea. Sometimes the owner, Nikos Psacharopoulos, a Sifniot who was a theater director in America, would be in residence himself. This was his family house, and although he lived mostly in the States, one would glimpse him from time to time, an elegant figure in white slacks standing on his beautiful old-world terrace. Mostly, though, he rented out the house; later, and particularly after his death, friends of mine often rented it for a week or two, or a month at a time.

In Exambela, even before I moved there, there were the Colemans, a British couple, he a judge, she a painter, and their two daughters. They had bought the old village "theater," a large hall with several attached rooms that had been turned into bedrooms. It was a charming, eccentric sort of house, the only problem being its loose un-stuccoed stone walls—shades of my old ruin. Indeed, one of their daughters was badly bitten by a scorpion. As with the Stars and the Mitarachis, I watched their children grow up and go through the changes of youth, many of which seemed heightened, perhaps, by these young people being removed from their normal worlds, but also by the charged atmosphere of the island, the combination of simplicity, even purity, and harsh rawness that gave everything a sexual subtext. I mean, I was always overstimulated there, and I can't believe they weren't turned on as well. The Colemans still go to Exambela, and one of the daughters, grown now, and her husband have bought the house next door.

Also in Exambela was Evelyn Laud, a very British lady who bought Serge and Roger's house, the one I had always been peering into. She had two pleasant if rather Horse Guards–y sons who visited from time to time. She fell victim to the sexual subtext of the island,

I think, eventually having a very painful love affair with an Athenian who had a house on the island. Over the years, lots of women came to Sifnos, lots and lots of them. Many were rather like those British women who headed to the Middle East or North Africa in the nineteenth century, seeking something else, something Other. Going to a Greek island wasn't going quite so far as to the "Wilder Shores of Love" or dancing with the Bedu, but they may have felt themselves at least partway there.

It was difficult, though, for women alone on Sifnos. The islanders didn't know what to make of them. It was assumed that they were loose women, and the village women no doubt saw them as a threat. One of them, Frossa, a sculptor from Athens, didn't help change that view much. She was a friendly, sexy (could-be) redhead who slept with men so openly and casually—so innocently, really—that she developed quite a serious/hilarious reputation. Men would joke, not unkindly, "Have you been frossed lately?"

There were also lots of young women, girls, who came to Greece for the same reason girls went to Italy, to Capri, or Portofino, looking for fun and sex in the sun with romantic dark-haired men. The bars and clubs of Mykonos and Santorini were filled with local (and nonlocal) lotharios, amateurs or professionals who could show these girls a good time. Sifnos had only the one, Andonis. Quite handsome in his youth, with his perfect, gleaming (albeit cap-toothed) smile and dark, slicked-back hair, he would wait for the boats in Kamares, legs crossed, leaning against his motorcycle. He had a good deal of success; more often than not, he emerged from the melee at the dock with a long-legged blonde on the back of his bike, and they'd zoom off up the hill to Apollonia or to the beach. Island gossip had it that he loved his motorcycle more than he loved his girls.

Another foreigner with a house in Exambela was Johannes Hoffman, who lived there with his wife. He was very small, she very tall, so at first glance they were a comical pair. He was a talented artist—both a painter and a violinist. Once, when I was playing a tape of my friend the singer Frederica von Stade, an early Mozart album, the sound sailing out over the village, Johannes materialized at my studio door, rapt, as if holding his breath. During a pause, in an awed, hushed voice he said, *"Was für eine Mozart-Stimme!"* What a Mozart voice!

He—not unlike a few foreigners on the island, or indeed on islands all over the world—was a terrible drunk, and he and his wife fought often. When I was at their house for dinner one evening, he took his violin and bashed her over the head with it. Still young, still Swiss, I completely freaked out; I had never known or imagined such a thing. His wife said, "Oh, that's just his artistic temperament!" His drinking got worse and worse, however. Luckily, I was able to buy a small drawing from him, a lovely thing, for soon after that visit to my studio his wife threw him out. He left the island and was never seen there again. I was told he died a few years later in Tuscany. His wife still lives on Sifnos in the summertime with her girlfriend, who presumably doesn't hit her over the head with things.

Among my favorite foreigners on the island were an American couple, Bob and Louise Keeley. A career diplomat, he was ambassador to Greece in the 1980s. Ardent liberal Democrats, they were outspoken, opinionated, fun. I enjoyed the sight of them arriving at any one of the tiny restaurants on Sifnos. They had no say in the matter, I am sure, but their security arrangements made it quite a show: first two or three black SUVs would arrive outside, then three security men would fan out from the door, whirling and twirling into the room, coiled wires hanging from their ears, eyes darting around, checking the place out while they whispered mysteriously into their lapels. Finally, a signal was given, and they would guide the Keeleys, looking a bit sheepish, to their table, where they would order the stuffed tomatoes and meatballs with the rest of us.

They had built a house in Kastro and loved it there—or loved it except for the goats. They had bought the property from a slightly mad old farmer who, when showing the land, simply chucked stones here and there to mark the boundaries of the property and, though he was very rich, continued to live in a kind of hovel below their house with his herds and herds of goats. The goats ran riot all year all over their property. No one was quite sure whether the old man encouraged it, herding the goats in their direction, or whether, as in *Elephant Walk*, the old Liz Taylor film, they had inadvertently built the house across some ancient goat path to water. The goats ate everything, every flower, every shrub, every vine, everything the Keeleys and their gardener, Koula, planted. The Keeleys would wake in the morning to find thirty or forty goats on the terrace, sheltering from the wind. Louise kept a bucket of stones by the door, and I loved the image of her with her always perfectly coiffed hair hurling stones at the goats to drive them away.

—

While my life on Sifnos seemed to me to be more and more settled, with me returning every year to the same room in the potter's hut in Platy Ghialos, my life in London and Switzerland—my real life?—was becoming more confusing. My time in London was winding down; I was to graduate in 1975, and I was not sure what was to follow. I suppose, for my age and situation, much of my confusion was perfectly usual (I can't quite say normal). As an artist I wasn't doing badly. I was having shows, selling pictures, even receiving some prestigious honors, such as the *Eidgenössisches Kunststipendium*, the Swiss Federal scholarship for Fine Art. I was obsessed by work and my career-to-be, by my pictures and their "direction," by being an artist and by Art itself. Excited, awed, sometimes moved to tears by the art I saw in museums and galleries, I could also be supercritical—and competitive. And always self-absorbed. Once, I visited an artist in her studio, and as I left, she chided me gently, saying, "Next time you visit a painter, try to talk about their work a little and not just about your own."

Still, more often than not I was frazzled and anxious and—as always, from my childhood on—quite literally *dépaysé*. I had been born in what was then the Belgian Congo to effectively stateless

Kastro

parents. As a Russian émigré, my father had only a Nansen passport, and when my mother married him, she was stripped of her Swiss citizenship, so we were all stateless—I was five years old before we had Swiss passports. I was totally confused by everyone in Africa speaking Swahili or French and, upon returning to Switzerland, everyone in Basel speaking German, so I just didn't speak at all. Then one day, when I was about four, my half-uncle walked by me and casually snatched off my head the cowboy hat I loved and always wore, and I snapped, *"C'est mon chapeau, du dumme Siech,"* that's my hat, you stupid jerk. As anyone who knows me can tell you, I haven't stopped talking since.

To top everything off, Basel was the tightest, clubbiest, snobbiest city in Switzerland (well, maybe after Geneva), and I was always an outsider. I never belonged, never felt part of my world nor even part of my own life.

What I loved about Sifnos was that there, I felt none of this distress: I was in a foreign country, but Sifnos was mine, my place, my invention. I was creating a life for myself there, even an identity of my own, young Christo. It was my escape, my sanctuary. On Sifnos I could escape my history, my family, my up-and-down career, my sometime lovers—all the distress and pressure I felt so often rising up in me.

The most tormenting of all these difficulties by far was my confusion about sex. I was obsessed by sex, baffled by my feelings and urges. But on Sifnos I felt I had some kind of control. At least there I had boundaries, even if self-imposed. Anywhere else, I was all over the place sexually—madly in love, yes, sometimes, but more often simply driven, with no self-control at all.

Kathryn Grody, an American actress friend who was staying with me in London, crashing (platonically) in my tiny flat in Evelyn Gardens, was in the West End one day, standing in line to get tickets for some Maggie Smith–Vanessa Redgrave smash hit, when she met another American, a tiny redhead named Melissa, an actress studying at the Bristol Old Vic. They got to talking, and somehow it transpired that I was fixed up with her, set up with Melissa. Indeed, Kathryn did such a good job on my behalf that the first time Melissa walked through the door, she started taking her clothes off and we had sex on the spot. And had sex and had sex and had sex, on that spot and any other that came to hand.

I hardly knew what was happening. I mean, she was adorable, and she had a wonderful credit card from her daddy in Texas that let us go anywhere and everywhere when we weren't fucking. She adored my cock and was a kind of sex slave, which I loved, but I knew I was out of control and had no idea where all this was going. At the same time, a fellow student at the Royal College, a dark-haired, green-eyed, incredibly sexy Israeli named Zaki, was having the same effect on me as I was on Melissa: all he had to do was enter the room, and I folded; I could be feverish, sick as a dog, and still I couldn't say no. I too was a sex slave.

Whether in London, Basel, or Zurich, I felt I was always about to lose control. Was I really? Perhaps not. But I was often swimming pretty far out to sea, and most of the time, homosexuality was the stronger current. That didn't bother me anymore, I didn't feel guilty about it, and I had no problems about sin or anything. That was never part of my makeup. But I knew that I didn't know what I was doing. I have never felt that homosexuality per se was decadent, but a lot of decadent people were homosexual, and in big cities, when you are young and good-looking, you meet them all too easily. And in the 1970s there was so much casual sex, certainly among gays, and such a premium on youth and beauty that it was easy to get into all kinds of trouble very fast. I knew I was at risk.

But all winter in London, Sifnos was always there in front of me, a place where I could take a step back, calm down, and work in peace. Even when, as it happened, the World came there to me. As for example, the summer when, to my delight and my absolute horror, Melissa came to Sifnos. I had a telegram that she was arriving, and suddenly there she was on the mole in Kamares with a great mound of hatboxes and cases spilling around her feet. Well, not hatboxes, perhaps, but lots of high-toned luggage to go with the starlet-in-the-making she was styling herself to be. But on Sifnos, even she didn't make me crazy, didn't throw me off my stride. We just had a wonderful time. And she actually burnished my image on the island: she was a girl, at last, which delighted the islanders.

And she was adorable. For years afterward, my neighbors on the beach would throw back their heads and croon in fond memory, "Ah Mayleessa. Maaayleeeeessa."

I wonder where she is.

—

Nineteen seventy-seven was to be a banner year for me.

I went back to Sifnos at the beginning of May. I was scheduled to have a big show in Basel that fall, my biggest to date, and planned to spend the first part of the summer on Sifnos preparing for it. As a result, or maybe because I had a premonition of what was to come, I brought masses of supplies with me, more than I had ever brought before, more than I wanted to take on a plane, given the overweight charges of those days, and more than I would ever want to lug home. So I decided to take the train and rather grandly booked a first-class Wagon-Lits compartment all to myself on the overnight train from Zurich to Athens, traveling through Yugoslavia and down the Dalmatian coast. The trip was beautiful but endless. And a lesbian couple in the next compartment made so much noise in their love-making that it made me nearly crazy.

Does it seem that I spend a great deal of time sleeping next to people who are having sex?

—

As always, to get to Sifnos, I had to go through Athens. Many people I knew who loved Greece and had houses there on one island or another hated the city. I always liked it. It had a kind of sleepy charm and was wonderfully cheap. Shabby cream and yellow apartment buildings covered with balconies lined the sunny streets. There was a new four-lane highway from the airport, but there was nothing flashy about it, from the get-go a broken-down road full of cracks and potholes. Dry, dusty bougainvillea struggled for life down its center strip, while odd stores—with huge plate-glass windows—that sold, as far as I could tell, nothing but crystal chandeliers lined both sides of the road.

I started staying in actual hotels, usually in Piraeus, to be ready to catch the early-morning boat. And I had graduated from cruising in the park near the Columns of Zeus to actually frequenting bars, or rather a bar in Plaka that was called Mikonos. It belonged to a painter named Aleco whom I liked very much and who liked me too. A couple of years on, it moved to Kolonaki and was renamed Aleco's Island, and it was filled to the rafters every night with men and boys. I went there just about every night too whenever I passed through Athens, particularly when I started staying in Kolonaki.

Which, as always, I found a delight. Named for the little column in the main square, Kolonaki was full of charming restaurants and had the best shops and galleries as well as wonderful museums, such as the Benaki and later the Goulandris. The center of action, the heart of Kolonaki, was the sloping shaded square just below Lyca-bettus Hill with its two *kafenia* side by side, then, as now, among the favorite meeting places of Athens, particularly for young people. Athens was and still is, I think, sexy—the heat, the good-looking people, everybody in lightweight white clothes, the sexy girls in short skirts, the dark-haired boys with their shirts open down their tanned chests—and I could sit quite happily in Kolonaki Square ogling them for hours. I didn't even need to set foot in Aleco's Island, but of course I usually did.

Finally, there was a new boat for the Sifnos-Mílos route, the *Ionion*. In reality, she was just another old boat. Almost all the Greek boats were bought second- or thirdhand from Norway or Sweden, where they had been ferrying cars and people back and forth across the Baltic for years, but the *Ionion* was a major step up from the *Kalymnos*, much faster and fitted out with a handsome paneled din-ing room that made it seem less like a floating trash bucket. It was still a long trip, though, with the boat dawdling from island to is-land, often breaking down, and either hours late arriving or uncer-emoniously dumping her passengers on one wrong island or another, stranding them there. Exhausted by my trip, I started taking a cabin to myself and slept through most of the voyage, only coming out for lunch.

The drive to Platy Ghialos was still magical for me—the soft air, the fields filled with flowers. Once arrived, I would settle into my room, the same room I stayed in every year, right on the beach. It was bigger than my potter's shed had been, with two adjoining rooms that shared the terrace. My parents, Axel and Dita, came to Sifnos too: on their very first visit they fell under its spell and started coming every year. They stayed in the same room, my room, and though at first we never overlapped, we all started leaving our things, books or sweaters, in the closet or on the shelves, and the room became a kind of second home. After a couple of years one corner of the room was filled with walking sticks carved by my father, none so fine as the one he had carved for me.

After unpacking, I went for a swim. In May, the water was still chilly, but after Swiss lakes and mountain streams, the sea was delicious, and I let myself float in the clear, crisp water, my body rocking in a steady motion, back and forth, slowly, evenly, like a heartbeat. I lay back, breathing deeply, staring up at the sky, the light, the air, clear and fresh, and imagined the days that stretched before me, blessedly uncomplicated, and felt the tight-knit weave of nerves and defenses, anxieties and self-justifications that had grown over me like a shell during the winter—a brittle case, a carapace—begin to dissolve and fall away.

—

From a letter to my American college friend Ola in May of that year, with no idea of the roller-coaster year to come:

. . . I have embarked on my Sifnos journey once again and I am slowly finding my way to a "new Christian," a whole and sane one carried by the love of this island that spreads its wings around me like a lover. Only Sifnos seems to provide me with this sensation and it is here my work blooms.

"Let the inward and outward man be one," Plato says.

[Still the heavy summer reading, it seems.]

On Sifnos this seems possible. I soar in my loneliness, solitude, timelessness. Physical loneliness alas I feel much too often and at night I long for some warm tender body next to mine.

I have started to paint and over twelve paintings are hanging on the otherwise pure white walls, along with some sepia and black-and-white drawings. Hope to start with oils soon, especially after lugging all this material with me this trip. The colors on the island are a sea of reds and yellows, mauves and silvery grays, and this avalanche of color goes right into my palette.

The days are intense, long and without interruption, no phone, nothing, only the gentle roll of the Aegean five meters from where I sit on my terrace. I work and work. The new pictures are alive and sparkling with sun and laughter, but also with a certain darkness I cannot explain. It is night now and I expect the full moon to rise soon. It has been quite impressive these last few nights as it glides up behind the mountains, a huge magical apricot salmon-colored ball.

Wanting someone to share it with. Although a little self-realization: maybe not quite all the time. Love to be alone and love to be free. A problem I am dealing with, with someone in Zurich.

Am reading Proust in French, Virginia Woolf in English and trying to learn Greek at the same time and it is all a bit confusing, but I try. Also some thriller stuff for the beach, Christo's special rock.

I worry a bit about the show in Basel this fall. It will be in a huge public space belonging to the city and a leading art critic will introduce me and the show, and it scares me a little. Some people though will come to the opening just because of him, which is great. I think the show has good karma. I will come back to Sifnos after the show comes down, do my horrible annual army stint and then, after a stop in New York, go on to Mexico, meeting my friend from Zurich there.

Standing invitation for you to come.

Love,
Christo

—

Lush in word and thought—fueled some by my youth, some by the moon that night as I was writing to Ola, and some by the person in Zurich who was making me feel particularly romantic and particularly alone. I had, you see, met a young man. Curiously, his name was also Christian, and I seemed to be almost crazy in love (again). Done with the Royal College and London, I was in the throes of trying to set myself up in a studio in Zurich, a new town for me, and hard at work on pictures for the fall show I mentioned. As if that were not enough, there I was in the middle of a major affair with a man, an affair that actually seemed to be going somewhere.

Always wanting to be in control, I was trying not only to have him be mine but to corral him into doing everything I wanted, and one of the things I wanted him to do was to come to Sifnos with me. I had always dreamed of having my lover, whether the real one of the moment or an imagined one, come to the island. Everywhere I walked or ate or swam or sketched, I imagined him there with me. I imagined how I would show him the island, the places only I knew, and I imagined how he would love it as I did. But in the end, Christian never came—work, bad timing, something, maybe my very insistence. Everything with me was always so urgent. Or perhaps he had a sneaking suspicion that as much as I seemed to want him, was indeed chasing him, I was also always dipping and weaving away, that as much as I said I wanted a relationship, I seemed equally intent on keeping my freedom.

But then, all kinds of other things were going on, and other shoes were about to start dropping all over the place.

The next to drop came only a week or two after my arrival on a beautiful evening at the huge *panaghia* at Chrissopighi, the most important festival of the year. I was standing in the courtyard in front of the old church when, across the crowd of pilgrims, I saw a slim, dark-haired girl with sparkling green-brown eyes and a beautiful tan. She looked radiant, I thought, full of warmth and sensuality. Was I looking at her or was she looking at me? Who knew? At any rate, in a matter of minutes we had crossed to each other and were huddled together talking.

Joanna—Jo, as she styled herself—was a South African who had left home because of her opposition to apartheid. As we talked, I learned that she had spent the whole winter on Sifnos, which I had never done, in a village called Cheronisos, where I would surely never have stayed. Cheronisos was all the way at the northern end of the island and was the most isolated, windblown place on Sifnos—a couple of one- or two-room houses on a barren promontory with the tiny monastery of St. George at the tip.

Jo had had an apprenticeship with the main potter there over the winter, and I was full of admiration for her knowledge of the island, her near-fluent Greek, and her courage and tenacity in having stuck it out for so long in such isolation. To get out of Cheronisos, she might have been able to find a fisherman to take her to Kamares once in a great while, but on top of freezing to death in the boat, she would have had to find a way to get back—probably on foot, as there was no road, walking four or five hours up and down rocky paths past abandoned silver and copper mines, the most desolate landscape on Sifnos, especially in winter.

I was, of course, always horny, and after her long winter alone in the nowhere, she was no doubt starved for affection, and we pretty much threw ourselves at each other that evening. She amazed me, with her independence and guts and intensity, and I became quite infatuated with her and saw her almost daily. By the time I met her, she was living in a tiny room off a chapel above the Kamares harbor; a long, whitewashed stone staircase that seemed to glow in the dark led up to her place. It was all extremely romantic, and our lovemaking in that little room is still vivid and moving to me.

But of course it was also wildly inconvenient. Platy Ghialos and Kamares are miles apart. I usually walked the quickest way, along the old goat trails over the hills, and would have to walk back that night or the next morning.

On the way, I would often stop at Lakis's for an ice cream, and it was clear that he knew what I was up to. So did the whole island. Jo and I became for that time a "couple," and the Sifniots were more than happy to see us together. Not just to see *to pedi sou*, their child, Christo, settled, but also to remove the unknown quantity of this young, single woman living alone. She too was well known on the island, and no doubt there had been a good deal of curiosity and gossip about her. Our being together put much of that to rest. I mean, some of the farmers' wives started making baby clothes for us.

I suppose I liked the heterosexual image, and she liked the position, the credibility, of being with someone. So we were happy to be or at least to play the couple. That was a total novelty to me. I would sit there at Lakis's, lapping away at my ice-cream cone, and Lakis would look at me with a sort of lewd smile, aim his glance at my crotch, raise his Greek eyebrows, and croak, "*Ah, vitamini, vitamini.*" And I would smile back salaciously, knowingly, man to man.

I was not only not alone anymore, I was one of the boys. A win-win situation, it seemed to me.

—

Meeting Joanna that summer was nothing compared with the clomp of the next shoe dropping.

High above the beach, close to the Xenia Hotel, lived a shepherd whom I visited every morning to buy his fresh yogurt. One morning a charming Athenian lady with a deep voice—they all had deep voices, it seemed—was there, also buying yogurt. She was lamenting that Sifniots were too stubborn to sell their houses or too secretive about it. She was desperate to find a house, she said, but there was nothing on the market, or at least no one would tell her or show her anything.

It was island xenophobia, of course, as she was from Athens, but in truth there was no real estate office of any kind on the island. Real estate transactions were strictly word of mouth, and whispered word of mouth at that—except for Francesco, the son of old Sofia at the hotel, who knew more than anyone about Sifnos real estate. I told her about him, but it seemed there was in fact nothing.

Over the years I had met several people, mostly Athenians like her, who were looking to buy property on the island, but the idea had never meant that much to me. I would have the odd fantasy about this or that house, usually one of the older, grander houses I couldn't possibly afford, in Artemona especially, one being a big old farmhouse with a windmill and an ancient palm tree. But now I began to really think about it. Was it the presence of Jo in my life that triggered my rather conventional Swiss yearning for domesticity? Perhaps a little. At any rate, a day or so later, over coffee with the handsome farmer Stavros, my neighbor on the beach, I casually mentioned that I was perhaps interested in a house to rent or buy, instead of just having the room.

Neither of us said anything more about it, but one beautiful Sunday morning a week or two later, he came over—all dressed up, having just come from church. He said he wanted me to come along to his village, Exambela, where he had something to show me. I had already half forgotten our conversation, but he was a good friend, and of course, if he had something to show me, I would go. He had a new little red Toyota pickup truck, his pride and joy. I climbed in, and off we went. He didn't say anything on the way up, just polite chitchat, but he seemed a bit nervous and full of anticipation.

Leaving his truck on the main road, we hiked up the back way, up a series of paths and steep steps into Exambela. After several sharp right and left turns we went up some more steps into a kind of dead-end alley where I had never been, and Stavros stopped in front of a small one-story whitewashed row house, a perfect Cycladic peasant cottage. It had a double grass-green central door with a pretty four-paned transom above it and long, green-shuttered windows on either side. The courtyard in front had a lemon tree in the middle and remnants of a vegetable garden, and an outhouse off to the side. The one-story house on its right was a little higher up, and the one on the left a bit below, down the hill.

Stavros told me, in a rather furtive way, that no one really knew about the house being for sale yet and then shyly said that if I wanted it, I could have it for 230,000 drachmas. My heart began beating faster, or perhaps it was skipping beats altogether. I wasn't sure I had heard right, wasn't sure I had understood; my Greek was still very shaky. "What? Really?" I asked. Had he said I could have the house? Gulp. "*How much?*" I asked, my voice rising in my throat. He repeated the figure, and I dizzily calculated what it meant: 15,000 Swiss francs, or about $7,500 in those days.

I was fuddled and muddled, but I knew something very special was happening. There was no bargaining—very unusual in Greece— maybe because I was a foreigner, maybe because I was a fool? Looking back, I think it was a "true" price, a true value, because he genuinely wanted me to have it. Years later, Stavros told me that he'd chosen me for that house because his family lived next door in the house below, and he wanted his old father and mother and his unmarried sister to have a good neighbor. But he said nothing of that then— thank goodness, as it would have been too much for me to manage. The house, the honor of his choosing me, it would have been too emotional, and I might have simply burst into tears.

My knees were shaking with excitement, but trying to be grown-up and sensible, I said I would think about it. And he gave me the name of a carpenter in Apollonia who he said had the keys to the house and represented the owners in Athens. We shook hands. Wanting to be by myself, I refused a ride back and rather shakily walked home over the hills.

—

Later that same day I found the carpenter with the keys and we opened the doors of the little house with the grass-green shutters. The proper entrance was on the street side, which I had not yet seen. This street was only a bigger path, the house set back from it on a slip of terrace. I inserted a huge antique key in the old wooden door, which had two windows with wrought-iron grilles over them, heard the key grind in the lock, and stepped into a two-hundred-year-old world where it seemed that nothing had ever been touched or fooled with. Maybe a bit of modernization in the 1950s, but not much.

The empty kitchen—indeed, the whole house—had rough stone walls that leaned and sloped every which way. To my left, next to the door, above an old marble sink, a big window faced the street. The sink and its window were all that was new in the room, and even they were from a long time before. In the far corner was a fire-place for cooking, with a rough, hood-shaped chimney above it and storage space for wood underneath. Beside the fireplace were the original molded spaces made for the huge water jars, once seen in every Greek house, that were carried to and from the well. All of it—fireplace, chimney, and shelves—was made from huge slabs of whitewashed schist fitted together into a single, flowing piece of sculpture. In the wall opposite me were scattered niches that reminded me of the windows in Le Corbusier's Ronchamp chapel, and straight ahead a door led to the next room, a high old wooden frame supporting the arch above it.

We went down a step into the main room, a long, rather narrow *sala*, with the door and the handsome shuttered windows I had seen from the back on the far wall. As we opened the shutters and the double door onto the little courtyard with its lemon tree, the room was flooded with late-afternoon sunlight and the smell of lemon blossoms. Opposite the courtyard door, an open archway pierced the thick, sloping interior wall and led to a small bedroom that was like an enchanted cave, the walls seeming to grow right up out of the stone floor. Crookedly carved into the far wall of this little room was a deep-set casement window that looked out across the street to a neighbor's ruined house and a garden full of hens and cockerels, which I fell in love with instantly. At the other end of the *sala* was another door to what must have been a nursery bedroom in the past. I knew instantly that this little space with no windows would be my closet and a place for a refrigerator and a "bar." Its back wall was one of the few straight walls in the house, so I could build bookshelves there. I was already planning how it would be.

On Sifnos, the floors of old houses, the terraces, and even the streets were made from beautiful big slabs of schist, and the plastered joints between the stones were whitewashed, giving the village floors and streets a remarkable spidery look, as if white veins or tangled roots spread across them. These intricate, seemingly organic white lines created designs that were as modern and elegant as any Brice Marden tracery. My floors—I knew almost immediately that they were going to be mine—took my breath away. They were the original stone everywhere, except in the main room, where they had been replaced with the cheerful red and ivory-white tiles I had often admired in other island houses.

The ceilings, astonishingly, were composed of the same huge irregular shapes of flat schist, a couple of layers thick, all held up by great, strong wooden beams—not just beams, really, but rough, twisty, knotted tree trunks. The flat roof was poured plaster. Every year, the surface got whitewashed with a solution that had olive oil in it to make it waterproof and to guarantee that the rainwater collected in the cistern was pure.

Outside, a staircase ran crookedly up the wall of the courtyard to the roof. From up there, almost the highest point in Exambela, the village stretched down and away around me, a warren of white houses, flat-roofed cubes locked together, fitted against, below, and on top of one another, with little paths and steps leading around and between them. The village ended abruptly at the Apollonia–Platy Ghialos road, and the land dropped farther down to a farm valley with a small dovecote and a stream, then up again through terraced fields leading to a tower built of enormous stones—perhaps the remains of an old windmill, or more likely, given the immense size of the stones, an ancient Cycladic tower, one of dozens that dotted the island. I preferred the latter. The earliest of these towers date to the sixth century B.C., the latest to the third century. (One of them—in the valley near Kastro, the Butterfly Valley—had a small chapel and a barn attached; for a time, years later, I wanted to buy it.) On the highest terrace, by the tower, stood an old gray mule, just standing, staring east toward the sea. It was Sunday, and he and his owner didn't have to work. Over the years, it would seem to me that that mule was always there at the end of the day, resting peacefully. Behind the tower were two mountains that rose up out of the terraces and orchards, each with a white monastery on its very top, to the left Agios Andreas and to the right Profitis Elias, the highest point on Sifnos.

The carpenter pointed down across the courtyard and the little path in back where I had stood with Stavros to yet another sort of miniature row house, a tiny building that, it seemed, also belonged to the house, an *apothiki*, a single room with a green door and a tiny window. This little *dépendance* had a worn-out bamboo ceiling of a kind I had not seen before on the island, and the walls had more little niches like the ones in the kitchen. It also had its own cooking fireplace and *nerochiti*, a basin for water. Attached to this little building was a strange whitewashed stone structure, almost like a stone tent, about five feet tall and five feet across, that was tucked into a corner between the *apothiki* and a neighbor's house. It had probably been used to store wood, the carpenter said. I never learned whether this was its purpose or not; in the thirty years I was to own the house, I never removed the stones covering its entrance, because I always thought of it as a piece of sculpture. Stavros had neglected to point it out to me, but I do believe that my guest cottage, as I already grandly called it, sealed the deal. I was determined to own the house.

Before all the villagers noticed us and wandered over to check me out, we locked up and I went home to Platy Ghialos. It was already dark by then, but sleep was out of the question. I had too much thinking to do. Should I see other houses? Was it a fair price? Should I ask an architect or builder to look it over? So many questions. But I never really questioned buying the house. It did not bother me that it was in the village, squeezed between other houses. I knew I couldn't live like Onno, somewhere out in the nowhere, or on the windswept shore. Nor did it bother me that the house was in serious need of repair, that there was no bathroom or running water, no water at all near the house.

It did not occur to me that it was a crazy thing for a twenty-six-year-old Swiss painter with no money to buy a house on a faraway Greek island. The little house was calling to me, and I had to follow my instincts. I could see it clearly. It all seemed quite simple. I was in love with the island, and the island would never lead me wrong.

—

Joanna was the first person on the island I took to see the house, but that wasn't until after I had bought it. Until then, I told no one what

I was doing. I never even went back to Exambela. I didn't want the keys. Part of this was a superstitious fear that somehow I might jinx the deal; part of it was not wanting anyone there to see me, a foreigner, looking about, or to learn about the house being for sale. I was terrified that someone else would come along and make a better offer.

Every day I became more fixed on owning the little house with the green shutters. I knew I had to have it. But how? A few years before, when I was at St. Olaf's, I had wanted to buy a picture from my art teacher. I had no money at all, but I got a job at a Jell-O and iced-tea packing plant called the Right-Way Packaging Company, an improbable name right out of a 1950s musical such as *The Pajama Game*. It was my first and only job, and I hated it. I worked the night shift, and every morning I came home with my eyes and nose full of powder. But I earned the money, bought the picture—and quit the same day. Obviously this would not work in my current situation. Fifteen thousand Swiss francs was a lot of money for me, and I needed it right away.

Finally I summoned up the nerve to call my parents for help. By then they had visited Sifnos often, so I knew they loved the island themselves and would at least have some understanding and sympathy for what I wanted to do. I walked to the post office in Apollonia, along the way practicing out loud what I would say, how I would state my case. I went to the counter and placed my call and then waited anxiously on a little bench near the old row of wooden phone booths until the ringing of the phone indicated that the line was connected.

"Hello . . . Axel? . . . How are you? How is Tchocky [our beloved Norwich terrier]? How is Mami? . . . Yes, yes, everything is fine." I fumbled and fumbled. "But, but . . . guess what?" I finally plunged in. "I found a house, a little house, an incredible house. In Exambela, you remember Exambela? My favorite village." Well it was, or it certainly was now. "And . . . and . . . and, yes, well, I can buy it very cheap. How much? Only fifteen thousand. Yes. Swiss francs. Yes.

Well. And I think I want to borrow the money from the bank. What do you think?" My heart in my throat. "Do you . . . do you think . . . could you guarantee the money for me? Do you think?"

My parents were not rich, my father's family's considerable industrial fortune having been lost a generation ago, my mother's family having been comfortable but never having had a fortune at all. As doctors, they earned decent money, but still, although I knew the house was cheap, it was a house in Greece, for God's sake, and fifteen thousand Swiss francs was real money. I knew perfectly well what most parents would say to their son in this situation: "Are you out of your mind? You must be crazy! Come home at once." But my father, without hesitation it seemed, in his wonderful Russian accent said, "Of course, Christian. If you found a house, it must be a good house, and I shall go to the bank and see that they send you the money tomorrow."

I knew that my father was extraordinarily generous with both his sons, but I realized as we talked that I had a sliver of advantage in trying to convince him. Early in my teens, already a bit obsessed by real estate, I played a kind of game, looking at newspaper advertisements for country houses for us. By chance, I had found a notice for a small house outside Basel, which I convinced my parents to go see. I was sure it was the right house for them, for us, and indeed they bought it and were very happy there for almost fifty years, until they sold it when they got too old to go there. "If you found a house, and if it is half the house you found for us, it must be a good one," my father continued.

Ecstatic—well, flooded with emotions, panic among them—I rushed off to the carpenter who had shown me the house. I told him I would buy the house, we shook hands on it, and the deal was done. Though no money had been exchanged, he promised not to show it to anyone else and said he considered the house mine. Looking back, I am sure my friend Stavros's "fine Italian hand" was at work here, since he had already picked me as his family's neighbor. But rather proud of my courage and the agent's willingness to trust me,

I rushed back to Platy Ghialos, threw a few things in a bag, and rushed back again in the other direction to Kamares and the night boat to Athens to get the money for my house.

—

June 1977

Dear Parents,

A quick note while running around sweltering-hot Athens, collecting money, checks and legal papers.

I cannot thank you enough. You cannot imagine what is going on in my head. That this little house is going to be mine is mind-boggling.

Buying a house here, though, and barely speaking the language, is no easier than you would imagine. The paperwork at the banks, the paperwork everywhere, the forms that have to be filled out and stamped and stamped again, the lawyers I have to see. It is insane. And in this heat. For some incomprehensible to me legal and tax reasons, I need THREE certified checks, and I run sweating from the National Bank of Greece in the center of town to my lawyers and back and then to a nice Athenian lady I met on Sifnos, who is giving me advice. Good advice I hope—she was trying to buy a house there herself and is green with envy at my luck, but very helpful. She has been offered ruins for twice as much money, where my little house is a move-in.

[Okay, I lied a little.]

The papers are all being drawn up and notarized here, but the closing will be on Sifnos. My new address will be:

Ch. P-B, Spiti 133, Klouvati, Exambela, Sifnos, Greece

Lots of love from your still-very-young-almost-owner-of-a-house.

Christo

PS I am booked to fly back to Zurich June 30th. Can't believe it. Hope I get all this done and can come home owning the house.

—

I did have to go back to Switzerland at the end of June. As I had written to Ola, I was having an exhibition in Basel that fall, which was a big part of why I felt confident that my parents would not have to pay off my loan. I was fairly sure I could make the money back. For the moment, though, the show took a backseat. The house was the only thing on my mind. Holding tight to my three checks, I returned to Sifnos as fast as possible. I had been too scared to cash them; 230,000 drachmas was a lot of cash to carry around.

Sifnos was so tiny still. There were no such things as bank branches, and I knew that my friend Thomas the grocer handled only small exchanges of money, but I had been told there was another, bigger grocery shop next to the police station that would cash the checks for me. I had never much liked the owner, *Kyrie* Iannis, a grim and serious man who never smiled. I never bought groceries in his shop, but I was told I should go there. The National Bank had given me the necessary information for exchange rates, and I marched into his shop sure, well almost sure, that I could handle this transaction.

After the series of Greek ritual greetings and the usual small talk, all rather stiff stuff with him, I produced the checks and my passport. He examined them closely, suspiciously, it seemed to me, and then disappeared in back. He reappeared a while later with a handwritten sheet of foreign-exchange numbers and, referring to it, told me how many drachmas I would receive in exchange. To my horror it was a number far lower than I had been told in Athens. "What? How . . . How is this possible?" I stammered in panic. "That's not what I was told in Athens." If he was correct, I couldn't pay for the house.

I reached for the sheet. "Please let me see," I begged, but he pulled the papers away, telling me I had the wrong information, this was the latest exchange rate. After a moment, stunned, paralyzed, not knowing what to do, I asked for my checks back, but he refused to give them to me. He just stood there, waiting. Then I noticed a date at the top of his sheet: it was 1975, two years before. And I realized that the man was trying to cheat me, giving me a two-year-old rate that would make him a good deal of money.

I went a little crazy, screaming and yelling, and then ran to the police next door. In minutes, my noisy, hysterical fit began to attract a crowd in front of *Kyrie* Iannis's shop, and I am sure he became as freaked out as I already was. This was not what he had expected. I was just a boy to him, and he was accustomed to dealing with trusting, docile tourists anyway. He was not prepared for my reaction and the commotion it was creating in the street. When I returned with the policeman, the handwritten note of exchange had disappeared, and a completely up-to-date printed version was on the counter.

I think the police did believe what I told them, but I was a foreigner and a kid to boot, while he was a Sifniot and a local businessman. When the policeman quizzed him about the numbers and the checks, *Kyrie* Iannis smiled, shook his head, and shrugged in wonder and incomprehension at this mysterious confusion, and the policeman in turn tried to convince me it was all just a misunderstanding. Of course I could have my checks back, *Kyrie* Iannis said. Another misunderstanding, he said, smiling widely. He didn't speak English, my Greek was poor, and so on and so on. I grabbed my checks and ran to my friend Thomas's tiny grocery store down the street. I was sure he would help me, and he did. And remained my friend for life.

I was in a state, though, no question. It was the first time anyone on Sifnos had ever done anything like this to me, lied to me or tried to cheat me, and on that particular day, in my excitement and happiness about the house and the island itself, the incident did more than just upset or infuriate me; it hurt me. I knew my experience with *Kyrie* Iannis could happen anywhere, of course, but I had not imagined such a thing on Sifnos. It was like a first unexpected quarrel with a lover, a slap across the face.

I had my money. But until the day he died, I never entered *Kyrie* Iannis's shop again, nor did I speak to him or greet him.

—

A few days later I found myself with my new carpenter-friend and old *Kyrie* Lemonis, the only lawyer on the island, in the Apollonia town hall for the closing. On the table were piles of papers—documents, forms, sheets of old onionskin, and faded carbons, the history of my house rustling in the breeze from the open window. The papers were covered with tight, mysterious, to me incomprehensible Greek lettering, strange postage-type stamps, and generously applied red and black rubber stamps. The lawyer ceremoniously read the whole deed to me. I could not understand a word, but staring out the window at the sunny Greek day, the rather beautiful words pouring over me, I became very emotional about this great event in my life, sniffled quietly, and surreptitiously wiped my eyes.

In spite of my experience with *Kyrie* Iannis, I trusted the lawyer and the owner's agent blindly—which, looking back, seems astonishing. I had no idea what was in the deed and later on never had it translated—a serious mistake on my part, as I was to learn. Now excited, teary, my heart thumping, I signed all the different papers, and they did too. More rubber stamps were brought out and applied to still more indecipherable documents. Finally, we stood and shook hands, pumping our arms up and down endlessly and beaming at one another. The house was mine. And as tradition would have it, in the absence of the seller I took the carpenter, his (sort of) agent, and the carpenter's wife for a celebratory dinner with lots of retsina and many toasts.

During my first official visit to the house, my new neighbors came by to shake hands and congratulate me—and to be sure I understood exactly what I had bought and, more important, exactly what I had not bought. They walked me around my tiny property, carefully showing me where my boundaries were. The structure of all these villages is incredibly complex, at times as crazy as a block version of pick-up sticks, all the houses and walls interconnected and interdependent, with rooms like my little *apothiki* literally part of another house. The villagers knew every inch of it, every wall, every stone, what belonged to me or to this neighbor and that one.

Following them as they pointed out corners and angles, drains and chimney stacks, all the quirks and puzzles and anomalies of my little piece of Exambela, I figured this was probably the best translation of the deed there was.

After everyone left, I just stood there and stared around me, exhausted, unable to believe I owned this house. I owned a house. I owned something. It was not La Bastide du Roi in Antibes, but it was mine, this little house, it was mine.

Maybe because of the vast property in Antibes and everything my father and the Brechneffs had lost, it seemed rather fragile to me, something not quite real that could be snatched away at any time. Or maybe it was simply having something of my own for the first time that made it seem so fragile. But for the next thirty years, arriving at my kitchen door after long journeys from Europe or America, I still found it hard to believe that this little house at the end of the world was truly there, and that it was mine.

3

Why did I buy a house in Greece? Curiously, no one ever asks. People act as if it were the most natural thing in the world—doesn't everyone want a house on a Greek island? Well, no, everyone doesn't, and I didn't. I had never before even thought of such a thing.

A house? Oh, I wanted the big Brechneff house I imagined in Moscow, or La Bastide du Roi, but those were fantasy houses of my childhood, places I wished I had grown up in, not anything I wanted for myself now. Nor had I ever dreamed of having a house in Greece. I thought I might want to explore it someday, maybe stay there, paint there, as I was doing, but nothing more. I guess, looking back, my real dream house would have been in Berzona, the tiny mountain village in the Ticino, the Italian part of Switzerland, where my family rented a house every summer that belonged to my father's friend Jan Tschichold, the famous typographer and book designer. Truth to tell, that was where I had wanted my parents to buy a house, not in the rather bland Jura, where I had helped them find "Le Sporlet," as they called it, but in those days the Ticino was a perilous eight-hour mountain drive from Basel.

There was certainly nothing bland about the Ticino. It was rough and wild, full of rushing rivers and snowcapped peaks, wildflowers and chestnut trees, dazzling, crisp sunlight and dense fog. The locals were rough and wild themselves, strong and hardy, their faces carved and lined by the strong mountain sun and the harsh winters. The

Christo's house

Ticino's charming Italianate towns had tall houses with wrought-iron balconies opening onto high mountain views, or there were simple mountain farmers' stone cabins, like the one we rented every year, where we huddled by the fires my father loved to build, playing cards while it poured rain outside.

Berzona was a tiny village. In fact, not just tiny but, like Sifnos when I was first there, actually shrinking. I looked it up. In 1795 it had 306 people; in 1850 only 235; 151 in 1900; and 84 just before we started going there in the 1950s. In 2000 there were only 48 souls. It was, though, a mecca for artists and writers, some of them famous, such as our landlord, or Golo Mann, Alfred Andersch, and Max Frisch, who lived right below us. I was to find that, curiously, the ex wife of Johannes Hoffman, the painter/violinist, had lived there for a time too. Small world.

I began to feel that for me, Berzona had been like a rough sketch of Sifnos, an early draft. Berzona was part of the reason I was intuitively drawn to the island, part of the reason I'd fallen for it on sight. It was as if I recognized it immediately. It was, after all, Berzona with a better climate.

I looked up "serendipity" the other day in *Roget's Thesaurus*. One of the synonyms was "happy chance," but my favorite was "dumb luck." It is said that we all make our own luck, and that is true in a philosophical sense, but there is also being just plain lucky, being in the right place at the right time. And the important thing is to know it when you see it, to know it is lucky, to know you are being offered something and take it. Or, even more simply, to get out of your head, to let go of your doubts and anxieties and hesitations, to get out of your own way and let it happen.

—

June 1977

Dearest Parents,

Thank you for all your trust in your younger son. After all one doesn't buy a house that easily. "Le Sporlet," though, has given your two sons and your friends so much joy, and I hope to repeat that, and to return your love and generosity with this house on this magical island.

I barely know where to begin. You can see from the plans, the sketches, I sent you. The house is one down from the highest house in the village, facing inland towards the mountains and totally protected from the meltemi winds and stormy sea weather. The actual entrance to the house, the door to the kitchen, is on a street, a glorified path really that leads up to a small square with views over Kastro and the sea. The courtyard with the doors to the sala and the lemon tree are on the opposite side of the house, completely hidden from nosy neighbors or wandering tourists in a tiny cul-de-sac. From the rooftop, the views are breathtaking, with sunrises to the East over the sea and sunsets to the West behind the mountains. The whole village of Exambela is spread out below me to the South and the little village of Katavati is right across the valley. Beyond the village, there are terraced fields filled with farmers planting their crops, the terraces climbing up and up to the monastery of Profitis Elias.

When I raved about my view to an old Sifniot, he turned to me and said, "Any view on Sifnos is beautiful. Even just a white wall." Of course he is right, but my view is pretty amazing.

The lemon tree in the courtyard is the heart of the house; the blossoms are full of bees and smell heavenly and I look forward to having lots of lemons for my gin tonics. We will have to plan the cistern and septic tank to preserve this little gem of a tree.

[Well, as I said, I may have lied a little when I told them the house was a move-in.]

I have chosen my builder, whom I believe I can trust. His name is Stephanos. He is an Exambela man with roots in Platy Ghialos. I love the way he looks and smiles. His wife is a bit more problematic, a bit grim, or sad probably. They have no children due to the malnutrition during the war when they were young. They have never been to a doctor about it as "God makes these decisions for us all," they say. I know him from island festivals and celebrations where he plays the violin. When I pass his house in the evening, I can hear him practicing. He will use local villagers for the work which will be more complicated than one would imagine—for one thing everything has to be brought in by mule from the road.

I am quite confident my show will be successful and I will be able to pay for the house and the work without any trouble. In spite of all these distractions, I have been painting nonstop, and have quite a lot of good work, I think. And my girlfriend Joanna has been a great help, and will be a great help with the house.

As soon as I have running water and a bathroom, we can all use "spiti apo Christo," Christo's house, as my neighbors already call it.

I am a very happy son and cannot thank you enough.

Love,
Christo

—

Though I hadn't told her about the house right away, once the deal was closed, Joanna was the first person to know about it and the first person I showed it to. And right away she was enthusiastic and immensely helpful. We would go to Exambela, wander through the house, and discuss what needed to be done. She was quite in love with the house and a bit in love with me, and we had fun playing in the house, imagining how it would be, making plans. The village was amused by this show of us being lovers and welcomed us both.

I suppose from the start this created a problem: I didn't want to share the house, and I wasn't at all ready to share it with Jo. I had to leave soon to prepare my show, and she said she wanted to stay in the house while I was away and start the work with Stephanos, who, by the way, was crazy about her. I said no. I didn't want her to. It was my house after all, and I wanted it for myself, and I wasn't ready to be living with anyone. I didn't say all that to her, of course, but I knew I wasn't ready to give over my house before I'd had a chance to experience it for myself. I didn't want the house, and the builder too, for goodness' sake, co-opted and taken from me. Nor, indeed, my independence.

In a kind of dazed scramble I put the house out of my mind as best I could and flew back to Switzerland to prepare for my show. This was important, and I knew I had to concentrate. There was work to be finished, framing to be done, invitations to be produced and sent, the opening to be planned. The city space where my exhibit would take place had a hanging committee, and a well-known curator would be working with me. I had to focus if I was to be ready.

Once back in Switzerland, I was able to recognize the tangle my personal life had become and how confused I was. The confusion began the moment I walked through customs at the Zurich Airport to find my . . . what? Lover? Christian was there to meet me. I was thrilled, but what was I to do about Jo, my . . . what? Lover I had left behind on Sifnos? What was I to do? What was I doing? I was once again "crazy" about Christian, but I believed I loved Jo too. And I actively encouraged her to come to Basel for my exhibition.

Jo did come to Basel, and she met Christian. They knew about each other—at least I hadn't been lying to them—and she wanted to meet him, she said. Indeed, during my opening they spent most of the evening together. That was so like Jo, I thought, but it made me crazy. I mean, I was already a nervous wreck from rushing around trying to glad-hand everyone and sell pictures, and at the same time I had to keep my eye on this couple with their heads together in the corner. What were they talking about? I wondered. I hated to think. Me, no doubt. And nothing good, I figured. Of course I had created this confusion, this little head-on collision, but I was relieved when the evening was over without any flare-ups or screaming matches.

I think that Jo finally understood everything after meeting Christian. She knew, no matter what I might say, that this was not just a simple competition, as it would be with another woman, say, the two of them duking it out on a level playing field, but that she was up against a whole other life, a whole other possible me. No matter how confused or confusing I was or had been, she had to sense that the game was fixed and somehow she had already lost. Whether I knew it yet or not, she had to know that if it wasn't Christian in my life, there would be some other man.

"I'm off to London," she said, cheerily kissing me goodbye. And, she promised, she would see me soon back on Sifnos. But she knew. Maybe better even than I.

—

From my diary, Exambela, October 1977:

My first night in my house. Happily alone. The house empty, nothing in it but my suitcase in the sala, and my Greek blanket tucked around me. I carried my water from the well, had a drink, or two, made some soup. My bedroom is filled with light even at night. The whiteness of the old walls is like the light of shining stars. I try to slow down, be still. I try to just be. I am happy, truly happy.

The house has to become mine now, has to become me. I must creep into every wall and niche and beam and stone.

The night is so quiet, surrounded by my own walls, total silence.

I am falling asleep . . .

—

The show was a success. It almost sold out—for me a triumph. I was ecstatic over the attendance, the reviews, and everyone's enthusiasm. And I was ecstatic about the money. I paid back my loan on the house in its entirety and in October headed back to Sifnos with pockets full of money for the construction work, which I hoped would get started immediately.

I could stay only about a month, since in November I had my annual military service and then I had a trip to Mexico planned with Christian in December. But right from the start there were all kinds of problems—a job Stephanos hadn't finished, workers busy on other sites, early rains, and even after a couple of weeks nothing had been started.

The biggest problem was the stranglehold that Greek bureaucracy had over everything. Neither Stephanos nor I seemed to get anywhere with securing the necessary permits—simple building permits to start with, but also permits for the cistern, the septic tank, and the bathroom, to say nothing of the permits required for work on an old house in a historic district. There was an endless maze of papers and forms and people to be spoken to, documents to be approved and, of course, stamped and stamped and stamped again, and we were getting nowhere.

The only saving grace was that I knew Jo was coming. Although in the summer I had told her she couldn't stay, I had changed my mind in Switzerland after my show and, rather grandly, I thought, offered her the house for the winter. She could have it after I left, I'd said, from November until March, when I would "need it myself," though I had no particular idea why. I was just setting boundaries, I guess. I knew she would be on Sifnos anyway during the winter—she hated high season—and I felt bad about my earlier denial and, I suppose, sort of guilty about everything.

It is also possible that I had had a premonition that everything might not go so well with the house, that I might need someone there I could trust, someone who could keep an eye on the work and push things along. And I knew Jo was just the person. She not only spoke fluent Greek but knew everybody on Sifnos, and the villagers loved her; she could gossip and laugh and cry with them. Indeed, to this day those who knew her remember her as an angel. I knew that Stephanos loved her and that she would have him tied around her little finger in no time. She knew how to act helpless and get men to help her, a major skill in Greece, and she was also practical and organized and very tough about money, much tougher than I.

—

So, incredibly frustrated but always the optimist—this will all work out, I thought, Jo and the house, everything, somehow—I decamped for Switzerland for my army stint and after that for the United States. I was to meet Christian in Cancún, Mexico, but along the way I planned to stop in New York and Los Angeles to visit old friends and make contacts and maybe sell some pictures. But before the trip had even really begun, my first week in New York, I was taken to a cocktail party, where I met a man named Tim Lovejoy, a playwright and filmmaker. He was dressed all in black, very seventies, but he had a huge smile and incredible blue eyes, and I was taken immediately. A group of us went on to another party together, and then he took me home.

In those days gays didn't really date. There were no bourgeois trappings to gay relationships, as there seem to be today. It was, after all, still illegal in most places and illicit everywhere. No gay man was seeking a spouse, certainly not intentionally. There were no such things as partners, no thought of civil unions, much less same-sex marriage. Even "longtime companions" were rarely heard of. I'm not sure that they really existed anyway until gay men started dying of AIDS in the 1980s and the obituary writers needed a label for people's lovers. There was no circling around, checking each other out; you dove right in and went to bed. Or we did.

It wasn't love at first sight, I suppose, but during the week I spent in New York, mostly with him, I knew this was different. I had never known anything like it. It seemed I was actually, truly, at last falling in love. Knocked sideways, I had no idea what to do or how to handle this or myself. I was on my way to meet my unsuspecting lover, for God's sake. What was I going to do? I thought I was in love, really in love, but was I? Was Tim? Was Christian? And what about Jo? What was *she* doing in all this? But I knew something had happened. And I knew I had to be honest, direct, up-front with Christian, and the sooner the better.

Arriving at the tiny airport in Cancún, I climbed down the wobbly rolling stairs from the plane into the blast of Mexican heat and walked across the tarmac. He was standing there, waiting for me.

"I've met—met someone—someone in New York," I blurted out. "I've met someone else."

"So have I," he said.

And he had. In Zurich it seemed, soon after I left. We laughed, we hugged, we cried a bit, and then decided to make the most of our days, traveling together as planned, and being very nice to each other. Then, after rather sentimentally parting, he returned home and I went on with my painting trip to San Cristóbal in southern Mexico and on to Guatemala.

When I flew back to New York, to Tim, I was a little nervous, I must admit; I mean, I wasn't even sure if he was still interested or indeed if I was. But even if we were, there were so many problems! I was in love, I thought, with a man who lived in New York, a dyed-in-the-wool New Yorker with a large, complicated world there of family and friends. He wanted to write plays but at that point was a filmmaker, and I knew he was unlikely to move to Switzerland to work there; he had a finished but undistributed film that had to be dealt with and a business partner and an ex-lover to be dealt with as well, and I could tell that having just begun to disentangle himself emotionally from that relationship, he had no interest in rushing into a new one. But he promised to come to Europe in May, promised we would meet in Paris and he would come to Switzerland.

And I returned to Zurich, nearly crazy in love with him, I was now sure. And nearly crazy that he seemed so standoffish, so uncommitted. And nearly crazy, I am afraid, with . . . well, jealousy, I suppose, of Christian, whom I had gone and "returned to sender" before I even had his replacement firmly in hand!

And definitely nearly crazy to learn that almost nothing had been done to my house in Greece.

—

By the time I returned to Zurich that winter, Joanna had already been on Sifnos for a couple of months, some of the time living in her place in Kamares or, once it was possible, in my little guesthouse-to-be in Exambela. But even though we both thought Stephanos was perfect for the job, she and he still hadn't gotten the necessary permits, and the work was barely begun; it kept stopping and starting and stopping again.

For the next few weeks we exchanged long letters about the house, letters about the permits that never arrived, and, even after they finally did arrive and work started in earnest, endless letters about the cistern, the kitchen, the new bathroom, the electrical wiring, cracked tiles, beams filled with dry rot. And endless letters about our now, to me clearly, shredded relationship—her letters twelve, fifteen pages long (I have them still), handwritten in flowing sepia script, filled with many underlined words, exclamation marks, and, above all, Emotions. Mine were hasty, tightly typed, unpunctuated, uncapitalized instructions about the house and equivocations or excuses about "us."

I told her about New York, and about Tim. Most people would have walked, but Jo kept at it, at the house and to some extent our relationship, or what was left of it. As she wrote in a letter from a table at Lakis's, "How many epistles have been written from here I wonder." Dozens from her that winter.

At one point there was a letter with the sad bad news that "our little lemon tree is very ill." It survived; our relationship did not.

—

I was a total wreck that winter. There was Jo and my unfinished house at the end of the world, and there was my growing anxiety about whether and when the elusive Tim would ever ever call, beckon me to Paris, give me the nod, and change my life. That was the worst. When I should have been on my way to Greece, I was just waiting in Switzerland, waiting for him to come. By May it had gotten so I didn't dare leave my studio for fear I would miss his call. I thought I would go insane waiting.

Finally Tim called and said to come ahead to Paris the very next day, a Monday, I think it was. Trying to retain at least a shred of self-respect, I replied that I was so busy I couldn't possibly come before Thursday, and then I sat there like an idiot, bags packed, for three days, sat there waiting by the door and worrying the whole time: Why had it taken him so long to call? Where did I fit in? What was I doing? Was this going to work or was it already screwed up? Maybe this was a big mistake, I thought. But when I finally got off the Trans-European Express in Paris and saw him at the end of the platform in the Gare de L'Est in a white linen jacket and dark glasses, that wonderful smile on his face—I had forgotten the smile—my heart did a little flip.

We stayed in Paris a few days; then I took him to Zurich, to my studio and friends there, and then to the Ticino. I didn't take him to my family; I am not sure gay people back then took their potential lovers home to Mom and Pop for vetting. Instead I took him to Berzona. Berzona would tell him everything about me, I thought, and seeing him there would tell me all about him.

We stayed in a friend's flat in a village not far from Berzona, a wonderful old-fashioned place with high-ceilinged, elegantly stuccoed rooms, where we ate breakfast on a little balcony on the village square, looking out over the mountains, and slept tucked up under heavy duvets at night. It was early May and still very cold. Days we drove up to Berzona, walked in the mountains, and swam naked in the freezing glacial rivers of my childhood. Or I did. Tim wasn't so sure about the icy water. But somehow it clicked for him, it seemed a go, and I knew that I would and could and had to move to New York. Which I did the following winter.

I knew this was it. I was in love, and I was in love with a man, and to my surprise I was perfectly happy about it. I had been in love with men before, I knew that. Looking back, I had always loved men more than I had ever really loved women. My sexual attraction to men has always been strong, direct, fulfilling—perhaps because it was about them and my truly wanting them. My attraction to women, I think, was more about me, my pleasure and my vanity—about them wanting me. I wasn't as interested in them experiencing real pleasure as I was in being the one who gave it, that is, in my sexual prowess: as Melissa was in love with my cock, so was I. Beyond that, my attraction to women had always been part of the conventional world I had grown up in. I was trying to please my parents, her parents, my friends, her friends, the whole city of Basel. I was being my father, I was being my older brother, I was playing a role. I knew that, I suppose, but I still thought I wanted it, wanted to be that Man.

Now all of that . . . that confusion and anxiety fell away—the worry about being with a man, how it looked, and what it meant about me. It just fell away, a monkey off my back. The question had been answered. Just like that. A page turned. What a relief! I was twenty-seven years old, and I was finally going to start to know who I was and what I was.

And with that settled, as soon as Tim left for New York, I raced to Sifnos to take on the work of the house myself.

—

Exambela, July 1978

Dear Axel and Dita,

Very excited by the progress on the house. All taking more time and cost-ing more than it was ever supposed to, but we are getting there. The courtyard is close to completion and turning out as planned. Paul, my Greek-American architect-friend, was by the other day. I wanted to talk to him about my idea for putting another story on the house someday, a studio-bedroom for me upstairs.

[Having made enough money to pay off my debt and pay for all this work, I was getting a bit cocky.]

Getting ahead of myself I know, but anyway . . . He thought I had done such a good job with the house, I wouldn't need an architect and should just design it myself.

The cistern is coming along, almost done, and soon we won't have to lug the huge water jars that Jo found in Cheronisos to and from the village well. Stephanos made me go down under the terrace to show me the splendors of my future water tank. Since water is almost a religion here, I had to go see, even though it felt mighty claustrophobic down there. On Monday, we shall fill the tank with water from the monastery at Vrissi—I love the idea of my cistern full of holy water.

Between the cistern and the septic tank is a double concrete wall to ensure the cleanliness of the water. Seems a little close to me, but Stephanos is very proud of all this work and assures me it is safe. All the digging was done by hand as we could not use any dynamite in the village because of the neighboring buildings, particularly the huge old Prisani mansion up behind me. Do you remember, with the ruined terrace looking down over Kastro?

Stephanos cannot always be here, so I am often the manager, overseeing all the workers, their schedules and work details, and overseeing all the mule transports. An amazing sight, that, a daily parade of heavily laden mules climbing up the steep steps and paths from the road. Everything has to come in that way, stone, lumber, sinks, the toilet, everything. Then, some still carrying their loads, they stand in a kind of circle in the path out front, eyes closed, heads together against the heat, shifting their weight from one hoof to the other.

Of course, there are always problems. One day the electrician doesn't come, the next the plumber, but everyone is very cheerful and smiling and I can't get too mad at them. The younger ones, most of them my age or only a couple of years younger, are envious, I feel, of my talent and possibilities in life. One particularly wonderful-looking twenty-two-year-old with giant black eyes and masses of curls lamented the fact that all he wanted to do was go to fashion school in Athens, but his parents, having no money, there was no way for him to fulfill his dream. Unfair world. I wish I could provide a scholarship.

[I needn't have worried too much; he became a successful photographer later in life.]

The most difficult part is explaining to them what I want—my Greek is improving every day but is still pretty bad—and convincing them that I am right. I have to fight for every niche and curve and beam and every old crooked wall. Yesterday, I caught them just as they were about to fill in a beautiful old arch over the door between the kitchen and the sala. Stephanos actually does understand what I want, but the workmen all want everything to look as new and straight as possible. If they had their way, everything would be tile, linoleum, brass, and plastic. Best of all would be marble of course, but even they know that would be a different house altogether.

My biggest battle has been with the tile merchant. The old outhouse is gone, replaced by a new bathroom. Tiny, but a bathroom, and with a shower. It has a new, real glass window toward the courtyard, but I am leaving the old open window as a reminder of past glories. From a grumpy but attractive tile man in Artemona, I ordered elegant gray tiles for the floor and the shower wall, matching the new color I have chosen for all the doors and windows and shutters. He kept pushing for screaming blue tiles, and I kept saying no, I wanted the gray. And he said the gray was not suitable, that he knew I would be happier with the blue. No, I insisted, I wanted the gray. Back and forth, back and forth we went, but I remained firm.

Joanna has left for London. She was here and did a huge amount of work, helping me enormously with the house. But we didn't do very well together. We try to remain as civilized as possible with each other, but it just doesn't work. She is too negative and complicated and intense for me and is driving me crazy. I am glad she has found someone else on the island whom she has started seeing, a Greek, a man from Athens. I guess we were kind of using each other. I hope we can remain friends.

Come to Exambela next year. Spiti apo Christo.

Never a cloud, magic light.

Your new architect son,
Christo

PS Two days later:

The very attractive jerk of a tile guy has delivered screaming blue tiles! With a dazzling smile, and great charm, he explained to me that he could not bear the thought of the ugliness of the gray tiles and that I shall be very pleased with the blue. Now I have no choice as I cannot wait for another shipment. Screaming blue! What a bastard!

—

Poor Jo. Short shrift, looking back. She had done so much work and helped me so much. But she was done finally, done with everything. With me going on about Christian, then Tim, she had seen the writing on the wall and over the winter had taken up with said man from Athens. Attractive and charming, he was a bit of a devil, a bit of a womanizer, moving through the ladies of the island, in the foreign community especially, like a hot knife through butter.

Whenever Jo was on the island, I would bump into them every-where, swimming, sunning, dining together, holding hands. I said in a letter that I was happy for her, but in truth it made me crazy to see the two of them together everywhere. I knew I had driven her away, but still. When she was not there, he, the new lover and I, were perfectly friendly—at least until a few years later, when I said something about how badly he was treating a recent conquest of his, a British lady, and he never spoke to me again.

Island life.

Jo came back to Sifnos from time to time. At one point she bought a ruin, but I don't know what came of it. She even came to see me in New York once and met Tim; curiously, she always wanted to meet my lovers. Then somehow, in time, she vanished from my life.

—

Over the past five years I had spent many uncomfortable nights on horrible thin Greek mattresses, and I was having none of it for *my* house. I swore I would have the best beds on Sifnos. And with my newfound wealth, I ordered fancy Swiss beds and had a whole ship-ment of household goods sent to Athens with them via a Swiss shipping company.

One day near the end of July, when the house was actually start-ing to get done, a telegram arrived informing me that my shipment was at a clearinghouse in Piraeus and I needed to go there as soon as possible to deal with it. It had never entered my mind to hire a bro-ker to deal with clearing my goods in Athens, and I had not a clue what customs might do to me. I rushed off to Athens, organized a truck to the boat, I don't know how, and somehow found the right place. It was on some strange industrial street in Piraeus, a huge, grubby, smoke-filled room jammed with men pushing and shoving. The fans turning slowly overhead had no effect on the unbearable July heat and the smoke-filled air, and it was miserable in there.

I pushed my way to the desk, *a* desk anyway, I had no idea

which, as the signs were all in Greek. I handed over my documents, which appeared to interest the surly man sitting behind the counter not at all, and was unceremoniously told to go wait, he waved vaguely, over there. Which I did. I waited and waited and waited, one hour, two hours, three hours, waiting for someone, anyone to help me.

I was nearly suffocating in the heat, and I was getting panicky. The *Ionion* was scheduled to depart very soon, and the truck I'd hired to take the goods from the clearinghouse to the boat was waiting outside, costing quite a lot of money. On Sifnos, another truck organized to haul everything from the dock to Exambela would no doubt soon be waiting. At Exambela, the mules to take everything up to the house would also eventually be waiting. But no one paid any attention to me or to my papers.

Just as I was about to either throw a fit or burst into tears in front of all these mustachioed, macho Greek truck drivers, one of them took pity on me, guiding me back up to the counter, this time to the right counter and this time the right man. As we approached the counter, my new friend leaned in toward me and whispered in my ear, asking me whether I had a couple of thousand drachmas, which I did, and of course, as soon as he passed the money across the counter, all the papers were suddenly signed and stamped, and I was on my way.

I hugged my handsome savior, excessively I am sure—I was grateful—and watched as my stuff was brought out and thrown onto the waiting truck. Breaking whatever speed limits there might be, we raced across Piraeus to the *Ionion* just in time to have my belongings chucked on board, not very lovingly, and pushed and shoved and squeezed into storage bins between the trucks and motorcycles— the new Sifnos—and off we sailed.

The arrival, about eight hours later, was somewhat less chaotic and nerve-racking, but not much. The little three-wheeler truck was there at the dock, and as soon as the passengers were off the ship and the trucks and cars had been off-loaded, my things were packed in the back and driven to the steps of Exambela, where the mules were waiting with their handlers. Everything was loaded, precariously, I thought, on the mules' backs—one, two, three mattresses, box springs, and several crates and packages—and the now sweating mules struggled up the path to the house. Though it was already quite late, to my surprise the villagers were still awake and watched curiously from their doors as our little parade passed by. Finally everything was dumped in the middle of the floor of the *sala*.

Now the fun began. The whole village, it seemed, had been waiting for this moment. They knew the house was basically finished, and after all this time they were dying of curiosity. They poured in, the women especially, snooping everywhere, helping tear boxes open, bouncing on the Swiss beds and mattresses, clucking and cackling like so many hens. Others practiced flushing my brand-new toilet, one of the first in the village, and spoke glowingly of my horrible screaming blue tiles—a particular hit, it seemed. "*Orea, poli orea*," they clucked and swooned.

What would they have thought of the gray, I wondered?

Suddenly there was a commotion as the kitchen doors were flung open and the village priest and his acolyte, a very young fellow carrying a censer and some olive branches, swept into the room. Even before the boy was able to wrestle the prayer book from the tangle of his robes, the priest had begun chanting and praying, and the rest of us arranged ourselves devoutly around the room. What were they doing here? How did they know to come? I saw Stephanos across the room, nodding and smiling at me. It was he, of course, who had told them, invited them: the house had to be blessed before I moved in.

The ceremony was totally incomprehensible to me, but very moving. It was my house, after all, and as usual in such a situation I soon found myself wiping away a tear or two. After quite a time of intense chanting and many asides to the acolyte, who seemed to have no more idea of what was going on than I did, the priest took the censer and lit the incense, and the room filled with the dusky smell of the island churches. Then, handing back the smoking censer, the priest took the sprigs of olive and a glass of, I was sure, very holy water that the boy produced. From where, I have no idea, another fold of his robe? What else was in there? I wondered.

The priest turned, and when Stephanos pointed out the owner, me, he dipped the olive twigs in the water, sprinkled some drops on my forehead, turned, and grandly toured the tiny crowded house, glass in hand, spraying holy water everywhere, on the floors and on my newly whitewashed walls, blessing the whole house while the boy trailed behind, swinging the smoking censer. The priest went everywhere, including my *apothiki*, sprinkling water generously around. He even went into the bathroom, where he flushed the miraculous toilet, carefully watched the water swirl down, and then flushed it again for good measure.

After that, we headed back into the house, where Stephanos whispered my name, Christo, in the priest's ear and he blessed me by name, and my house. *"Spiti apo Christo,"* he intoned grandly. After a nudge in my side from Stephanos and another low whisper, this time to me, I thanked the priest and promised him a donation for the church. With a rather self-important nod to me and the assembled guests, he and his bumbling acolyte swept out. And so did everybody else, the whole village leaving in a wave of smiles, backslaps, and handshakes.

By then it was eleven at night. I collapsed onto one of my new mattresses and fell asleep.

—

Although I had friends in Exambela, I knew very little about it or its history when I bought the house. I had been drawn to it by its proximity to Chrissopighi, with its wonderful swimming, and to Platy Ghialos and all the friends I had at the beach. Since it was quite centrally located, it was a fairly easy walk to almost everywhere on the island. Still, it had a feeling of isolation, set off the road as it was, with no cars and no streets, just the narrow stone-paved paths.

There were no restaurants and no shops except for a few shelves of basic groceries in a small house near the entrance to the village and *Kyria* Olympia's even smaller corner *kafenion* in the center. Even today, with a real grocery store out by the windmills and a couple of little restaurants on the main road—they open, invariably fail, and close—the village is so off the beaten path that one can go through high season without feeling so much as a ripple from the influx of people.

Old guidebooks about Sifnos tell us another side of Exambela. George Moussa's sweet, clunky, old-fashioned guidebook from the 1970s says:

> *Walking through Exambela nowadays, one can hardly believe that the place had at any time been full of jollity. The apparently calm habitants of today . . . were once so notorious for their zeal in mischief and fun-making that the Turks coined the term* Aksham Bela *(trouble in the evening) to apply to the town . . . Consequently the village became known as Exambela. It seems that in the old days, no evening went by without a misdemeanor being committed by the village rowdies . . . Among the customers of Café Vasselos were some of the most marvelous and strange characters. Many of them excelled at dancing the* zebekiko *and often grabbed the nearest wooden chair or table (!) between their teeth and whirled it around in their warlike dance.*

I rather loved the idea that I had landed in a village with a rowdy, risqué past, though it was hard to find so much as a trace of it now. It was remarkable, though, how welcoming the villagers were once I had my house there. My neighbors were not at all standoffish, but hospitable and very curious. This was unlike anywhere I had ever lived, perhaps a bit like St. Olaf but certainly not Basel or London. I was still a *xenos*, a foreigner and a guest, but owning a house gave me a stake in the village, and the village, I suppose, a stake in me. I thought it was a little like going from being in love to being married. I was not one of them, of course, and never could be, but they took me in, adopted me, made me a kind of honorary citizen of their world.

In the days after I moved in, villagers steadily trickled through my house, welcoming me and exploring every inch of the place. Sometimes there was quite a crowd: one day I found myself with two Floras, one Chrysoula, one Rhodope, two Popis, one Despina, and one Calliope—how I loved their names! They carefully examined and commented on everything, turning over cups, rubbing fabrics, or running their fingers along shelves, all the while telling me stories of the previous owners, how so-and-so had been born in my bedroom, how this one or that had played there as a child. To my amazement, it appeared that a family of seven had previously lived in my tiny house.

The price I had paid for the house—somehow my new friends knew all the details—was a major topic: "*Tst, tst, tst. Po po po, para para para poli, para poli lefta,*" much too much money, Despina cried, throwing her chin up and clicking her tongue at my foolishness. "I could have gotten it much cheaper for you," clucked Rhodope. Indeed the price of everything was discussed and criticized. They examined my kitchen chairs, which I had bought from *Kyria* Olympia, who was closing her *kafenion*, old cane chairs, the real thing, with handsomely carved backs. Too expensive, was the judgment. They bent down to inspect the underside of an old table I had bought in Apollonia, shaking their heads in dismay at the traces of woodworm, the curse of the island, and at how much it had cost. Worst of all was how *old* everything was.

With much shaking of heads and wagging of rough, chubby fingers, I was told that I had to replace all the old stone floors, the wooden arches over the doors, the marble sink. "What was Stephanos thinking?" they fussed. Everything had to be torn out and rebuilt; it was that simple. "*Christo, christaki mou,* these are so ugly," one said, pointing at my beloved Corbusier niches—when we had broken into the walls, to my delight we had found even more. "You must cover up all this. You must replace the dirty marble sink. You need plastic containers for the water, not these old pottery ones." And so on.

I tried to explain that I liked it that way. "But," said Maria, "no lady will want to work in such an old-fashioned room." Dodging that particular bullet, I said they would see, one day the old styles would be popular again, people would collect old things, and they would be very valuable. This happened everywhere, I said. And indeed, once word got out that I was looking for old furniture, they all wanted to sell me stuff. I would be shyly, more often slyly, beckoned into a house and shown some dusty heirloom or other. I loved these visits to local houses and found, besides a few smaller pieces, a fabulous *canapé*—a long wooden bench with high carved back and arms, a classic piece of Greek island furniture—for the end of the *sala*. It needed to be totally restored, but the village carpenter was eager to take on the job, and over a long winter he returned it to its former glory. But they continued to think I was a little bit *trilli*, crazy, and shook their heads over me.

And what was I going to do about the windows? my ladies continued. Didn't I need curtains, blinds? I did not. Very impractical on such a humid island, I thought. And anyway I had shutters. I said I wouldn't mind some of the old embroidered curtains I saw in many village windows, but they snorted with disdain; they would give me no privacy and would just collect dirt. I knew the islanders slept sealed in their rooms, windows and shutters closed, terrified of drafts and the Damp. Maybe they had learned this from their long-ago Venetian rulers.

I tended to leave everything wide-open, a fact the village seemed to be well aware of. It didn't matter to me, as it was not easy to see in, except for the kitchen. If a passerby wanted to look in anywhere else, and they all did, she would have to walk by very slowly, embarrassingly slowly, and awkwardly crane her neck, and even then the steep slope of the path would take her on down the hill, too low to see anything. I had to laugh at the acrobatics as people walked past on tiptoe, trying to peek into my little bedroom.

Courtyard at tou Vounou

I was to find that few of the villagers had any interest or affection for the old houses they had grown up in, no matter how charming. These houses were loved by foreigners only, and maybe nowadays a few Athenians. I had a sneaking sympathy for their preference for the new, though, and not just among my ladies that day, but also the carpenters who worked on the house—in fact, all the islanders. Why should one expect them to go on living without plumbing and the other amenities we took for granted just so we could time travel back a hundred years or more when we visited? The magnificent stone floors of the Sifniots' village houses were murder to clean and in winter gave them crippling arthritis, the beautiful old beamed ceilings could be filled with scorpions and almost always had dry rot, and those beautiful old jars I was collecting now that I had a house reminded them of the years and years they had had to lug them, filled with water, from the village wells. For them, the primitive was all too recent, the past all too present.

Those first days, people dropped by all the time. One day, an old lady who clearly was very *trilli* burst into the house and walked through all the rooms, her hands clasped in front of her large, heaving bosom. "*Orea, orea, poli orea,*" beautiful, beautiful, she kept repeating, tears in her eyes. She had grown up in the house, it appeared, and told me about the babies born there, the babies who had been sick there, the babies who died there. Finally she held me at arm's length, shook her head, then kissed me sloppily on both cheeks and left. I never found out who she was. And as much as I loved all the "old" about my house, I decided that maybe I didn't want to know too much of its history. It was very grim, I suspected. I needed to live and work in these rooms, and I didn't want to know where all the dead babies were buried.

Among my new neighbors there in the village was Rhodope, the daughter of the very stout *Kyria* Kathe, who tended the church and monastery in Chrissopighi, and whom I adored. Rhodope was the housekeeper for the Millers, the American family who lived in the large villa above the church. At that point I didn't think I needed a full-time housekeeper—the house then really was so small—but I did want someone nearby to have the keys to my house and keep an eye on it. Rhodope seemed perfect for the job, and over time she became more and more of a real housekeeper for me and started to oversee the opening and closing and the airing and annual whitewashing of the house.

—

Living in a Cycladic village is a very intimate experience. You are living almost as a family in an endlessly extended house, a cluster of connected, abutting, adjoining boxes with shared walls, roofs, and terraces. It is almost a lost art to build in this way, the villages running on and on, up and down and over the hills like some kind of organic creature. One has the feeling that if you tapped out a message on your wall, it would travel the length and breadth of this wood and stone organism and be heard at the far end of the village.

Streets, paths, and steps weave between the houses, turning corners here, dead-ending there, forcing you to turn back as in a maze, more Eastern, literally Byzantine, than European. Here and there a house stands alone in its walled garden or orchard; here and there is a church with an ancient cypress or palm towering over it, here and there a strange, inexplicably shaped windowless and doorless space, probably the back ends of two or three village houses . . . Whose property is it? It must belong to someone.

Exambela was not nearly so hivelike as Kastro, where the villagers lived on top of one another, but still, windows looked into neighbors' kitchens and over their terraces, and housewives gossiped from window to window. You could hear everything—conversations, quarrels, even lovemaking, I am sure. My little row house stood a bit above and apart, out toward the edge of the village, and I didn't live there all the time, but I and it were surrounded by close neighbors, our terraces, our walls, and our stairs adjoining one another's. The stairs to my roof were built right into one of my neighbor's walls, and the low wall I sat on to eat breakfast at my outdoor table actually belonged to another neighbor. My house was part of the village's woof and warp, its weave, or I felt it was and wanted it to be.

From day one, old Popi, my neighbor, was my favorite person in Exambela, and indeed on the island. Meeting and getting to know her was alone worth having bought the house. She and her second husband, Georgos, were for me, and later for Tim once he started coming to Sifnos, the heart and soul of Exambela. They lived on the other side of my back courtyard, across the alley that ran along it, in a single room above their daughter's house. Popi and Georgos had moved out and upstairs when her daughter Simone had married, and Simone would move out herself to make room for her daughter (also named Popi). My little guesthouse was tucked against this larger house, and the two houses were so close it felt as if we shared the same roof terrace and could talk from roof to roof without even raising our voices.

Stout and as sturdy as an oak, Popi usually wore a scarf wound tight on her head, the tails of the knot hanging down her back, giving her, with her naughty, leering grin, a slightly piratical look. She had glasses as thick as Coca-Cola bottles and a muddle of slightly cockeyed teeth interspersed with gold. She always carried a heavy walking stick, which she used freely to gesticulate with, banging it on the floor for emphasis or using it to whack your legs when she got to the punch line of what was usually a dirty joke, wickedly grinning with what was left of her teeth as she bit down on her suggestively waggling little finger. She watched my every move from her house, and if anybody arrived, she would appear instantly in my *sala*, dying of curiosity. She adored my parents, who soon began coming every year, and it came to seem that as their child, I could do no wrong.

One evening, slightly nervously, I told her that my new friend Tim was coming to visit Sifnos for the first time—to warn her that someone other than my parents was coming for a visit, and a man at that. At that point I had never had a friend come to visit my new house, and I was rather anxious about how we might appear to my neighbors. How would we pull it off in this tiny village where everyone knew everything about everybody? Would we have to sneak from room to room, slink around in my own house?

I felt it was nobody's business, but telling Popi was like sending up a trial balloon. I told her a bit about Tim and told her that he would be staying in the *apothiki*, tucked there below her terrace. Frowning, she smacked her stick crossly against my calves and announced, with all the authority of a four-foot-eight despot, that I would do no such thing. Whack! Under no circumstances should *avtós to Tim*, this Tim, sleep there all by himself. Whack! It was my duty as a good host to offer to share my bedroom in the main house.

Well, whew. If the highest of village royalty said it was okay to share my room, it was okay, and indeed, no one ever questioned the two of us sleeping there together.

Regal she was, that little fireplug of a woman, a natural aristocrat with innate authority and, with her radiant smile and wicked sense of humor, very charismatic. She was a classic island figure of a type that is now almost completely gone. She had a simplicity about her that was a kind of wisdom, uncomplicated, straight, and clear. I have no intention of getting all Rousseau-ish about her or that older generation of islanders, speaking of them as noble primitives, but I have to admit that in the years to come, something was lost in the shuffle from those simple, sturdy islanders I knew when I first got there to the flashy youths of today with their motorcycles, open shirts, and gold chains.

For Tim and me, Popi was the best of the village; she represented its quality and essence, its vital force and genius, its anima (shades of my Jungian mother). But she was also simply my best friend on Sifnos, a warm, hilarious little fairy godmother living next door, keeping her eye on me, on us. I was her *Christaki mou, pedi mou*, a kind of honorary son, and she loved Tim too from the moment she met him that summer, always jabbing him in the ribs and winking, the two of them, though Tim spoke not a word of Greek, somehow communicating, somehow always in on the same joke.

Every evening Popi would sit on her little bench on her terrace, her chin resting on her chubby freckled hands folded together on the head of her stick, looking out across the valley to the village graveyard, contemplating her future inevitable journey there and beyond. Cemeteries in the Cyclades often overlook the sea or some beautiful vista, and this one was no exception. It sat on a high slope facing back toward the village and then straight down and out over Kastro to the sea and the distant islands. To get to this enchanting little graveyard, you had to go down into the valley below the village, then up through a beautiful grove of cypresses, which was quite a steep climb. The villagers joked that on the deceased's last journey he at least didn't have to walk there, then or ever again.

—

Parting from my simple village life every year to go to bustling Manhattan was hard. I had moved to New York a year after meeting Tim, and once he started coming to Sifnos, we often came together, sometimes for a month or more, early in the summer. I would most often leave with him, but sometimes I stayed longer, and I always returned in the fall, with or without him, if only to close the house. And when I left for the year, Popi would come over with homemade cheeses and fresh eggs to put in my suitcase. Stinking *mizithra* cheese and several-days-old eggs made for quite an effect if you had to open your suitcase for customs inspection in New York, I assure you, so I usually gave away her offering as soon as I left the island. We always cried a little bit together, she and I, and then she would point her stick across the valley to the graveyard. "*Christaki mou*, when Christo comes back next year, he will find his Popi over there."

Given the harsh, raw Cycladic winters, the damp, and the bone-chilling winds, I often thought she might be right, but she was tough and lived well into her eighties. But one year when I came back, she was gone. And that summer I often visited her grave with Georgos, who had been devoted to her. We would laugh and cry a little, remembering stories about her. He was a few years younger and outlived her by a good many years, but after Popi's death he was never the same, almost a shell of himself. The only thing that gave him pleasure was Popi's great-granddaughter, Maria, a tiny little mite of a thing who lived downstairs with her mother and father, Popi and Nico. An only child, she was lovingly spoiled by everyone in the family, especially Georgos. But without Popi it seemed as if nothing really held his attention anymore, and soon it was he who sat on that little bench up on the roof in the evenings, waiting to join his wife in the graveyard across the valley.

At one time, Georgos had been quite a celebrity. In 1943 a Wellington bomber was hit by German flak and ditched in the sea half a kilometer from the rocky shore of Sifnos. The British captain and his crew made it to land in a dinghy that popped out of the sinking plane. They were cold and exhausted and hungry, but worse, they said later, their cigarettes were all wet and ruined. They slept under some olive trees, where they were discovered in the morning by Popi's daughter and Georgos's stepdaughter, Simone, riding on a donkey. She immediately went to fetch Georgos, who arrived with a Sifniot who miraculously spoke some English. He made sure that the six beached airmen were English, not German, and then Georgos took them back to the house he and Popi lived in, the one next to mine, and gave them water and bread, which was all they had. The airmen, equally suspicious, would not eat or drink until he and Popi had eaten too.

The men were hidden up at Agios Andreas, the mountaintop monastery across the valley. Their presence was kept from the village children in case they unwittingly tipped off the Italians who were occupying the island or the Germans who came from nearby Milos several times a week. The British captain recalled, "During the war, over one hundred and eighty people died on Sifnos because they didn't have enough to eat, but the locals made a big fuss over us, bringing food and cigarettes. The men spent ten days in the monastery, while a stream of very hungry people climbed the steep path to bring them bread, cheese, figs, retsina, and a handful of precious and rationed cigarettes." The Sifnos chief of police arranged for a fisherman to get them to the neighboring island of Sérifos, where, housed in a cave that was used as a goat pen, they found five British commandos spying on German troop movements. Eventually they were all rescued and taken to Cyprus on a Royal Navy gunboat.

The captain kept in touch with Georgos after the war, visiting Sifnos in 1966 during the making of a television documentary, when Georgos was their guide. And in the early 1980s he was flown to London to receive a Medal of Honor for helping save the six men's lives. He was very proud of the medal, carried it everywhere with him, and pulled it out of his jacket pocket and told the story whenever he got the chance. Popi, as long as she lived, would give him a whack with her stick and scold him, pretending to tell him to stop showing off while beaming with pride. Sometimes, as he sat alone on his terrace in the evening, after her death, I would see him take the medal from his pocket and stare down at it.

The way of death on Sifnos, and all Greek islands I expect, is as of a passage that comes to everyone. The motorcycle accident that caused the death of my young neighbor in Platy Ghialos was unusual, freakish, and so the grieving that followed it was unusual too, over-the-top. Normally the islanders, sturdy and tough, as flinty as the miles of walls and steps their ancestors built all over Sifnos, lived to be very old. And as with Popi and Georgos, most of them died during the long, cold, desolate winters. I would come back in the spring and there would be another one gone, taken. And I missed their funerals as well.

One that I did attend was the funeral of an old, old man who lived a few houses down from me. I knew him and his many sons, one of whom was a priest, and his many grandchildren. I went to visit him before he died. He lay with his eyes half closed in the hot, stuffy sickroom, his family sitting and standing awkwardly against the walls, hats in their large, bony, sunburned hands. It was late July,

The tower

and a child, a grandchild I assumed, sat by his head, fanning him and swatting at the flies that buzzed around him.

A small man, he was tiny in death. When he died, they dressed him in his best black suit and a brand-new pair of shiny black shoes for his next journey—to heaven—and he was placed in a small, plain wooden coffin, bareheaded for probably the first time ever during the day. His bone-white brow above the tan line peeped out through wreaths of jasmine that had been piled in the coffin to cover the rising smell of the body in the summer heat.

After the church service I watched from my upstairs terrace as his sons, as tradition required, carried the coffin through the river of people below for a last goodbye to his village and his neighbors, the coffin parting the crowd like a little rowboat in the Nile. Finally, as the smell began to get worse, the sons started literally running with the coffin, hurrying to get it to the pickup truck down on the road that would carry it, closed at last, to the graveyard. Sweet, touching, vaguely comical when they desperately threw the coffin onto the truck, it was all part of a way of life, a tradition older than memory.

Over the years I lived there, the islanders started dying younger, often from cancer, particularly lung cancer. They all smoked like chimneys, at first the men but eventually women too, though in my early years on Sifnos I never saw an island woman smoke. More and more often the islanders began to disappear to hospitals in Athens, flown out by helicopter in emergencies. Its noisy clatter soon became the sound and symbol of calamity, and a communal shudder would cross the island. People would rush to their windows to watch the helicopter rise clumsily from the landing field, turn, and disappear while they waited for word of who had been carried off this time.

—

Popi's daughter Simone, the girl on the donkey who found the British soldiers, was a near neighbor for many years, living across the way below Popi and Georgos until she herself moved out to make way for her daughter. Always and in all things a little jealous of her mother, she was determined to be an intimate friend of mine too. No longer a girl, she was now shaped much like her mother, short and heavyset, but she had none of Popi's charisma or loopy charm. She was, however, an assiduous friend and a determined presence, popping in and out of my house at all times of the day with questions, gossip, bits of food, any excuse to come by.

Whenever I came from Switzerland or America, I brought gifts to my village friends and neighbors, or brought them things they had asked me for—effectively ordered—such as a watch or a piece of jewelry for a grandchild, things they couldn't get on the island and doubted they could get from Athens. They seemed to prefer that these gifts come from abroad, preferred the glamour, I suppose, of saying they came from Zurich or New York City. Given Simone's kind of neediness, I was always careful to bring her a gift, and would rack my brains to be sure it was something special.

The islanders were very strange about these transactions. When I handed Simone her gift, for example, she wouldn't look at it or open it in front of me or anyone else. The gift would swiftly disappear under a baggy sweater or into a fold of her skirt, and head down, she would scurry off home on her chubby legs. Even if this happened in her own house, she would not so much as glance at what I'd given her, but hide it away under a piece of sewing or a cushion. And she would never even tell me if she liked the present unless I asked.

At first I was a bit discomfited by this, but I learned that there was nothing personal in it; it was simply the way they were. Thinking back, it occurs to me that the explanation might be the Evil Eye, that they didn't want their neighbors to see their gift for fear of provoking envy and hence bad luck.

At any rate, many of my neighbors would in turn leave sweets, fruit, cheese, or vegetables, even little bouquets of flowers from their gardens, on my steps. And whenever I arrived in Exambela, often late at night, exhausted by endless flights, delayed boats, and jet lag, my neighbors would appear as if from nowhere, stopping in to say hello when they saw my lights, often with gifts or something to eat, rightly presuming there would be no food in the house. A farmer neighbor would stand there in his rough tweed jacket, shyly reach into a pocket, and pull out a tomato, which he would set carefully on the table, and then reach into the other pocket and bring out two fresh eggs or a homemade cheese, usually a smelly but delicious one.

Simone was married to a gentle, soft-spoken man named Aristides, who knew all about gardens and plants and took care of my few pots of lavender and jasmine and especially my beloved little lemon tree, which often seemed to be ailing. When, as it sometimes did, the tree would suddenly, inexplicably start to turn yellow and lose its leaves, Aristides would come and prune a little here, clip a little there, and then rub *azvestia*, the chalky white base for white-wash, into the trunk. He would talk to the tree all the while, making little jokes for its pleasure, as gentle and caring with it as a physical therapist with a sickly hospice patient. And wonder of wonders, a few days later the tree would perk up, put out some new leaves or flowers, and flourish again, at least for a while.

One day Tim and I went to Simone and Aristides's house—I can't remember why, but maybe we had just arrived and I had a gift for Simone. Anyway, she was making lunch for Aristides, frying three eggs in an enormous iron skillet filled, but *filled*, with olive oil. As she scooped and ladled hot oil over the eggs to push them along, she banged on about this and that—she was always a major talker—while Aristides sat quietly and patiently at the table, waiting for his meal. When the eggs were done, she scooped them onto his plate and then, to our openmouthed amazement, poured all the oil from the skillet over them.

Cardiac arrest in the making? But then maybe not: olive oil is, after all, mother's milk to island Greeks and has been shown to have many health benefits. Meanwhile, their son, Nikos, a sweet young man, had come in. To our ongoing astonishment, now verging on horror, he was casually holding a huge rabbit by the ears, the soon-

to-be meal dangling completely still, alive but mercifully in cata-
tonic shock, its stunned eyes staring straight ahead.

Too many insights into Greek cooking for one day.

Simone's brother Alekos and his wife lived near me too. They
had a son, Ianni, whom I watched grow from a little boy to a young
man. Like any little boy, he was always out wandering the village or
playing with friends. When it was time for meals, his mother would
call him to come in. "Ianniiiiiiiiiiiiiiiiii!" she would scream, as only
Greek village mothers can scream. *"Iannnniiiiiii!"* Her voice would
sail out over the village, the valley, the island, the sea, the universe.

By his late teens Ianni had become startlingly handsome, with
green eyes, olive skin, ruddy cheeks, and thick, curly chestnut hair.
I always wished Popi, his grandmother, had lived to see him during
the Summer Olympics in 2004, his (and Greece's) great moment.
He was one of the folk dancers in the little island stadium, dressed
in the full Greek army regalia worn by the Evzones, the guards of
the Royal Palace, now the President's residence, in Athens.

It is an amazing costume. Each guard wears a red cap with a long
tassel; a beautifully woven vest covers a white shirt with wide, puffy
sleeves; then comes the *fonstanela*, a kilt made up of four hundred
pieces of cloth representing the four hundred years of hated Ottoman rule. The outfit is finished off with white stockings, and black,
tasseled knee garters, and heavy clogs with enormous pom-poms.
Dressed in this astonishing, near–comic opera rig, Ianni and the
other young men danced traditional Greek dances while the islanders, especially his neighbors, clapped and cheered them on. I could
imagine the damage his grandmother would have done in her pride,
beating out time with her stick, whacking the calves of everyone
near her.

All the villagers were enthusiastic about performing in rituals
and ceremonies, dancing, singing, often acting in roles they had
played for years in various festivals. *Kyria* Olympia was a figure in
the village, a kind of elder, like Popi. She owned the tiny *kafenion*
where I bought the caned chairs that provoked so much disapproval.

In truth, her place was more like a strange kind of salon than a *kafenion*, where the men of the village trooped in of an evening to sit and smoke and gossip with her over a retsina or an ouzo. Having had polio at a young age, like quite a few Sifniots, she had a pronounced limp, and I suppose there seemed no threat to the village women in their husbands' spending the evening with her. Besides, she was the cantor at Agios Nikolaos, the main church, a leading figure and consequently above reproach.

Pascha, or Easter, the high point of the Greek Orthodox religious calendar, was Olympia's great moment. At the midnight service on Easter Eve she played the role of the Devil, trying to break into the church and prevent Christ from ascending to heaven. There we would be, the congregation, safe inside the church, the doors locked against the dark night and the evil outside. Suddenly there would be a loud banging on the doors—the Devil, *Kyria* Olympia, pretending to try to get in, a deafening noise compounded with Olympia's screaming and yelling. It was genuinely chilling, and the younger children would bury their faces in their mothers' laps.

At midnight the Devil would "give up," the priest would intone, "*Defte lavete fos*," come and receive the light, and the doors would be flung open. Lit candles in hand now, we would all chant, "*Christos anestos, Christos anestos*," Christ is risen, Christ is risen. And we would leave the church and parade through the village, its white walls aglow with flickering candlelight, and head home for *mayiritsa*, a special Easter soup with which the Greeks break their forty-day Lenten fast. It is made, I fear, from lamb offal, but is quite delicious, especially after fasting.

The other great moment in the church year was three days earlier, on Kali Paraskevi, Good Friday, when the priest and the whole congregation walked the *epitaphios*, a shrouded cross (in some places it was buried in a casket), around the church and through the village while the priest blessed the houses. The first year I saw this happen, I had no idea that you were supposed to leave all the lights on in your house, and candles too, since otherwise it was assumed your house was not occupied and wouldn't be blessed. Halfway through the service I had to run home through the village, throw on my lights, and frantically search for matches to light my candles. Then I waited proudly by the door for the priest to come by. While everyone watched, he made a cross above my door. I went back in, turned out all the lights, and joined my neighbors, feeling very much part of the village as the procession worked its way, house by house, back to the church.

—

My immediate neighbor to the north, our walls adjoining, was Aphrodite, who had also been my neighbor in Platy Ghialos. Her husband, Georgos, had died suddenly, and too young, the year before I moved in. As always, she kept her two houses down by the beach and lived there, renting out rooms in the summer, moving back to Exambela for the winter. Every year when I got to Sifnos in the spring, she would be there in her house next door, but by June she was back at the beach for the summer, which was a blessing for me as she was really too close for comfort: her house sat higher than mine and her terrace looked directly down into my little courtyard. But I was fond of her, and when she started living in the village year-round, in her old age too frail to go to the beach, I tried to be helpful, bringing her things, as she could hardly walk, and a few times even breaking into her house to help her when I heard her moaning after she had fallen. Most of the time, her nephew and his family took care of her, especially in the winter, and she lived there next to me, uncomplaining (highly unusual for islanders), for the next twenty-five years.

From the start, I was fascinated by the trickle of people, mostly men, who went past my courtyard to her house. Eventually I learned that Aphrodite was famous all over the island for being able to cure sunstroke, and more important, remove *matiasma*, the Evil Eye. An ancient superstition that is strongest in and around the Mediterranean and the Aegean, the Evil Eye is, they say, a negative power we all carry in ourselves. It is not necessarily intentional but springs from envy and can be activated simply by looking at something for too long—a beautiful child, a fine animal, a flowering fruit tree. A childless woman, watching and admiring a newborn baby, can rouse the Evil Eye in herself, and the victim, the child or mother or both, will suddenly get a headache, grow faint, fall ill, maybe even die.

In Italy and Greece and Turkey, people may say they don't believe in it, but the Evil Eye is in them somehow, ingrained, almost bred into people. And in all these countries, the ancient ways of warding off the Evil Eye—talismans, amulets, and traditional gestures—are everywhere. The blue beads worn by women, the blue eyes painted on the bows of boats, the famous gesture of pointing your index and little finger at someone, and men simply grabbing their genitals are all ways to fend off the Evil Eye.

There are all kinds of cures, some complex and esoteric, some ludicrous, running the gamut from long, mumbled recitations of prayers to spitting in the evildoer's face. Aphrodite's technique seemed benign—at least she skipped spitting in your face. It was a traditional, ritual exercise combined with secret incantations passed from mother to daughter for generations. She would offer some coffee, chat for a while about her visitor's problem—a financial deadlock, a bad crop, the man's health, his prize mule's loss of weight—and then, with some ceremony and great seriousness, draw out a length of no doubt incredibly special old string. She would tie a knot at one end, hold the knot on her knee with her elbow, and begin measuring out the string in lengths—here was the key thing—always leaving a certain magical amount left over. All the while she would mutter and chant repeated verses or prayers, unintelligible of course, since if the words were actually understood, she would lose her powers.

The same was true of her mysterious behavior with the string. She would give no explanation and certainly not demonstrate how she did whatever in the world it was she was doing. She would measure out her length of string over and over, and if it didn't come out right or even—whatever right or even was—she would gasp, throw up her hands, and sit back dramatically in her chair, shaking her head.

Not good. If it didn't match, you see. If it didn't come out right, it meant someone had put the Evil Eye on you. And then she would go through the whole rigmarole again and again until the magical measurements somehow came out right, at which point you were released, cured.

I went through this with her a couple of times myself because I was curious and also, at one point, because I imagined that someone had put the Evil Eye on me. But that is a later story. My Jungian mother was so intrigued by all these goings-on that she insisted on visiting Aphrodite. After going through the ritual of measuring out the string, Aphrodite turned deathly pale. She measured out the string again, almost frantically, disbelief all over her face, then dramatically pushed her chair back from the table as if to rush away and, pointing her finger at my mother, announced that *she* had the Evil Eye, the Awful Gift.

Although she went through Aphrodite's endless cure with the lengths of string, I wasn't sure that my mother really wanted to give up her newly minted witchdom without a dry run, at least one turn around the dance floor, as it were, with her horrible newfound power.

Opposite Aphrodite's and adjoining Popi's house and my *apothiki* was the Karella house, one of the few grand houses in Exambela. The huge entrance gates and grand facade were on the far side of the house, along with a private chapel and a dreamy terrace shaded with ancient pines; from there, the house looked east toward the sea, the view stretching all the way from Kastro in the north to Faros in the south. This was truly one of the great views on Sifnos, and I would often tiptoe across the broad, flat roofs of the Karella house to watch the sun or moon rise over the islands of Páros and Foligandros.

The Karella family had made their fortune in the nineteenth century in the garment industry, but by 1977–78 the family fortune was largely gone, and two spinsters in their eighties—sisters, perhaps, no one seemed to know—lived there, pottering around alone in the lofty rooms of this grand old house. Whoever they were, these two old ladies thought themselves the aristocrats of the village, and though they had no staff, they certainly knew how to keep up appearances.

They dressed to kill whenever they ventured out. They never left by the front gates—too heavy, or possibly simply too far to go from the front all the way around to the village proper—but instead, passing through the huge pantries and vast kitchens, they would slip out the back door into the alley opposite my house, locking the door behind them with a huge key that they hid carefully, as everyone in the village knew, under a large stone by the door.

When they went to church on Sunday mornings, one of the few times one saw them, they were always in the same outrageous gold and silver high-heeled shoes, not very high heels, perhaps, but heels—unheard of in the village. They would teeter and totter past my courtyard without ever looking up, worried no doubt about falling on the uneven stones, a purse clutched to a bosom in one hand, a walking stick in the other. Both had significant mustaches, but their outfits and coiffures were well worth waiting for, so as soon as I heard the key turning in the lock, I would call my guests to witness this little ritual *passeggiata*.

Their annual *panaghia* in the family chapel was their great social event and only real public appearance. Like ladies of the manor greeting their serfs, they would wear every piece of jewelry they owned and of course the gold and silver shoes, and would sparkle like Christmas trees as they nodded and smiled gravely at their visitors. I always went, dressed in my best clothes, which I otherwise never wore anywhere on Sifnos. Once, they actually invited Tim and me in, a first, and we wandered through those large white rooms with their tall shuttered windows, all slightly fusty and airless, everything covered with sheets. A few rooms were still lived in, filled with dark nineteenth-century furniture, tables covered with brica-brac and family photos, and mosquito nets drooping from the ceilings to the floors around the beds.

For a time I had fantasies, both Tim and I did, of owning the house—talk about *folie de grandeur*.

When one of them died, who knew which, the other moved into a smaller house in the village, where she stayed until her own death, and for a time the house was empty. But it has recently been sold to a rich Athenian family who have restored it—or rather more than that, having put in a swimming pool, an unheard-of luxury, and an air-conditioning system.

The Prisani mansion next door, which forms the end of the alley behind Aphrodite's, has sadly fared less well. In the early twentieth century one of the Karella daughters married a Mr. Prisani and was given a piece of land adjoining her family's house as a dowry. Very nouveau riche, Mr. Prisani clearly set out to top his in-laws and proceeded to build a huge villa that covered the entire property, every square inch of the land his wife had been given. The whole village worked on the construction of this palace, as it must have seemed to them, its high stucco walls and long shuttered windows towering over the village, even over the more traditional Karella house next door.

In the summers, the two families and their guests would arrive on their yachts and ride teams of donkeys and mules packed with luggage up to the houses. Many villagers worked for them from time to time, and the older ones would regale you with tales of the entertaining and laughter that went on there. The greatest feature of the Prisani house was a vast raised terrace that stuck out from the house to the northeast, with servants' quarters and kitchens below and spectacular views over steep farm terraces down to Kastro and the sea. It was straight out of a Visconti film; one could imagine ladies with parasols sitting or strolling about, surrounded by tubs of flowers, at least on the days they weren't being blown away. The Prisani house was the quintessential badly situated grand villa on Sifnos, totally exposed to the wind and weather.

But disregard of weather and pretentiousness were not the only faults in Mr. Prisani's house. Maybe he and his architect were both showing off. The house had been built in the 1920s with the newest materials of the day, including iron beams instead of wood to hold up the ceilings and floors of the immense rooms. By the late 1950s the family had lost its wealth and stopped coming to Sifnos. Neglected, abandoned, the house began to lose its windows. With all the wind from the north and winter rains blowing in, the iron beams began to rust, making them heave and twist, and the ceilings started to fall in. Soon people started looting, pulling out the old hand-painted tiles, the carved interior doors, and the ornate metalwork. It became a total ruin, with windows and doors gone, marble floors littered with glass and plaster.

Some years later I was offered this falling-down mansion, without a square foot of land, just the crumbling walls and the vast terrace, for fifteen thousand dollars. I thought of buying it, tearing it down and building a studio, but Stephanos, my trusty builder, assured me that tearing it down would cost at least another ten thousand, and then I would have to remove it all, he said—nothing could be saved—so I lost my nerve and gave up. But the house has had various owners since, including the University of Athens, which purchased it for their Drama Department. They bought it through a Greek friend of mine named Phoibus (he later helped me get my gallery in Athens). As far as I know, it still belongs to the university, but it is now also under landmark protection, which infuriates most of its direct neighbors, such as my friend Maria, who lives in its shadow, since it is amazingly dangerous even just to walk by it, stones and tiles and bits of plaster often coming flying down. In fact, the whole broken-down thing may simply collapse on someone someday.

In the early days, Tim and I would slip over there on wind-still evenings with our drinks and something to nibble on—it was only a few steps from my door. We would walk past the high stucco walls of the house, with their perilous, heavy, overhanging moldings, go around the corner and through the rusty, creaking iron gate, and—

after spooking about the broken rooms, imagining how it must have been—sit on the low wall around the vast terrace and watch the fading light on the far-off islands.

—

Tim came to Sifnos for the first time in 1979. I had come on ahead and was waiting impatiently for his arrival. By that time, a neighbor had a phone, the first phone in the village, and she got everyone's calls and would scream out over the village. "Christoooooo," she yelled, and I ran down the street to her house. And there was Tim, in Athens as promised. Because of a late plane, he had missed the boat that morning, but he was all set, he said, to get on the *Ionion* the next morning. I had to break the news that the *Ionion* had broken down as usual, and he would have to stay in Athens yet another day and then take a boat to Mílos and connect to yet another boat to get to Sifnos. I would be there, I said, and I would meet him at the harbor.

"What if you aren't there?" he shouted down the line—everyone shouted on the phone, you could hear every conversation all over the village, sometimes both sides of it—"I mean, this is already all screwed up. What if you aren't there? How do I find the house?" This was fast becoming my favorite question. "Just ask anyone, anyone at all," I shouted back. "Just say 'spiti apo Christo,' and someone will bring you here to the house."

It all worked out, and indeed I was there when he got to Kamares—hours late, of course. He arrived late at night, in the pitch dark, just as I had the first time, the same black mountains rising up on either side, the same tiny harbor with its strings of fairy lights reflecting in the water. The best arrivals are always at night, in the dark, certainly the most romantic and the most intense. Since you can't really see, you are struggling to make out what you are looking at, and everything is more mysterious and extraordinary. And bigger. Those mountains looming on either side of the harbor always seem enormous in the dark.

We hugged, piled into the same old rattling bus I had taken on my first day in Sifnos, and rode up the same, barely improved road to Apollonia. I watched Tim as he peered out at the landscape, its farm buildings and dovecotes glowing ghostly white in the moonlight. I was hoping he loved it as I did, loved it at first sight, as I had. I was crazy to have him love Sifnos. I would show him everything, I thought, take him all over the island, take him to all my favorite spots and to visit all my favorite people. And I did. Over the next few days I walked his feet off, guided and toured him half to death, pointing out the island's many beauties and curiosities. Finally, one day, as I was banging on about the wonders of this or that—"Look, look over there!"—he stopped dead in his tracks and said, "Why don't you stop trying to make me love this place and let it come to me?"

It wasn't easy; I wanted him to love it, and me, so much, but I sat on my mouth and backed off. And he did love it, the wild, barren island, the walls and terraces, all of it to him like a sunny, blue-skied Ireland, a place he had loved when he was young. He loved the churches and monasteries and didn't even mind being pinched by the mad, lonely monk at the monastery at Vrissi. He loved swimming off my rock at Chrissopighi and lunching under the pines at my favorite taverna on the beach. He loved Exambela with its twisting alleys, and he loved the villagers with their polite, smiling ways. He would say it was impossible to be depressed here. All you had to do was walk out into the village, with everyone greeting you, asking how you were, and you would cheer up right away. *"Tikanis?"* they would ask, smiling, How are you? And as he said, you can't answer, "Oh I don't know, I'm really kind of down." He especially loved Popi, and the affection was mutual, it seemed. She came over even more than usual, cackling, jabbing him in the ribs, whacking him with her stick, quite frankly flirting with him.

He loved all the smells and sounds of village life in Exambela, many of which I was just learning about myself—I had barely had the house for a year, after all—and it was fun to experience these things together: the smoky morning fires in my neighbors' kitchens,

Monastery of Vrissi

the chickens clattering and roosters crowing outside my window, the women screaming out the door for their children or husbands— "Ianniiiii!" The best, though, was the sound of the donkeys carrying the farmers to their fields in the morning, the donkeys' hooves, rapid, dainty, mincing clicks on the stones outside my window, the men whistling to their dogs trotting along behind.

Aristo, the bread man, was probably our favorite. We listened to him from our room every morning as he came clopping along on his beautiful white mule, which was laden with baskets of all kinds of bread. We could hear him approaching, calling to the women of the village, "Popi! Rhodope! Calliope!" He would park himself in the little square just beyond my bedroom window. "Maria! Popi! Despina!" he would call. But no one came. It was a kind of game, but on a daily basis a slightly sadistic one. The women would wait in their houses till the last possible moment, till he swore he was bloody well leaving. Then, just as he started loading his mule, they would appear from their kitchens, chattering and gossiping as they came, innocently strolling up the street.

—

For Tim, no doubt the most amazing part of that first visit was that he started to paint, or rather draw, setting off daily with pad and pencils, plopping himself down around the village or farther afield, drawing the streets, the houses, the village churches, doing tiny, delicate views of Sifnos. At that point he had no thought, I am sure, that he might take up painting. He was very much a writer, though he had in fact done drawings before, architectural drawings mostly, pen-and-ink drawings of peoples' houses, done on commission and for the money, which he always needed badly. But the following winter in New York, trying to generate some business, he started to do watercolors, little jewel-like pictures based on his drawings from Sifnos, and together we cooked up a show for him in New York at a beautiful little gallery. It was Tim's first exhibition, and a sellout. "Hmm. Let's do that again," he said when it was over.

In part because of this, for it was clear that Tim would come again to Sifnos and draw—the next year and, I hoped, from then on—I decided to go ahead with some more work on the house. From day one I had known that in the long run it would be too small, and I had always envisaged a real studio to work in instead of trashing the *sala* every day, and a real bedroom as well. With the thought of two men living there, both of them painting, I decided to get started as soon as possible.

The only place to go was up, and I knew that this new construction would be complicated and costly. According to Stephanos, my beloved contractor, to put a room as big as I wanted upstairs, concrete columns would have to be poured into the existing walls; and both roofs, the existing one and the new one on the room upstairs, would have to be built with concrete as well. Fortunately, Stephanos found the whole project wonderfully challenging, and together we planned out my new room. The upstairs, which would suddenly give me real views over the village, we planned as a thirty-square-meter room that would sit toward the northern, back end of the house, abutting Aphrodite's, with a terrace in front looking south. There would be a window to the east facing over the Karella house and the sea, a window to the west overlooking a ruin and the main village path, and another window and a pair of French doors to the south, giving onto a terrace, with a view of the village and the two mountains across the valley, each with its monastery at the top.

In order to push the plans through, I knew, I needed a Sifnos architect with good connections in Mílos, where building permits were given out. I didn't want a repeat of the endless waiting I had gone through before. Today it would be more difficult to push through the addition I planned—they are stricter now about changing historic village houses—but even now I think I would probably be given permission, as there was already a very tall old house across the street, a two-story ruin directly opposite my kitchen, and of course the Prisani mansion towering over the village behind me, so my upstairs room, now as then, would not actually change the

Profitis Elias church above Kamares

Exambela "skyline." In any case, it turned out that there wasn't much of a problem. Mr. Koressi, the architect, just drew up the basic plans Stephanos and I had made, I paid all the proper fees, and we obtained the necessary permits on the spot.

The hitch, though, was that once again I had to leave for the winter. But I knew Stephanos well by now, and with all the permits acquired, I was fairly confident that he could handle the project himself. I left for New York, planning to return the following spring and move into my brand-new room.

Exambela, May 1981

Dearest Parents,

Driving along the road from Apollonia to the entrance of Exambela, I could see my house, the top of my house, my new room, for the first time. It sits very handsomely and if you didn't know, you would say it had always been there. But it is all completely different. It is really a much bigger house now and the villagers call it "to manhattan"or "to villa," as any two-story structure is by definition the home of a rich person and thereby a villa.

Standing in front of my house, it is not just my tiny little house anymore; it is a real house. And it is perfect.

Stephanos paid attention to every detail, even adding niches like in an old house. I now have a big square room upstairs with a red-tiled floor and a beamed wooden ceiling, great tall windows that flood the space with light all day and large French doors with wonderful views to the mountains. From my (future) bed, I shall look straight out at the church of Agios Andreas across the valley. The window beside my bed looks down into my courtyard, out past a little church, to the roof of the Karella house and the sea beyond—a view I shall have to paint.

I can reach my new roof above the bedroom on a wooden ladder. From way up there (quite scary and dangerous really—Tim will hate it, he hates heights) I can see rooftops and mountaintops, islands, sea and sky. If it weren't for the high wall of the Prisani house rising up behind Aphrodite's, the view would be 360 degrees with a direct view down to Kastro. Just incredible. Someday I shall have a little staircase built to be able to go up there more easily.

[Which I did in the early 1990s, copying an old metal spiral staircase. It led up to what was by then a roof terrace with cushioned seats built into the walls.]

Stephanos proudly showed me the work in the sala, where the concrete pillars were built inside the old walls. It must have been a very difficult job and an amazing mess. But you can barely tell where the walls were opened up and the concrete poured in. He even managed to keep the pitch and slant of the walls, and the seam between the old and new is almost invisible.

All has been paid up. I am so proud I can pay for this with my own work. Of course it was all twice the agreed amount, but I believe it is still cheap. And very well built. The whole thing seems solid and like it will last, earthquake proof.

The lemon tree survived a winter hail storm and all the construction and dust, and is full of blossoms and smells heavenly.

I am very moved by it all. Now I must go to work and paint the very best pictures possible in my new atelier.

With lots of love,
Christo

—

Owning a house on Sifnos had already begun to change my life, the amount of time I spent there, the amount of time I could spend there, coming and going as I pleased. Now, though, the house had several rooms, a real studio I could work in, two guest rooms, my beloved courtyard, and a large new upstairs terrace. For the first time, I had real space. It all seemed quite grown-up to me—and to the islanders too, I think; they were only half joking when they called it *to villa*, the villa. But of course I was still very young, only twenty-eight. And though I may have felt more of a player now that I owned property, for them I was still a boy. They admired me and my work and were proud to have a Swiss artist living among them, but my persona, the Christo persona, was more or less that of *to kalo pedi*, the good child. An image that was only reinforced when my parents started coming to stay with me.

I don't think I bought the house to impress my parents—as I say, I had never imagined even buying a house—but it did feel a bit like a feather in my cap. Like most people, I think, much of what I did was somehow done for them, and this was no different. I remember Tim saying years later, when his parents died suddenly just at the moment when it looked as if we might get a book of drawings published, how amazed he was that almost his first thought was that his parents would never see it. But I knew my parents had grown to love Sifnos, and with this house I could give them happiness there in return for all their love and support. And indeed they came and visited every year.

On top of being a place they loved, the house filled a practical need for us all. I now lived for most of the year in New York, and as often as I went to Switzerland for exhibitions or family events, and as often as they were to come to New York, Sifnos was the place I would see my parents the most. We never stayed a long time together, but we always overlapped, often with Tim there too. And it was a wonderful place to see them and for them to see me, and us. One had all the time in the world, it seemed, time to talk, time to just enjoy being together.

Enlarging the house also made it possible to have Tim on the island, just as I knew it would. My dream of having my lover there with me had come true, and I knew I would never be as lonely there as I had been in the previous years. And of course the house also changed Tim's life. He had been writing plays and had made a film, but after that first show, he started drawing and painting seriously on the island, and in the next few years he began to paint full-time. For him as for me, Greece became an inspiration, a muse, but for him it was also the trigger for a whole new career and a whole new life. As he has often said, "If someone had told me when I was thirty that ten, twenty years later I would be making my living as a painter, I would have laughed in their face."

Tim started to come to Sifnos every year for at least a few weeks, sometimes a month or more. Arriving together as we often did, we would sleep and sleep for the first few days. It was not just because of exhaustion from the trip, though that was often terrible, or from our lives, which were busy but not that busy. It was the silence of the place, of the village, the absolute quiet surrounding you after the roar of New York. Oh, in the morning you heard the neighbors, the women especially, chatting, sounding exactly like the hens that lived in their yards, but in the afternoon it was quiet, the quiet of the whole village napping. And at night the silence was absolute, and we slept as we never slept anywhere else. One of the most wonderful qualities of that house and that village over the years was its power to recharge you, almost reconstruct you, your mind and your body.

After the first few days we would settle into a rhythm. We were up early and had breakfast on my new terrace. We rarely used the courtyard terrace anymore; the views upstairs were so spectacular, and it was so completely private. Then Tim would set off with his paper, drawing board, and folding stool, his pencils and paints in a blue-and-white-striped shoulder bag, a "Sifnos bag" of a kind that one saw everywhere on the island among the locals, and I would go into my studio and start working, my music blaring out over the village.

The way Tim described it, he would head off, walking all over the island, sketching or perhaps starting a watercolor. He would take along crackers, fruit, and water and would stop somewhere in the shade to eat, then go back to work and come back about five with a tiny corner of a drawing or watercolor laid in, only to find that I had done two gouaches, gone to Chrissopighi for a swim, had lunch at the taverna, spent a couple of hours reading and swimming and sleeping on the rocks, and was just getting up from a proper nap.

This was partly true. Tim worked very slowly. His drawings back then were small and tended to be incredibly detailed; "how many angels you could get on the head of a pin" was how a friend described his work. I always worked much faster, and with my new studio, the pictures poured out of me. In the early 1970s my work was still that of the young *malender Gymnasiast*, Jungian eyes and birds, and the paintings, even those of the Swiss mountains, were pretty monochromatic. But over time I became more at home with the Sifnos landscape and colors.

I had always been overwhelmed by the fields of flowers on Sifnos in the springtime, but it was only after maybe my third summer that all that color finally started to sink in and become part of me, become mine somehow, mine to use. It began slowly enough in 1977 with four small Tree Paintings, as I called them, olive trees with masses of red poppies around their roots. But soon all my pictures started to be flooded with color—gouaches done there on the island and large oils done from them in New York. I based the paintings on sketches and drawings and from memory, as usual, but now I also painted directly from my open studio windows. I would stand in the corner of my wonderful new room and paint and paint, intensely, rapidly, in a rush of enthusiasm and energy, until I was exhausted. And by the end of every visit to the island, the walls would be covered with pictures I'd hung with clothespins from strings that went from the ceiling to the floor, dozens of them, all these intense splashes of color against my white, white walls.

—

Evenings, after drinks, Tim and I would usually walk to Apollonia for dinner. The return, all uphill—hundreds, literally hundreds of steps—was a sure way to stay fit and return home dead sober. In the early days we ate sometimes at Sofia's but more often across the street at Kaliope's; her *keftedes*, which Tim loved as much as I, were still the best. Sometimes we would go as far as Artemona, which had some good restaurants, but it was a real hike there and back, so often we would take a taxi home. As the years passed and more restaurants opened, we went farther and farther afield, and once I had a car, we could go anywhere, avoiding all the tourists and backpackers in the village restaurants in high season.

Sometimes we stayed at home. We would go to Katerina's market, which eventually moved to a much bigger space, a real supermarket, just below Artemona. There you could get chicken, lamb, sometimes fish, and all kinds of vegetables, and we would cook up different dishes in my funny secondhand pots on my tiny gas stove. It was pretty eccentric cooking, in that there were no cookbooks in the house and back then neither of us had much of an idea what we were doing. It appeared that Tim had a heavy hand with the garlic. One night, walking through the village after dinner, we ran into Stephanos, who started back, away from us—a Greek overwhelmed by someone else's garlic breath! It was hard to imagine.

A wonderful custom on Sifnos enabled the village women to attend church on Sunday but still have a hot meal for the family afterward. In every village was a *furno*, an oven, where the village bread was baked. On Saturday evening a family member would bring the *revithia,* chickpea soup, to the oven in a specially designed ceramic pot. The man in charge would be firing up the oven with dried brush and shrubs and wood, and a wonderful smell spread over the village. You would leave a few drachmas for him, and leave the pot—mine marked "Christo"—in the oven overnight, and after church the next day you would collect the pot, still hot from the oven.

Everyone always knew which pot belonged to whom, but I am sure that some of the ladies checked out one another's pots to see whose soup was best. It was not always plain chickpeas. I often threw in chicken, onions, carrots, any vegetable I could find, and filled the pot with wine instead of water. The *furno* was a major gossip center, with everyone standing around chatting, and I felt very much part of the community when I collected my soup on Sunday morning. I would carry my still very hot and heavy pot by a string handle and walk home over the rocky paths and steep steps, careful not to spill even a drop.

—

Over the years, we often had guests, friends of Tim's and mine or family members. We liked having guests, though obviously it was more of an effort when I was there alone, as I often was, and couldn't share the work of keeping them entertained. But even when we were both there, after a while we were apt to tire of visitors. The problem was that Sifnos was so far away, so hard for everyone to get to, that people—unless they happened to be traveling in Greece, and Sifnos was on their way somewhere—would come for a week or more. We ourselves always said it wasn't worth the trip if you didn't stay for at least ten days.

Some guests were fine, self-starters, like my parents, who took care of themselves completely, leaving in the morning and walking all over the island. But there were those who would hang around waiting to be told what was happening next, what we had planned to entertain them that day. It was particularly difficult because most of the time we both wanted to be working, at least in the mornings, and people sitting around tapping their feet, even metaphorically, could be tedious. Part of the reason that our guests clung to us, to me, was that almost none of them spoke Greek, and almost no one on the island spoke anything else, so they could do very little without me. So as often as we invited friends, and as much as we truly wanted them to come, we were both secretly thrilled when they found that for some reason or other they couldn't get there.

Also, even with the new room, the house wasn't very big, and there was only the charming but tiny cavelike guest room and the little *apothiki* for guests. An excellent solution was our persuading friends to rent the Psacharopoulos house in Artemona. That was wonderful: they could stay indefinitely, which was fun, and Tim and I in our little house in Exambela could get a taste of what we thought of as *la vie du château*.

—

It was a full moon, incredibly bright, light pouring in through the open French doors and the window above my worktable. The room was almost as bright as during the day, the white walls glowing in the reflected light. You could see everything outside—the neighboring houses, the terraces and hills, the village of Katavati tucked there at the base of the mountains across the way, and the gleaming monasteries perched on top.

The night was cool and pleasant, almost still. My drawings and gouaches hanging on the walls barely stirred on their lengths of string, making only the slightest scraping sound against the rough whitewashed plaster.

The problem was the dog. A farm dog in the village of Katavati, it seemed, barking at the full moon. And neither Tim nor I could sleep. We knew that no villager was being bothered by the dog, even its owner, as they all slept sealed in their rooms, windows, shutters, and curtains closed. But our windows and doors were wide-open.

And the dog barked and barked and barked, the sound echoing

across the bowl-shaped valley south of Exambela. Once in a while it would stop, and we would begin to think maybe it had gone to sleep. Then it would start up again, barking and barking and barking.

It was one, then two, then three in the morning, and we tossed and turned. We tried reading in order to be exhausted enough to sleep, but it didn't work. We tried closing the doors and windows, but then it was too hot.

Finally we couldn't stand it anymore. We decided we would find the dog and its owner and maybe kill them both. We got up and got dressed and then, bone tired and angry, staggered down the steps and down the path through the village to the Platy Ghialos road.

We didn't need a flashlight, because it was so bright; the newly whitewashed spaces, the veins between the stones were luminous, almost electric. Even when we crossed the empty, silent road and plunged down the path into the valley, it was as bright as day, the dovecote with its red gate and little red door perfectly clear by the side of the path.

Even going down farther into what we called the Snake Valley, down the dirt and rough stone path toward the stream and the shade of the trees there, we could see everything. We were a little anxious about snakes—we had run screaming from a viper stretched out in the sun across this same path only a week before—but we assumed that they were asleep. "Just let's don't step on any," said Tim.

And always in front of us the dog was barking barking barking.

"I think it's coming from there," I said, pointing at a house up and a bit to the left in Katavati. We started to climb up the path to the other side of the valley.

We climbed and climbed toward the house, and then suddenly, strangely, it was quiet. Silence. Maybe the dog had heard us, we thought, though surely it would bark even more. Why had it stopped? It should have been barking like crazy now.

We stepped up on the path that ran along the edge of the village and stood for a minute and listened to the dog, which had started barking again, barking barking barking. Barking like crazy. And we stood there exhausted, dumbfounded, listening to it—or to the echo of it, who knew which anymore. It was barking across the valley in Exambela, where we had just come from. And we gave up and went home.

—

Away from Sifnos, my life was changing, had changed to some degree. I was living in New York and had shows and sold pictures there and in Basel and Zurich. After the first couple of years I had moved into a large loft, and this, combined with my house in Greece, made me feel, I fondly thought, quite different from the boy banging on the closed doors of the city of Basel. And I had Tim. In reality, though, when I was in Switzerland, I still had many of the anxieties I had grown up with, still felt largely an outsider there as an artist and even as a person, and it would be several years before that began to change. And New York, while wonderful, was also a completely frazzling experience for me.

For a boy from Basel, New York was amazing, and for a gay boy from Basel, it was like nothing else on earth. Rock and roll was gone, but in the late seventies and early eighties, sex and drugs were everywhere. It was still a bit dangerous to be gay in New York, but for the first time it was also fun. "Bliss it was to be alive," we all thought, as Wordsworth put it, and "to be young was very heaven." Young and good-looking. Gone was the hiding and skulking around. For gay men, New York was like some kind of sexual frontier town, filled with clubs, discos, bars, and baths, and people went crazy in them. Which is of course part of why so many died in the next few years.

Even though I was with Tim, the city often had me by the throat. The clubs and streets for someone my age and with my looks were like a kind of buffet; there were available boys and men everywhere, all of them out and about, for the first time openly and publicly gay, and it made me almost crazy. Add to that the availability of drugs among the young people my age and the astonishing social mobility of the city in those days—something that no longer exists—and

I was flying. I worked and worked, had shows, hustled collectors—I lived totally on my work always—went to dinner, went to Studio 54, experimented with drugs, had sex, you name it. And after a few months I was usually at the ragged edge of myself and beginning to yearn for the peace and quiet of Sifnos.

—

Traveling to Sifnos as we did every year, no matter where we came from, New York or any number of other places where we would go to paint, we had to pass through Athens, and because of the hopelessly disjointed plane and boat schedules, we often had to stay awhile, sometimes several days.

Fortunately, Tim liked Athens too. We both liked it enough to even think that we might take a flat there for a winter and go back and forth to Sifnos. To start with, we both thought Athens was kind of sexy: sunny, hot, full of good-looking half-naked people. But we also loved the city itself, the food, the little restaurants we found in Kolonaki, and the two *kafenia* in the square where the young met and hung out. I had a favorite antiques dealer there named Dimitri on a little side street in Kolonaki. I would always go and see him and sometimes buy things from him or trade paintings for some of the wonderful antiques he had, all Greek things, often island things of the kind my village ladies objected to. I had a little crush on him too, which made it even more fun to go, but at some point he and his shop just vanished.

We loved the museums too, the great ones like the Benaki or the Museum of Cycladic Art, but perhaps even more, ones we searched out, such as the little Tsarouchis Museum, which had been the artist's house, at the end of a sleepy, dusty little street in what must have once been suburban Athens, in his day almost the country. Yannis Tsarouchis was our favorite Greek painter. He painted mostly in Piraeus, sketching sailors, having them back to sit for him, often naked except for, curiously, their shoes: a young sailor, for example, from the back, sitting completely nude, doing up his boots. In other pictures the naked young men had wings. They were wonderful, sexy, homoerotic, yes, at least to a degree, but beautifully painted and full of fantasy.

We also loved the St. George Lycabettus, a nice hotel that sat right at the foot of the forested Lycabettus Hill in Kolonaki, with its rooftop pool and amazing views, and maybe even more, the hotel we started staying at in Plaka, the Elektra Palace, which also had a rooftop pool that was right below the Acropolis. Swimming up there at night, floating in that pool, the water glittering with the reflections of the lit-up Parthenon was an amazing fantasy.

During these visits, Tim got to know some of the people I had met in the city during the years before I knew him, or people I met on trips when I went through Athens alone, as when I would go in the fall to close the house. Some I had met in what might be called respectable ways, some not. With a partner at home, I'm afraid I still went to Aleco's Island whenever I passed through town. But even without setting foot in there, I often had some pretty eccentric encounters. Once, staying at the St. George, swimming and sunning on the roof terrace, I noticed a young man whistling and waving at me from the penthouse terrace of the building next door, the only other building that high up on the hill, both terraces with views out over the city to the Acropolis. He was waving me over and yelling, "Penthouse elevator, penthouse elevator." And over I went. He was a fashion designer named Phillipos, quite successful and well known in Athens. He was not old at all, but he lived with two even younger men, one Swiss, one German, a rather confusing household, I thought, and Tim did too when eventually I took him along there and introduced him.

Phillipos is dead now, of AIDS. Though at first one thought one was safer in Greece somehow from the terrors of AIDS, it was of course not true, at least not in Athens. After New York and Los Angeles, anywhere seemed safer in those first years of the AIDS epidemic; in New York we all just thought we were going to die. Even if you were tested, a big issue, there was no cure, none at all. And

I suppose everybody else thought we were going to die too; for some, we deserved it. A member of my family, flippantly, offhand-edly, without thinking much, told me one day, "Well of course you are going to die of AIDS." In the early days, my reaction was often denial: I wasn't going to let this run my life, ruin it. But come the mildest cold, a case of the sniffles, what seemed like the slightest symptom, and I wasn't so sure.

On Sifnos you could put it out of your mind, but not in Athens. Even though the epidemic was slower coming there than to New York, it was still in the news—Athens had the news, after all. I was in bed one day with a young man in his flat in Kolonaki, and the television was on, CNN, and I remember sitting bolt upright when they announced that Rock Hudson had just died, and they showed footage of him on a gurney being wheeled onto the Air France 747 he had chartered to take him home to die after a hoped-for cure at the Pasteur Institute in Paris had failed. That footage, that moment, more even than what I had been witnessing in New York, was the end of the party for me. It brought AIDS home to me, and to many others, I suspect, and probably helped save my life. There would be no more nonsense about unprotected sex, or imagining that I was somehow immune to this disease.

I was beginning to realize how lucky I was to have found my house in Exambela, how lucky I was to have found somewhere so isolated and private. I hadn't thought much about it at first; there had been no need, so few people came to Sifnos.

Even by the time I bought the house, there still weren't many tourists, but they were starting to come in high season—tourists and summering Athenians. It wasn't really that there were so many people yet, but the villages, the beaches, the buses, the restaurants, the whole infrastructure of the place was so tiny, so antiquated, and so sleepy that you felt even the slightest influx of visitors. The bus to the beach was suddenly hot and crowded, you might have to wait for a table at Kaliope's, or they had run out of something you wanted at the market, little irritants that made you dislike newcomers and off-islanders. And I suppose I felt that owning a house on the island gave me a kind of seniority—I was here first—and as a result, I found myself getting huffy and grumpy and standoffish with people who came there.

I was particularly snobbish, as one is apt to be, about my compatriots, the Swiss. I would groan and roll my eyes as soon as I spotted them in their clumsy hiking boots and dull-colored clothes, and I shuddered at their accents. My parents and their friends and I were different, of course, but all I had to do was hear "*Grüezi*," and I would cringe and turn down any street to avoid them. If cornered, I would pretend I didn't speak Schweizerdeutsch, or any kind of Deutsch, and speak only English at them, and very plummy English at that.

One fall, coming to Sifnos alone to close the house for the winter, traveling on the *Ionion*, I noticed a Swiss family onboard whom I had seen on Sifnos over the years. They had far too many children for my taste, and it seemed to me they were always screaming in Swiss-German as they piled in and out of way too many rental cars at Chrissopighi during the day or at Kaliope's restaurant in the evenings. I never wanted to know their names and stayed out of their way. And that year I was particularly careful to steer clear of them on the boat, as one of the daughters and I had spotted each other in Zurich. She was on the tram and I was walking across Paradeplatz, and I knew she recognized me and that my faux-Britishy cover was blown.

In the autumn the weather was often windy, and this seemed a particularly rough and stormy crossing. All the cabins were full, everyone hiding belowdecks. I knew I would probably be sick if I went below, so I stayed outside in the air. It was so rough, though, that no one was moving around much, and I buried myself in a book well away from the Swiss family. I thought I was doing just fine when over the loudspeaker the captain announced that the ship, surprise, surprise, had engine problems and we would be sailing directly to Mílos, the boat's final destination, without stopping at Sifnos.

This was very bad news indeed, as I was traveling with masses of art supplies, very expensive handmade paper, rolls of canvas, and boxes filled with tubes of paint. Everyone started rushing around, consulting with one another about what to do, and my heart sank as I saw the Swiss girl from the tramway point at me and then lead her tall—I had to admit, rather handsome—father across the deck toward me. Curses, I thought, like some character in a melodrama. They introduced themselves, and knowing, they said, that I was on my way to Sifnos too and no doubt spoke some Greek, they wanted to know what I thought they should do, where to stay on Mílos, or whether there was a chance of finding some other boat to Sifnos.

To my surprise, they turned out to be charming—he, Michel, a photographer, his wife, Elizabeth, a writer—and we promptly put our heads together to try to solve our problem. For them it was serious: they had their rented house on Sifnos for only ten days, and if they didn't get there soon, their holiday would be ruined. I knew there was no other boat, but as the weather was improving a little, I thought it might be possible, with the right amount of money exchanging hands, to hire a fishing boat. But on arrival on Mílos, the harbor police made it clear that no such undertaking was possible. "*Tst, tst, oxi*," they said, not even deigning to turn toward me, only lifting their chins. It was out of the question. There had been a past accident with tourists being injured or maybe drowned, and now renting a fishing boat was against the law. We would simply have to stay on Mílos and wait for the new parts to arrive from Piraeus, something I knew could take forever, particularly in the fall, with the winds often blowing steadily for days.

Totally depressed, all of us, we piled into two taxis—there were seven of them, and I had all my supplies—and rode to the nearest hotel. There, I found myself sharing a room with my new friends' seven-year-old son, Philip, who alone among us was having a fine time with all this unexpected adventure. I found it was utterly impossible to be gloomy for long around this cheerful, upbeat soul, and we chatted away, him telling me *all* about his family, their marriages and divorces, all about his siblings, his stepsiblings, everything. I was to learn that his parents could hear all this from their room and were listening, ears to the wall, in hysterics.

Suddenly I thought I heard a knock at the door. I did hear a knock, a tiny tap really, and then another, a little louder this time. *"Pios eine?"* Who is it? I sighed, already expecting more bad news. No answer. Irritated now, my bad mood returning, I yanked the door open to find a handsome young Greek standing there. He stepped hesitantly into the room. "I hear you asking early before about a boat to Sifnos," he whispered, actually whispered, looking nervously from side to side. "You can be ready tomorrow morning at five the early morning?" he asked. "Two taxis picking you up and take you to a secret place with a boat waiting for you." He went on in his charming broken English, all very hush-hush and James Bond. I could see Philip's eyes glittering with excitement at this turn of events; even if he couldn't understand, he could tell that this looked like fun. "You must tell no one, not even hotel people," said the young man.

What was all this? A car will be waiting at sunrise? A secret place? What was I getting into? Could I trust this young man? Was there a boat, or were we being tricked into something? "Greeks bearing gifts" and all that, I thought. He told me, this young young man, this boy really, that he would be our captain, and he needed an answer right away. Highly suspicious, hands on my hips, I looked sternly (I hoped) down at him, and he suddenly smiled, this huge smile, a wonderful smile, and I decided on the spot to trust him. We haggled a bit, but soon agreed on a price and shook hands. I assured him that we would be ready, and he turned, opened the door, and, after flashing one more quick smile, looked both ways down the hall and vanished.

My new Swiss friends, the parents, were a bit more cautious, but they were desperate to get to Sifnos, and they finally agreed. Philip and the other four children, all totally overstimulated by now, let out a cheer, and we all had a very jolly meal together, confident that we would get to Sifnos the next day and that their holiday would be saved and I would not be stuck on Mílos till the end of time.

At four in the morning, alarms ringing, we adults dragged ourselves awake. Philip was already awake and raring to go. After checking out and, as promised, saying nothing to the sleepy, indifferent desk clerk, we were relieved to see two taxis waiting out front in the early half-light. Good grief, this was actually going to work! We stuffed what luggage we could into the car trunks, tied the rest on the roof, piled into the taxis, and our little caravan set off in a huge cloud of dust.

Mílos is a fairly big island, and we drove on and on in the predawn light, bouncing over unpaved roads, up and down hills for well over an hour without seeing another car or any people. I didn't know Mílos at all, we had no idea where we were going, and the drivers were totally silent. But turning a corner and dipping down toward the water, the taxis lurched to a stop at a small dock on a tiny bay. We were told to climb out, and our luggage was piled on the ground. One of the drivers said, "Boad come zoon," or we hoped that was what he said, and then both men got back into their cars and drove away, leaving us staring out to sea into the Mílos sunrise.

Only after a silent twenty minutes or so did it begin to occur to us that we could be waiting there forever. This was long before cell phones, and we felt—and maybe were—totally stranded. After a while, though, we heard a *tschut, tschut, tschut*, and little puffs of smoke appeared behind the hill sloping down to the mouth of the inlet. Suddenly a caïque appeared, and we saw our young captain in the stern waving and (happily for me) smiling his excellent smile. We all jumped up and down like idiots as he pulled up to the dock and then, losing no time lest anyone see us, we threw all our stuff on the alarmingly small boat, climbed aboard, and set off for the southern tip of Sifnos.

It took us a while to calm down. It had all been pretty nerve-racking, but we were saved! We were going to Sifnos! It was going to happen! Only as we headed out into the open sea did we realize there was more, possibly worse, to come. The winds were very strong, *"Buffo pende,"* wind speed five, the captain said, wiggling the fingers of his right hand and giving us one of his smiles—a very rough sea indeed.

The boat, already a bit low in the water for my taste, rose and fell sickeningly. Now I could certainly see why it was illegal to rent this kind of boat for this trip. I was filled with admiration for the way my new friends handled their children, keeping them calm and happy as we lurched about in the middle of the Aegean; of course, calming them may have been a way of calming themselves. I, on the other hand, stood holding on to the mast the whole way, clutching my precious paper and hoping I would not be swept overboard and drown. Only our captain and his mate were calm and happy, smoking constantly and singing into the wind and sea spray, delighted by their unexpected windfall of drachmas.

Five hours later we slunk past the harbor in Kamares, hoping not to be seen by the binoculars of the port police, something not very likely, in truth, but it made a sort of game for the children. Finally we arrived at the small dock in Chrissopighi, perfect for my new friends, whose rented house was one of the new houses on the hill above the church. No one saw us arrive, but as we disembarked, a bit shaky and unsteady, we swore total secrecy to the captain, who gave us one more dazzling smile and turned his boat around and headed back to Mílos.

We struggled off to the taverna on the beach and had a delicious, overexcited, boozy lunch, the adults anyway, all of us glad now to have made it through alive. And rather braver after the fact. All a bit stunned, almost stoned by our excellent adventure, we became lifelong friends.

—

I was still often alone on the island. I would come earlier than Tim, stay later, and usually come back, as during that trip, to close the house in the fall. I was constantly grateful that I had bought a house in the village. On a cliff by the sea or off and alone in the nowhere like Onno, I would have been lonely, I was sure, and vulnerable to all kinds of moods. In the village, surrounded by these smiling, friendly people, their children and grandchildren, all these lives being lived around me, it was almost impossible to become lonely or depressed. I felt sheltered there, with neighbors who looked after me. Most evenings I would walk through the village on my way to Apollonia for dinner. Back then, in those years before television and long before computers or cell phones, my neighbors would be sitting out in front of their houses, chatting, gossiping, smoking, playing music. I would stop and talk with them, all of them warm and welcoming, a small, supportive world, I felt, holding me somehow in the palm of its hand,

Yet there were a few shadows lurking. As in any small community, there were cruelties I learned of, the petty meannesses between quarreling neighbors or the barely understood but always remembered feuds that had gone on through generations. And in a village on an island, where there was apt to be tremendous inbreeding, there were all kinds of strange characters, *trilli*—crazy ladies like Mad Katerina, for instance, who stalked around the village in a mysterious rage (and who became the title of a picture of mine); or the always barefoot man who wandered the streets reciting Shakespeare, in English, no less; and the young man who exposed himself at Poulati and tried to climb into my bedroom.

Opposite my kitchen window was a romantic ruin, an old falling-down two-story house with a ruined olive press and a small walled garden filled with weeds, a tomato plant or two, and a few gone-wild artichokes that still managed to flower beautifully every year. My builder Stephanos's sister Agape kept her chickens there—it was some kind of complicated family property—and she came to feed them every day. She was definitely pretty severely *trilli*, and one could hear her from far away, singing and mumbling to herself, greeting neighbors, and letting everyone know what they already knew, that she was on her way to feed her chickens. From my studio window I would look down at her mop of wild, curly red hair as she unlocked a series of completely useless padlocks that dangled all over a wonderful old gate of banged-together boards.

Struggling with the locks, she would scream at her chickens, telling them what *they* already knew, that she was coming. Finally opening the gate, she would let them loose, the chickens rushing and clucking around her feet as she lovingly fed them, muttering to them in some kind of chicken talk, baby Greek, asking about the health and state of mind of each of them. None of them paid any attention of course and just pecked at the ground till the food was gone. After checking inside the henhouse for eggs, locking her chickens in, and securing her loopy gate, she would stop in the path and scream up at me in my window, offering me fresh eggs to buy. Though unmarried, she was no innocent maiden and would flirt with any man within reach in her deep, actually rather sexy voice. As it happened, she had a bit of a crush on me, and when I came down—I loved fresh eggs—she would giggle and snort and bat her eyes at me from under her waggling curls.

A few years on, I noticed a daily pile of human excrement and paper in a corner among the artichoke plants and tomatoes. I suspected who the culprit was but had no proof unless I caught him in the act, which I assuredly did not want to do. My friend Jeff from Los Angeles was visiting at the time, and we decided the best solution was to dig up the whole garden, plant shrubs and flowers and vegetables, and hope that whoever it was would stop coming. Buying everything from the new small island nursery, we planted the garden by flashlight overnight. The "public toilet" stopped immediately; mission accomplished. But Agape was not amused: "*Po po po, panaghia mou, panaghia mou,*" she wailed when she saw our handiwork. The two of us watched from upstairs as she glared around her, swearing and gesticulating and shaking her fist at the village at large. Somewhat cruelly, we thought it all very funny. What we didn't know was that under Greek law, if you occupy a property and cultivate it long enough, you can claim it as yours, and Agape was in a panic that someone was after what she thought of as her property.

The next day, Agape arrived, marching along ahead of a cousin

Vassilis, a cook

who was carrying a roll of heavy metal fencing that they clumsily put up around the garden. I was not allowed in, she yelled up, seeing me in the window. Nobody was, she yelled to the surrounding houses. Worried that she would let the plants die, I was relieved the next day to find her lovingly watering them, rather proud of her new roses and fruit trees. Having bought them, though, I felt slightly entitled and so would slip in once in a while through her ever-ridiculous gate—she never changed the locks—and pick some roses or maybe pluck an apricot. Agape would notice and scream bloody murder, yelling up at me that she had been robbed, and I would cluck sympathetically from my window, a bowl of divinely smelling roses on the table behind me.

Over time, as much as I wanted to be accepted, I realized that being a *xenos*, a foreigner, had certain advantages. You had more freedom, a bit more leeway in how you lived, and you could keep yourself apart from the stricter customs and crueler verdicts of the islanders. But if you were from the village or married into it, you were forced to obey, to live according to neighbors' ways and rules. I came to be very grateful for my amateur standing. There was a woman in the village, though, who was less discreet, if you will, who just could not or would not knuckle under, and at least for a while, she paid the consequences.

Her name was Melina. She was from the island of Foligandros but married to a man from Exambela. She had two daughters and two sons by her husband, who worked as a cook on one of the big ships and was rarely home. Having their husbands away for long periods of time was very hard on the wives who were left behind. Not only were they alone, but they were expected to live almost like widows. They were to stay at home behind half-closed blinds, not even going to village feasts, and only close members of their families were allowed to visit them.

Instead of following the rules, Melina continued to very much *live*, and eventually she moved in with the very handsome Panagiotis— the young man with the forget-me-not blue eyes I had watched dancing with the Cretan girl in Platy Ghialos years before—and lived with him in a tiny shed right smack in the middle of the village in plain sight of everyone, in their faces, as it were. As handsome and sexy as Panagiotis was, Melina was even more extraordinary; not only was she beautiful, there was an animal quality about her, and she exuded sexuality. She had dark—almost black, to Swiss me—Arab eyes, dark red lips, and gleaming white teeth. Her long, dark hair hung straight down over her shoulders, which was very unusual for married island women, whose hair was normally tied up or covered.

I found her sensual and beautiful and had real sympathy for her and her unconventional situation. Her neighbors found her shocking and were horrified by her behavior, and they would have nothing to do with her, with either of them. To make matters worse, after a few months she gave birth to a son. It was unclear who the father was, but most people assumed it was Panagiotis, not her husband. I was relieved to find that they didn't stone her to death, as I remembered from *Zorba the Greek*. I am sure they never thought of such a thing, but they assuredly ostracized her. As I say, I liked them both, and as they needed money, I gave them small jobs in and around my house.

One day, the husband came back, and Melina fled on the first ferry to Athens, deserting her children. She even deserted her tiny son Iannis, which was shocking, unforgivable to the villagers, even though they thought he was illegitimate. I was told that the husband chased Panagiotis off the island with a gun. I don't know about the gun, but Panagiotis was certainly gone.

A few years passed, and there were lots of rumors about her whereabouts, but no one really knew. And then one day she reappeared. By coincidence, I was in Kamares when she returned, and I found myself on the same bus back to Exambela with her and her daughters, who had come to the harbor to meet her. She looked well, even prosperous, and was still beautiful. No one knew what she had been up to, and she wasn't telling; she was always a law unto herself.

Then, for a while, her life seemed to change for the better. Her husband was off on another ship, and back in Exambela, she moved in with an elderly widow and took care of her. The childless old lady had land and a big house, and when she died, she left everything to Melina. With the instant respectability of property, of course, the village forgave her; and her husband, on his return, took her back, though in fact they never lived together again. Even Panagiotis was able to come back, and he worked as a roofer and whitewasher in the village. To repay me for my faithfulness, Melina offered me a very desirable piece of land to build a studio on, but her husband and children blocked the sale, also repaying me, I suppose, for having been nice to her and Panagiotis.

Time passed, but it seemed Melina could not help straining at her leash, the harness of village respectability. One morning the postman, bearer of all village gossip, whispered leeringly in my ear that Melina was having an affair with my housekeeper. The two, indeed, appeared to be inseparable, always smoking and whispering and laughing together in her kitchen door or on a secluded path down the hill at the edge of the village, and it occurred to me that for once, the postman might be right. It certainly didn't bother me, though I worried about her children and my housekeeper's son if their mothers were having an affair. What would the village make of that? And then, almost overnight, she was gone again. Unable to stand the confines of island village life, she vanished and was never seen again.

Dimitri and Despina were close neighbors. Already elderly when I arrived, Dimitri was tiny, wiry, and tough, with thick white hair that stood straight up and a bristly white mustache, his face and hands tanned and weathered from his work in the fields. When I first knew him, he was a total charmer, with a ready wink and a smile, a sort of poster-boy, cute-as-a-button, ruddy-cheeked, smiling Greek peasant in his smart tweed jacket and cap. Despina was handsome, but more severe looking, usually frowning, almost grim, though when her smile did appear, it was wonderful. They had several grown sons but only one daughter, still a child then, born late in their marriage.

Dimitri, like all true Sifnos farmers, rode his donkey out to his distant fields every morning. He had big herds of goats and sheep, and he was particularly proud of the *mizithra* cheese he made from their milk. He was a great favorite of mine in the village, and sometimes I would hike out to some faraway field to milk goats with him and one of his sons. I was a favorite of his too, and I think he may have fantasized that I might one day marry his daughter, which of course was not so very likely. Whenever I arrived from abroad, he was the first to come to my door, smiling shyly as, like a magician, he pulled a tomato or a couple of eggs or a whole cheese from his pockets. Like many of the village men who joked about sex all the time, he would wink and point at my crotch and ask if my "clock was still at five to twelve" or, like his now, "always at half past six, hahaha."

But then something happened. Another story, another small village tragedy. Suddenly the now-grown daughter vanished to Athens and got married there, unusual in those days, and then divorced almost immediately—worse and worse. Soon after, Despina vanished to Athens as well, never to return. Well into his nineties by then, Dimitri was mostly alone—even his sons rarely came—and he would sit on the little terrace in front of his house, complaining about his wife and daughter, how they deserted him, about his loneliness, his fate. But I always suspected something happened between him and his daughter when his clock was not at half past six.

"They are just *trilli*, like that one over there," he would say, pointing across the path to my neighbor's house, my other neighbor Aphrodite, the maiden sister of Stavros, the farmer from Platy Ghialos who had shown me my house. By then Dimitri and I both had feuds going with her. I didn't know what his was about, but I knew they didn't speak. Moving his hips obscenely, he would tell me, "All that one needs is a good, serious fuck, but she is so ugly, no one in the village will ever volunteer."

And I would look across the little path at Aphrodite's closed shutters, knowing she could hear every word, that in fact she was probably standing there by the window listening.

—

Curiously, both of my immediate neighbors were named Aphrodite. Old Aphrodite, with her length of string to fend off the Evil Eye, lived above me; Aphrodite, the unmarried sister of Stavros, below me. I shared walls with both of them, my kitchen wall with Old Aphrodite and the wall of my courtyard with Young Aphrodite. When I moved in, her parents, Andonis and Evangelia, were still very much alive. They actually had two houses, a larger one for Aphrodite on one side of the path and, across the way, abutting my house, a smaller one for themselves. Perhaps Aphrodite already had the larger one as a way of making her a more desirable catch, but it was clear that she was well on her way to spinsterhood.

Andonis was quite a character. As handsome once, I suspect, as his son Stavros, he was a very sociable old boy, always out visiting neighbors during the day. But come sunset, Evangelia, who ruled him with an iron fist, would let out an extraordinary, loud, shrill whistle you could hear throughout the village and across the valley, and wherever he was, old Andonis would come running home. He could be sitting on my terrace, drinking and gossiping happily, and he would hear that whistle, jump to his feet, and run down the steps to his house, the tails of his old jacket flapping behind him.

His relationship with his daughter was very close, and I always felt he was the only man she ever loved. He died a couple of years after my arrival, in 1981 I think, about the time I completed the new upstairs room. One day soon after that, Evangelia and Aphrodite appeared in my courtyard, at the foot of the stairs to my terrace, and Evangelia asked if they could come up and see my addition. They clambered up the perilous stairs effortlessly, as the villagers always did, and after a bashful glance into the bedroom, the big bed being directly opposite the door, they settled on one of the built-in seats on the terrace.

After a little awkward idle chatter, Evangelia launched into a recitation of how many houses, terraces, olive groves, and lemon trees, even how many cows and sheep they owned. After a moment's confusion I suddenly realized that my expensive addition had turned me into an eligible bachelor, a village mark—an alarming thought. Then, out of the blue, as her mother went on talking, Aphrodite, not so young anymore and never pretty, started to unpin her hair and let it down, shaking it out over her shoulders, a fairly terrifying sight, with her mustache and this long, thick graying hair, a grim, dark-faced wild woman, half Medusa, half Madwoman of Chaillot.

I can only wonder what she saw pass across my face, behind my eyes.

I knew I was in trouble right away. I had always suspected that those little anonymously left bouquets might be from Aphrodite. And I knew that the litany of properties and the unwinding of her hair were intended as inducements to marriage. How was I to get out of this? Operating on some kind of animal instinct, I jumped up, ran into the studio, got my camera, pretended that this strange, haunted, distressing performance was a sort of photo op, and took a series of pictures of them both. This somehow deflated the original purpose, changed the subject, and we drifted back to idle chatter. Aphrodite silently pinned her hair back up and covered it with a black scarf, and after a few more moments of polite talk the two of them went down the stairs and, without a backward glance, walked silently home down the street.

Talk about a life of quiet desperation.

Though not quiet for long.

Aphrodite, I am sure, never forgave me for whatever she had seen there on my face, or for simply dashing her hopes for probably the last time. As long as Evangelia was alive, we never had a problem. We didn't speak, really, and she lowered her eyes when we passed each other in the street. When the mother died and she was left alone in her two houses, though, she became more and more peculiar and difficult, not just with me but with everyone. The shutters were never opened, and I could hear her rushing back and forth between her houses, slamming doors, muttering to herself, or sometimes yelling to herself in a strange, high-pitched voice, almost like keening, more and more unhappy, and somehow wilder and madder as well.

She started having arguments and fights with everyone in the village. With me, she took it into her head that my *vothro*, the septic tank that Stephanos had built with all the permits and inspections in the world, had been built incorrectly and was now leaking into her house. An unattractive possibility, granted, but one that I knew was almost impossible; the location of the tank was deep enough and far enough away from Aphrodite's house that it would have had to drain horizontally, if not upward, to leak across the courtyard. Besides, one winter I had the tank cleaned, and Stephanos proudly assured me that it was so well built and drained so well that I could have a picnic down there.

Nevertheless, Aphrodite continued to fuss and complain and argue about it, yelling "Christooo, Christoooo" outside my window all the time, or even coming into the courtyard or the house itself to harangue me, and soon not only me but whoever was in my house. In New York I would get calls from my niece, Francesca, who was staying there, or from mystified tenants about this disheveled madwoman who would come in while they were having breakfast and start screaming at them. Once or twice, fortunately, I had a Greek tenant, Vassilis, a friend who lived in London, who yelled right back at her and threw her out. But then my plants started to die—two jasmines and my pots of lavender. At first, almost treating it as a joke, I began to think it was the Evil Eye, and I went to Old Aphrodite to have her measure out her magical lengths of string. But pretty soon I figured that Aphrodite was coming into my completely open courtyard when I was away and poisoning them.

Finally I went to her brother, my old friend Stavros in Platy Ghialos, for help. He admitted that she was getting crazier and crazier, but out of family loyalty, I suspect, he tried to convince me that a leak was, after all, possible. Not much of a help to me. But the following year, when Aphrodite decided to have her bathroom redone because of all the humidity I was supposedly causing, the plumber, who described the scene to me later, removed, on her orders, all the old tiles from the wall adjoining my property and announced that there was no moisture whatsoever, that it was all solid, dry concrete. Furthermore, he discovered that the humidity was coming from her floor, from the more than thirty-year-old leaking pipes that had been run in, illegally it seemed, under her bathroom.

After this, the insane screaming and accusations slowed, but her obsession with me never really stopped. She would come in waving a piece of root at me that she said came from my lemon tree; she said it was eating through her wall. And I began to think that she would start poisoning my beloved lemon tree as well as the jasmine. It was all slightly hysterical on my part too, I admit, but after more than ten years of this, the vibrations that came from her house and all the anger and misery directed at me began to make me crazy too, and I decided to build a high wall along the path at the back of my courtyard, with a heavy gate, a bolt, and a lock. At least that would keep her out.

And it did. And it seemed to end the whole thing. As she was unable to come into the courtyard, I think even she realized it would be silly to stand outside the gate in that tiny alley, yelling at a wall. And soon I found I was able to ignore her and even forget about her. In retrospect though, I think Aphrodite's hysterical carryings-on—the sense of living next door to a near or, more probably, flat-out psychotic who seemed to hold me responsible for all her misery—was the beginning of the end of my love for the village and my life there. I felt her hostility, her hatred really, all the time, in Exambela and, because of all those phone calls, even in New York, where it was almost worse, for I felt responsible for my guests or tenants and couldn't do anything about it. It began to eat at the pleasure I took in my house and the delight with which I would look forward to going back.

4

"My rock" was a perfectly flat shelf of stone, about the size of a large bed, sticking out halfway down the rock face at the far end of the point below the church at Chrissopighi. There was a bit of rock above me that hung over just enough to shelter me, hide me from sight, but not enough to cast a shadow, even through the long afternoons I would spend there. Around behind me to the left was a rough, rocky stretch that led back to the beach and the taverna; ahead of me and around to the right was where "everyone," all the other foreigners and off-islanders, swam and lay sunning on the rocks.

I went there every day, every afternoon for thirty some years, often lying naked on the rock shelf, reading and sleeping and slipping in and out of the water for long swims far out into the gently rolling sea. The young son of a cousin of mine who came to visit would always ask me in his piping French if I was going to my "*rocher secret.*" But of course it was no secret at all, as I was as regular as clockwork, going there day after day at the same time. Everybody knew. Once in a very rare while, an unsuspecting tourist would discover my rock and settle in there, and when I arrived, I would huff and puff and noisily move to the next, far less desirable rock, breathing loudly through my nose and sighing audibly, hoping he would get the message and push off.

My kitchen

One day, lying there naked on my stomach, reading, the sun beating down on me, the water slipping and slapping noisily in and out over the rocks below me, I thought I heard a sound, a very faint rustle above me. In a sort of trance from the sun and the water and the salty air and the book I was reading, something ponderous and wonderful like *Anna Karenina*, I paid no attention. But then, there it was again, and I felt a dusting of sand or grit on my shoulder.

I heard a voice. I couldn't make it out over the sound of the water, what it said. I was dazed and confused. In all probability I had been about to drift off to sleep, and I was irritated at being interrupted and woken up. Letting out an annoyed sigh, I rolled back onto my elbow, my back to the cliff face, and twisted around to look up and behind me. I was staring straight into the sun, the glare, and I had to put up my hand to shade my eyes. And there against the sun, lying on his stomach a few feet above me, leaning over the edge of the rock, was a young man, a rather ugly young man, in truth, almost a boy really, but with a very muscled arm and thigh, his elbow and knee sticking out over the edge. It took a moment, what with the sun, but then I saw that he had this amazing red hair, screaming red hair, peaked up on the top of his head by the water and the wind, and, judging by the glimpse I had, more red hair all over his chest. He must have been lying there watching me. And he was smiling and saying something to me. This boy. This Pan.

"What?" I muttered. "What?" Irritated, in a daze. "What!"

And Pan said, "Can I fuck you?"

—

After Popi's death, Tim came to Sifnos less often and didn't stay as long. Her death left a huge hole for him, as it did for me of course, but his connection with the island wasn't as broad or as deep as mine and he felt the change to the village more immediately and acutely. More critical, though, was that after a few years he stopped painting the island and even other islands we visited. He was painted out there on Sifnos and in Greece, and he started working farther afield, building his shows from work done in Italy, Egypt, or India. As a result, he found it more and more difficult, and sort of nonsensical, really, to come all the way to Sifnos, lugging all the supplies he needed for work, just to shut himself in downstairs in the *sala* and work on pictures of, say, Rajasthan. We started tying some of our visits to Sifnos to these other trips, coming there from Naples or Cairo, but over the years I began to find myself alone there more and more often.

For me, though, for the time being at least, Sifnos seemed to be a gift that kept on giving artistically, and I could still spend weeks there working. And I loved my new expanded house. With or without Tim, I would settle into a happy, almost blissful pattern. The downstairs, the *sala* and my old bedroom, became a large guest suite. I was in the kitchen in the morning, of course (and the bar in the evening, of course), and in the afternoon I sometimes napped in the cool dark of the little cavelike bedroom that I loved, but otherwise I lived almost totally upstairs.

I ate breakfast on the terrace up there and then worked in my studio, painting at my table in the corner between the two windows. I would climb to the roof from time to time to admire the view over to the mountains to the south, or down to the sea in the east. As I said, I had a copy of an old cast-iron spiral staircase installed in the corner of the terrace, and I loved to go up there for drinks in the evening. Sometimes, if it was too hot in my sunny room, I would nap on a pair of rescued old deck chairs in the shade of a bamboo pergola I had had built.

The only problem I had was that for some reason the house, with its new terrace and cushions facing the warm, sunny south, became the favorite spot for village cats—dozens of them—who would come and sleep and breed and fight and mark their territory. It was a war I could never really win; I just had to be sure my cushions were put away and locked in my room at night or when I was away.

I had a tape deck and a huge collection of classical tapes that I would lug with me from New York, and the whole village would have to endure my love for opera and string quartets, with an occasional Leonard Cohen album or (I confess) Françoise Hardy thrown in. I was put in my place more often than not by some neighbor setting his Greek bouzouki music or the latest Yanni album even louder than my *Norma* or *Così fan tutti* or my total favorite, Maria Callas, singing anything, and I had to give in. A few times neighbors would appear from their houses wanting to hear better, such as Johannes wanting to listen to Flicka von Stade, or Panagiotis, who, after Melina had finally vanished for good, appeared one day across a neighboring rooftop where he had been whitewashing and asked, "Christo? Mozart? Mozart. Can come in?" and then sat completely still, listening to the music while I painted.

In those first years, quite a few of my village neighbors would come by to visit. They were all dying to see the new room—for many of them it was probably one of the biggest rooms they had ever seen in the village, and brand-new, of course. Some of them were also curious about my paintings, about what I actually did up there, how I earned my money, and what the pictures I made were like.

There was no such thing as a gallery on the island then, so paintings were unknown to most of the villagers. A few islanders, such as my old friend Iannis from Platy Ghialos, had taken up painting over the years. They painted naïve scenes from their lives for the most part, and sold them to tourists and foreigners on the island. But the only real paintings the islanders knew or valued were the highly stylized altar screens or gold ground icons from the churches. This was no doubt the reason why Iannis's heirs simply threw out his charming pictures when he died; for them they were just something a little bit silly the old man had fooled around with.

My visitors would yell up from the street or the courtyard below,

"Christo! Chriiiiiisto!" I had a phone by then, but it took some time for a lot of the villagers to get phones or to become comfortable using them for anything but emergencies. And they all loved to yell anyway, screaming one another's names from one end of the village to the other. Popi, when she was alive, would have been halfway up the stairs by the time she called my name, but few of the villagers ventured up there without permission. They knew the upstairs was private.

Once invited, though, up they would come in a rush. Having spent their lives climbing stairs like these, even the oldest among them would practically skip up the terrifying outdoor steps to my terrace. Built against the wall down below, and uneven and tippy enough there, once the stairs reached the height of my bathroom roof, they became the wall itself, a maybe eight-inch-wide crenellation that rose several dizzy-making feet above the surrounding houses. After living there a while I got used to running up and down them too, but my foreign guests would often have to climb up on all fours, their hands on the steps above them, their eyes straight ahead, not daring to look right or left. Finally, when I missed a step coming down and had a bad fall, I installed an iron railing.

Once up there, on the terrace, they would go through the ritual "*Orea, orea, poli orea*," beautiful, very beautiful, as they admired the view or pointed to different angles of the village. Then they would nudge and butt one another into my room and gaze around at my new casement windows, the large double bed from Switzerland, and the antique wood dresser. "*Orea, poli orea*," they would continue, staring at the views out the windows, stroking the dresser, testing the firmness of the mattress, or ogling the dozens of brushes and the rows and rows of paint tubes spread out on my worktable.

Finally, they would turn to my gouaches, hanging on their long strings from the ceiling. "*Orea*," they would continue, politely but tentatively, as they stared around uneasily at the pictures. They wanted to like them, if only so as not to hurt my feelings, and they wanted to like them because they wanted to believe they had a famous or at least successful artist in their village, but these pictures were confusing to them. Not really abstract, but certainly abstracted, sort of figurative but surely not realistic, the pictures were a mystery. What were those red churches? And red houses? What were those flowers that seemed to be on fire under the olive trees? But wait, those were olive trees. Is that our village? Is that *my* house? And slowly, peering and pointing, they would begin to decipher the pictures, begin to see their world, their island in them. But I don't think they ever really understood what I was up to. What they wanted was for me to paint pictures for the church; that would have made sense to them, would have made me a real artist in their eyes.

—

After I was done painting for the day, I would make my way to my *rocher secret*, usually trying to avoid the crowd swimming and sunbathing together around the corner. I knew most of them, was friends with many of them, Greeks, Greek-Americans, and foreigners with houses on the island. But I preferred the privacy of the rock, only socializing a bit when I went for lunch at the taverna on the beach. But even there, I more often than not ate alone, going into the kitchen and choosing from the food laid out there in the Greek way, stuffed vegetables, potatoes, eggplant, or sometimes ordering a delicious chop or a piece of fish. After lunch I returned to my rock to read some more and nap and then would climb back to the bus stop on the road or, once I had a car, drive back to Exambela.

As I have said, no tourists ever came to Exambela. Even in August it was possible to spend weeks there and have no sense at all of the people coming and going on the island, a greater and greater advantage as the years went by. I could live in the village as in a cocoon, especially once I had a car, only creeping out to go to the beach or to the most remote restaurant I could find for dinner, and then slipping back into my sleepy village.

Living in Exambela, I was able to keep the changes on the island at a distance. And there were changes by now, changes of attitude, mind-set, and values, changes that had started coming years ago to the mainland and to islands such as Mykonos and Santorini and Rhodes, but were now even spreading to islands as remote as Sifnos.

But I was changing too. I wasn't really running away to Sifnos anymore. Over the years, I began to make peace with Basel; I showed there regularly at Daniel Blaise Thorens Fine Art Gallery, and to my astonishment I realized that I actually had many friends there. One of my secret joys has been that a cousin of my friend Martin's in Basel has moved into what was his family town house in the center of the city, a palace to me in my youth, with almost forty rooms. I remember his family on the balcony above the entrance during Fasnacht, Basel's Carnival, watching the crowd below—us, the people—like literal royalty waving down at us. Now I go there for dinner. I ring the bell and am secretly delighted when anyone sees me going in through those tall carved doors.

And I was happy living in New York too; I had a life I liked there, not one I was hiding from on Sifnos. If anything, I was more inclined to carry my baggage to Sifnos with me, problems with an art dealer where I was showing or a love affair that obsessed me.

The phone had a lot to do with this. The coming of the telephone changed the island forever. As I said, it took a while for the islanders to get used to it at all, and even I didn't call up and "chat" much from Sifnos, but suddenly all the nonsense of one's life was only a dial tone away. It was all wonderfully convenient of course, but it made escaping oneself more and more difficult. And with the coming of the cell phone, it was worse (or better?). People could call me from Madison Avenue and reach me there even on my *rocher secret*. Curiously, the islanders seemed to get used to cell phones much faster; in Athens everyone had one long before they became so ubiquitous in New York, but even on the island it rapidly became commonplace to hear people wandering around screaming into *to mobile*, their cell phones.

The island I knew was changing, maybe already gone. So perhaps was the boy who went there in 1972. But I still could not come into the harbor in Kamares, sail in between those two mountains without a wave of tenderness sweeping over me. It was still home, I felt, part of myself.

—

It was Kamares that was the most different, naturally, I suppose, as it was the island's chief harbor, its conduit to and from the outside world. It was still a small village, just one street with almost nowhere to stay, but the harbor itself was becoming unrecognizable. There were very few cruise ships, but the little harbor was starting to be packed with boats, sailing yachts and power boats, and the waterfront, though still tiny, was lined with *kafenia*, tavernas, and boutiques.

There were a few times that I myself had friends who came through on yachts. At one point a lady friend of mine with whom I once had a serious walkout, who remained a close friend in New York all through her marriage and divorce, came through on a sailboat with a couple of her sons. Sailboat is a misnomer; it was pretty seriously a yacht, and it was a huge treat for me to sail off with them for a little touring or a picnic. And coincidentally my stock on the island went way up when a few people I knew saw me nonchalantly strolling on and off her boat.

But that yacht didn't hold a candle to the one that belonged to the Suleimans, Saudis who were friends of the sister of one of Tim's and my best friends, Nadia. I knew that Nahed, the sister, and her husband, Amr, were cruising the Aegean with the Suleimans and their friends—Tim was not there—and I was prepared for them, but I was not prepared for the boat. Nahed called up on her cell phone (you see?) to tell me that they had arrived, and soon a huge fleet of taxis, all the Mercedes on the island, were ferrying the Suleimans and their guests up to Exambela. Telling them to "ask anyone" for my house—my old *spiti apo Christo* trick—was not going to work on this occasion, so I went to the edge of the village to meet them. The

Kamares

cars twisting and turning up the road from Apollonia to Exambela reminded me of the parade of cars off for a picnic near the end of Orson Welles's *Citizen Kane*.

Everyone was on his or her cell phone as I led them through the village and even during the visit to my house, the men especially, each of them in different corners of my terrace, all talking importantly to London or Paris or Jedda. After drinks, we all got back in the cars and I guided them to a favorite restaurant of mine named Christo (!), an old Sifnos taverna high up in Artemona, where we had a classic island meal served by the family of the owners. The Suleimans had probably never seen anything like this little Greek restaurant, and the owners I am sure had absolutely never seen anything like the Suleimans and their friends.

After dinner, the Suleimans, to my delight, insisted that dessert would be onboard their yacht, and our parade of cars headed back to Kamares, me staring from the car window down to where the biggest, whitest yacht I had ever seen sat gleaming like a floating Tivoli Garden in the harbor, light streaming across the water from it in every direction. Everyone back on his cell phone—I am only sort of kidding—we poured out of the cars and made our way to the boat. Glancing right and left, I was tickled to see several islanders I knew gaping as they watched their Christo climb the gangplank of what must have seemed to be the royal yacht of somewhere or other or one of the Niarchos or Onassis boats—the Greeks after all are not beginners when it comes to yachts. I had to scoop my own jaw off the deck as I stepped on board: I don't think they actually piped us aboard, but a huge crew all in dazzling white lined up to welcome us and to serve us—to my astonishment and infinite disappointment—on this naturally "dry" ship—rose-petal tea.

—

The Greek islands are places that people always say they are dying to visit, just to wander from island to island, they say, or to take a house and really spend time, to get away "for real," to lose themselves or, for that matter, to find themselves. But most of the people who say they are coming to Greece, who swear they are coming, never get there.

Lady Jeanne Campbell was different. When I ran into her one day on the corner of Seventy-second Street and Second Avenue, near where she lived, she told me that she wanted to come to Sifnos, and I knew she meant it. An old friend of Tim's and by then a great friend of mine, she was the daughter of the Duke of Argyll and the granddaughter of Lord Beaverbrook, the lover of Henry Luce, and the ex-wife of Norman Mailer. With such a provenance, I knew she was not given to idle promises, or indeed idle threats. She had been going to Foligandros, a nearby but even wilder and more primitive island than Sifnos, renting there for a couple of years, and she wanted to come to Sifnos and rent my house. This was back in 1980, before I had added the upper floor, and possessive as I was about my brand-new house and Sifnos itself, I was still easily talked into having her stay. She was a good friend, and she would be a very amusing and glamorous tenant. And I needed the money. So it was arranged for her to take the house after Tim and I left.

As planned, she arrived in July, overlapping with us at the end of our stay, before we left to visit friends on Patmos. She came with her daughters Kate, later an actress, and Cusi, now a writer, but then both only in their teens. Jeanne was crazy about the house, and everyone was charmed by her and her girls. Popi was the first to arrive, of course, to check out the new arrivals, and was in a frenzy of winking, leering salaciously, and nudging Tim about these very attractive girls, though they were still obviously children. That didn't seem to bother her at all.

As I took Jeanne through the village to meet her soon-to-be neighbors, I was suddenly aware that she would just smile and nod at whomever we met. Good Lord, she doesn't speak Greek, I thought, something I had not realized nor thought about, but I worried about it now. Nobody spoke a word of English in Exambela or much of anywhere on the island. Standing, beaming silently at *Kyria* Kathe at the gate to her rough stone hutch on her barren, wind-swept hill, the sheep in the background, Jeanne seemed, as Tim was to say, a bit like the Queen Mother on a royal visit to the Outer Hebrides.

She was no snob, though. She was to slip into the village with ease, and I rented the house to her for years. After that first visit, though, I learned a major lesson about renting, a lesson maybe not so different from what one learns when lending money—just give it, then let it go. Tim and I had moved out, but the day before we left, I went over to show Jeanne something about the house, and stumbling into the kitchen, I found her cleaning the floors with one of my best hand towels, a house gift from my mother, Lady Jeanne's aristocratic foot whooshing the damp bit of handmade linen around on the rough stone floors. There were also a few extra mattresses around for guests—paying ones, I soon found out—but I decided to mind my own business and let her live as she wanted. My house-keeper could see to the rest.

Over the years, I learned that there were "guests" everywhere, anywhere she lived, including there on Sifnos. She was always short of money and struggling to make ends meet. How this was possible for Beaverbrook's granddaughter was one of the great mysteries, but clearly none of his fortune had made its way down through her mother to her. In the mid-eighties, when Tim was working, paint-ing in Rome for a while, he saw quite a lot of Jeanne, who was living there, studying to be a lay nun—she had many lives. She had moved there with her younger daughter, Cusi, and lived, Tim said, in a wonderful, sprawling apartment near the Campidoglio. Every room, though, was rented out, mostly to young people, and Jeanne was cheerfully camped out on the living-room sofa.

One of the problems with having lots of people in my house was water. Water was always an issue everywhere in the Greek islands. There was more water on Sifnos than on many other islands, but we were still very dependent on rainwater. Thanks to Stephanos, my house had a cistern to collect the water, and a pump, i.e., running water—something many of the village houses still didn't have. But even in my house that first day, everyone practicing flushing my toilet was a short-lived delight. Normally to flush the toilet, we used the shower water, which was carefully collected in a plastic bucket we stood in to bathe, and my unhappy plants had to live on the water we washed the dishes in.

I had to watch my own guests like a hawk, insisting that they turn off the water while they soaped up. But a houseful of people, often careless people used to big-city plumbing or tenants who all thought they were owed at least one hot bath every day, was an invitation to disaster, and in New York my dreams were haunted by images of clogged-up septic systems or burned-out water pumps on Sifnos. Jeanne, of course, ran out of water most summers and the cistern always had to be refilled, a fairly complex and costly exercise.

I finally stopped renting the house to her when, arriving one summer after an endless journey from New York, I found a young man installed in my *apothiki*, living there happily, he imagined, for the summer, having rented it from Lady Jeanne. He cheerily referred to my guest room as "the coffin," which is what he said they all called it, and he clearly thought the house belonged to Jeanne—a bit of a misunderstanding. As politely as possible I tried to convince him that the house was mine and, as firmly as possible, told him he had to leave.

I think my real problem was that renting the house regularly to someone made it in a way their house too, or not quite mine anyway. Jeanne was very sociable and always having people in, and I found that it bothered me when total strangers told me how much they loved my house, my bedroom, my things. People I scarcely knew would come up to me at parties on the island and ask where I had found such and such an object or piece of furniture. Worse, though—or, for me, more unsettling—were people I heard referring to my house as Jeanne's, someone once saying to me, "Oh, you live in Lady Jeanne's house." If there was anybody who was determined that his house was his alone, it was uprooted me.

I told Jeanne diplomatically that my nieces and nephews were of an age now and were planning to use the house in the summers, which in fact they were and often did, and that it was impossible to go on letting her the house. Though she may never have quite forgiven me for making her leave Exambela—there were no houses available in the village at that moment—the timing was actually right, as she was writing her memoirs and had a handsome advance with which she was able to buy a small house in Artemona and fix it up.

I always loved knowing that Jeanne was on the island when I was there, that she was nearby. I would run into her on the rocks at Chrissopighi or in the taverna there. Our long lunches and cozy impromptu dinners were unforgettable. "Sweety," she would begin— she called everybody Sweety, in this sort of high-pitched little-girl voice, her eyes and smile filled with mischief—and she was off on some bit of gossip or some extremely personal story or a memory about Norman or Randolph Churchill or a murder suspect of the day whom she knew in New York: "Well, Sweety, of course he's a necrophiliac, everyone knows that. He would knock her out with pills, do it, and then just lie there reading till she came to." Or it might be some intense conversation about Life, religion, death, her writing, my painting.

When I ran into her, it wasn't just that it didn't matter how long it had been since I had seen her, it wasn't just the old saw about picking up where we left off, I literally could not tear myself away. I would be on my way to my rock or on my way home to paint. Stopping for a moment, I thought, in the street, I would immediately find myself deep in conversation, and the next thing I knew, it was hours later and we were sitting in a *kafenion* over an empty bottle of retsina. Creative and imaginative, she inspired me in my work, and I think her writing took off whenever she came to the island, though I have no idea whatever happened to her memoir, whether she ever finished it.

She stopped coming to Sifnos in 2000 owing to failing health, and for me Sifnos was never really the same. By then a few other great friends had started to disappear or die, islanders and *xenoi* as well, and I was beginning to feel rather old myself—my God, by then I was fifty. She died in 2007 in New York.

—

My original, beloved housekeeper Rhodope died of cancer very soon after I moved into my house, and I had to search for someone to replace her. Almost immediately I met her sister-in-law, Chrysoula, a tiny mite of a thing with short-cropped, wiry hair and a pointy little face. Hardly feminine, she was a sharp-tongued, feisty little toughie who favored leather jackets and loved her motorcycle more than anything. She had a mixed reputation in the village, but I liked her right away, and I had always liked her husband, Michalis, who would do all the whitewashing and help around the house. Together they had a then very young son, Dimitri. I knew she had worked hard for low wages for some quite rich people on the island, and I thought this might be a sort of break for her, a good job for a change, and that she would be pleased and work hard for me.

On a Greek island your housekeeper is crucial. Not a servant at all, she literally runs your house, not just cleaning it, but taking care of it all year long when you are not there, opening and closing it, airing it in winter, having it whitewashed in the spring, having the roof redone, seeing to repairs, hiring and firing workpeople, and paying the bills as they come in. In Chrysoula's case, I didn't even have a key of my own; she opened and closed the house when I arrived and left, and it was practically her house. She loved having *to klidi*, the key, and it was looked upon as an honor in the village, particularly once I added the upper floor and she found herself in charge of *to villa*.

And she did her work, certainly at first. Whenever I arrived from abroad, she would be there waiting for me, the house aired and everything whitewashed by Michalis, the whole place sparkling.

There would be flowers on the kitchen table, the fridge filled with fruit, water, eggs, cheese, and a bottle of her own wine. We would kiss with real affection. Then, still totally out of breath after dragging my luggage up from the road, I would have to follow her around as she strode through the house in her beloved leather jacket, this little skinny boy-girl, showing me all she had done, telling me all she had had to do.

Of course every year there was more, and in truth, after the new studio upstairs was built, the job was bigger, but over the years, the recital of all she had done, everything she had to take care of started to become almost a tale of woe, a classical lamentation. She would tell me how she struggled through the wind and rain to get to my house and air it during the winter, how difficult it was getting the right people to do different jobs, how everyone was greedy and conniving, and about her Herculean efforts to bargain them down on my behalf. I couldn't help smiling. For me it was a sort of comedy act, a star turn, mind you, but an act. For starters, I knew perfectly well that she hardly set foot in the house in the winter, and she always hired the same people, her pals, her cronies.

Then would come the presentation of *to logarismo*, the Bill, a mostly incomprehensible list of her expenses, with a variety of equally incomprehensible slips of paper attached, this one the electrician's bill, she said, or that one the man who repaired the broken shutter, all in Greek and in the Greek alphabet, all to be taken on faith. Particularly in the early years it was hard to complain; the house was clean, repairs were seen to, and in truth, it was pretty cheap—I had friends on other islands who paid their housekeepers far more. And I knew that in her eyes I was wealthy. Over time, *to logarismo* began to get more painful. But I never really questioned it; I always just counted out the money, which she immediately hid somewhere inside her jacket.

Finally, I would present her with her gifts, her bottle of Bayer aspirin, her Nina Ricci perfume, a watch for her husband, or some excellent Scotch, all things specified by her. Scotch was a serious affectation of hers. Most islanders didn't drink hard liquor, but she was determined to have Scotch in the house. For her it was the drink of the rich. As with the money, she would hide these things all over her person, and head down, discreetly, she thought, invisible to her neighbors, she would hurry down the path to her house.

I was always generous with Chrysoula. I not only paid the bills without arguing too much—you had to argue a little—but I also quite often helped her out. Whenever she came by, to work or just to visit, she always had a story about some problem or other, and after I had left in the fall, I would get long phone calls in New York about her health, her husband's job problems, the motorcycle she crashed and the cost of repairs, or the price of a new coat for her rapidly growing son. I paid for the motorcycle repairs. Eventually I even gave her some money for a new car. And I sent her L.L.Bean winter coats—at some expense to me, as the coats were often flown back and forth when she didn't like the color.

Although I knew I was being somewhat "had," I truly cared for her. The idea that she might possibly be having an affair with the village bad girl, Melina, even just that they were best friends, and the fact that she had burst into my room and caught me in bed with an Air France steward (oh, the shame; well, he was a first-class steward) and never said anything, and that she had never so much as said boo about Tim's presence there every year for weeks at a time made me feel we had a kind of special bond, and I forgave her everything.

And I suppose I spoiled her and let her think she could get away with anything.

One day in New York I received a letter. This was long before e-mail but was still something of a surprise, as nobody wrote letters much anymore, even from Sifnos, and it made me nervous. If someone had taken the trouble to write, I feared it was probably bad news. It was from the Colemans, my British friends in the village, the ones living in the old theater. I read with mounting dismay how it seemed that a Greek family of five had been living in my house for the previous four or five weeks, and they, the Colemans,

View from my terrace

were fairly sure that these people were neither friends of mine nor tenants.

In my house? Strangers living in my house? Had they broken in? I knew better than that. But what to do?

After I calmed down a bit, I dialed Chrysoula's number. She answered, shouting, "*Ne*," yes, in her raspy voice, and then hearing me say "Chrysoula," she promptly burst into tears. I sternly, I hoped, asked her who those people were in my house and what she thought she was playing at. After a bit more transatlantic sobbing, she went into a long rigmarole about a doctor from Athens who treated her only (as if I didn't know) child and the huge medical bills she couldn't pay. I knew she was probably just renting out the house, but even if all this nonsense was true, it didn't make it any better. I cut her off and told her to get these people out of my house at once, that we would discuss this in September when I got to Sifnos, and I hung up.

I was amazed, shocked that she could have abused my trust in this way, especially after I had been, I felt, very good to her. I had recently been quite royally screwed by a crazy lady art dealer in New York, who in fact eventually went to jail. That had been a nightmare, but for me this was even more upsetting. I was hurt that the person I trusted with my house, a person I thought of as a friend—

and, most of all, someone from my wonderful village—had betrayed me. And, worse, that my neighbors must have all known and kept silent. I wondered if she had done it before and no one had told me. And wondered about what that said about my place in the village.

I dreaded the journey to Sifnos. I hated confrontations and certainly didn't want one on my beloved island, my sanctuary. And I had no idea what to do. Should I forgive her? Fire her? Never talk to her again? All unthinkable ideas in my tiny village. Our meeting was of course horrible, me in the bogus role of injured employer, she like a child caught lying—embarrassing all around. Wiping away imaginary tears, she rattled out the same hard-luck story about the doctor and then, head down, with a great show of shame and remorse, offered to give back *to klidi*, the all-important key.

I acted stern, authoritative, and pained (the pained part was real), the tough boss, but I didn't really want her to go. I knew that she was genuinely poor, could barely read or write, and worked very hard to support her farmer husband and (famously) only child. And I hated the idea of finding someone else. I also knew Exambela was her village. I was just a guest there, and I didn't want to humiliate her in front of her neighbors. And in the end I think the villagers were glad I didn't fire her. I said she should keep the key, but the letting of the house had to stop, never again, and there would be no more Christmas bonuses or presents for her. At least for the time being.

I already knew I would have trouble sticking to that, pushover me.

We had a patching-up moment, both of us teary by now, both greatly relieved that this was over. And truly grateful, I think, at least for the moment, she promised the moon, and indeed never did anything of the kind again. Soon enough, everything was back to normal, with her doing her work and squeezing presents and bonuses out of me, almost as if nothing had happened.

But actually something had happened. We played much the same game every year when I arrived, and I went on paying, maybe overpaying her, but for me something was broken between us that couldn't be repaired. I never chuckled at her grand tragicomic act anymore. I had been permanently disappointed. I would never fire her, I knew it and she knew it. If I were ever to do it, I should have done it then. But though she would never make the same mistake, she became more and more difficult over the years, grumpier and more complaining, almost as if we were an unhappy couple who couldn't get divorced. I began to joke about it in New York, saying I would someday have to sell my house to get rid of my housekeeper.

But even then, when I did sell the house, I promised to pay her a pension, and I pay it still. I couldn't help it; I was that fond of her, especially now that she didn't work for me anymore.

—

I soon learned that my experience was not uncommon, that many of the key holders to foreigners' or off-islanders' houses were making money renting rooms on the sly, and Chrysoula must have known about it. It must have seemed that everyone was making all this easy money off the growing tourist trade, the foreigners and the rich Athenians who came there, and she must have decided to give it a try herself. Even if she didn't have rooms of her own to rent, she had access to mine. Everyone was doing it, after all, weren't they?

And it must have been tempting for her and all the islanders. All this money, all these things people had nowadays. How you gonna keep 'em down on the farm after they've seen Paree? Only in this case, Paree was stuff. It wasn't as simple as saying that greed had come to the island, but it was certainly true that the islanders had begun to think less about their terraces and crops, their old ways and traditions, and more about motorcycles, SUVs, televisions, and cell phones. Sadly for the Sifniots, most of the new hotels and boutiques and discotheques that opened on the island were owned by people from Athens and the mainland. And it must have often seemed that, while making more money than they ever had, they still had to make do with the leftovers, renting rooms, tending bar, driving taxis and buses, or waiting tables.

Obviously there had always been greedy people on the island; witness the shopkeeper who tried to cheat me on the exchange rate when I was buying my house. But the bargaining over taxi rides, food, carpentry work, or the few things one could buy on the island had seemed innocent fun, part of the culture. I had to bargain with Chrysoula a little; she wouldn't have understood if I hadn't, but now there was real money around. There was a high season, a tiny, maybe two-month window of opportunity to make money, and not only did people "work" it, but their mood for the entire year was based on how well the season went. And of course it never went as well as they hoped it would, not for any of them. Villagers would prepare rooms in their houses to rent and no one would come, and even those new boutiques and bars and restaurants opened by all those Athenians had a nasty way of closing after a single summer.

My most startling brushes with this new money "madness" had to do with real estate. By the mid- to late eighties I had begun to think of expanding my world on the island, perhaps having a separate studio. And I spread the word. Melina, as I said, offered a couple of very desirable terraces below the village, but her husband vetoed it in retaliation for my former friendship with her and Panagiotis. A bit later Stelius, the husband of my first housekeeper, Rhodope, offered me some land for the—to me—unheard-of sum of a million drachmas. It was a bit far from the village, but still accessible by mule for construction work, and even though the price seemed astronomical, I had the land surveyed. By my doing so, Stelius instantly thought the sale was a done deal, and he got overexcited. In the end I decided it was too remote and didn't buy it. Needless to say, Stelius was very upset, but I learned a day or two later that he had just bought the land himself for 22,000 drachmas and was hoping to flip it to an ignorant foreigner. This did not endear him to me; 50,000 I could have swallowed, but 1,000,000 was outrageous.

My friend Apostolos, the taxi and bus driver and eventually my partner in a car on the island, had an old friend who was selling some land way in the north behind Agio Anna, one of the most remote villages on Sifnos. It was windy and barren there, and the garbage dump for the island was not far away, so it was not what you would call a prime location. And though goats and sheep lived there, no Sifniots did. But the new road to Cheronisos made the area accessible for construction, and some building had started there. The rocky terraces with their few bent-over windblown olive trees overlooking the sea were quite amazing, and there was a giant Henry Moore–like stone standing twelve feet high that dominated the land. I fell in love with the property, and in spite of all the problems, I began to imagine a studio planned around that remarkable stone.

I went to see the old farmer who owned the land, and he invited me into his stone hut behind a small chapel there in the back of nowhere, where he lived while taking care of his animals. After some small talk, some ouzo, and some smelly cheese, the island I-am-not-really-selling-my-land, it-is-you-who-wants-it ritual, I finally asked him to tell me his price. Without blinking, his sharp blue eyes looking straight into my eyes, he demanded ten million drachmas. I tried not to blink myself, but I was deeply shocked. It was *not* a Henry Moore sculpture, and I was never going to pay such a large sum anyway, but I smiled, said I would think it over, and got up and left. A few months later he died in his little hut with his ten-million-drachma dreams, and I gave up on my plans for a studio away from my house.

—

One of the greatest changes taking place at that time, a revolution really, was the arrival of immigrants in Greece. For generations Greek men had fled the islands, many on ships, some to the mainland, and still others emigrated, mainly to the United States and Australia. And by the sixties and seventies in some places there seemed to be hardly any grown men left. With the implosion of

Yugoslavia, the Balkans—Greece's backyard—was thrown ass over teakettle, and the whole region was suddenly flooded with émigrés desperately fleeing the wars between the Serbs, the Croats, the Bosnians, and the Kosovars. The Albanians especially spread out all across the region, even as far as Italy, boatloads of them trying to land on the Italian coast. They poured into Greece as well, seeking asylum and looking for work, any kind of work, including the most menial. And with Greece's eventual acceptance into the eurozone, the number of immigrants just kept growing.

Even little Sifnos had its share of Albanian immigrants, men and women. I was very aware of them. You couldn't not be; they were everywhere. But also, I was particularly aware of them because many of the men were incredibly handsome—I cannot tell a lie, or not about that. Handsome and very sexy. Chrysoula, like many other islanders, loathed them. A flat-out racist, she trusted none of them; according to her, the women were whores and the men were thieves who were taking work away from Greeks. Most of them, of course, were desperate for jobs and extremely hardworking, but as is true wherever there is massive immigrant labor, that didn't count for much with her.

At one point I decided to have all my windows and shutters painted. I was going to use one of my Exambela neighbors, someone I had used in the past on Chrysoula's recommendation, and had him over to give me an estimate. He had a reputation for being expensive, but he did good work and I liked him, and I adored his parents, who lived nearby. He took a quick look at the house and asked three thousand euros for the job. This seemed a large sum to me; in fact, it was a large sum.

At the same time, the woodwork on a neighbor's house was being painted by a young Albanian named Victor, whom I had noticed. One day, passing by, I asked him if he could come and give me an estimate on my windows and shutters. He came over after work, inspected all the woodwork, measuring and studying everything, and then shyly told me that he had to ask at least six hundred and fifty euros! I felt totally "had" by my neighbor and, to Chry-soula's horror, gave Victor the job. From then on Victor did all the work on the house, repairs and whitewashing. Chrysoula's husband had been too old to work for some time. Victor was wonderful, helpful, and charming, but Chrysoula would have nothing to do with him.

Another effect of the collapse of Yugoslavia and the bloody wars that followed, and one that affected me directly, was the rise of a new, virulent anti-Americanism in Greece. The Greeks, like the Russians, were pro–Orthodox Serbia, and they were enraged by American and NATO bombings there. America had been hopelessly compromised, certainly to left-wing Greeks, as far back as the Greek Civil War and then again because of their support of the much-hated Colonels, and now the United States was siding against their Serbian brothers.

Anti-Americanism was something I hadn't experienced before, in part because in the days of the Junta, or even several years after that, I didn't have an American passport. Nor had I any particular feeling back then about the States, other than that I loved going to school there. Now I lived in America, in New York, and had an American passport and dual citizenship. In Athens, obviously, but even on faraway Sifnos, it got to be impossible even to go out for dinner without this coming up, everybody turning on me as an American and screaming and yelling about how terrible the United States was. Gone were the days of a Sifnos that barely knew the Junta had collapsed. Newly plugged in, with everyone by then having television and laptops and access to blogs, the islanders, like the rest of Greece and Europe, could sit and watch NATO bombs falling on Belgrade. And there were several very difficult, unpleasant years there for me. I couldn't escape it.

—

I would tell Tim about this anti-Americanism whenever I got back to the States or on the phone from Sifnos. I was shocked by the chauvinism and the insularity of it all, especially for a country yearning to be a part of modern Europe. And I suspect it made Tim not particularly interested in coming to Sifnos again. By the late eighties and early nineties, having stopped painting there, as I have said, he had started coming less and less, but in 1989 we bought a house in Connecticut, and he became obsessed by his garden and didn't want to go anywhere in the spring unless it was explicitly for work. He came once in a while, for my exhibitions in Athens or when we had guests, but not often. And in truth, "stuff" happened that started to keep me from coming as often myself—a show in Switzerland, a work trip, sometimes just being too lazy to make the effort. I loved Connecticut too, and traveling all that way to Greece for only a couple of weeks twice a year was beginning to wear even on me. Obviously it had been easier to keep up that kind of schedule when I lived in Switzerland.

During those years we had also started visiting our friend Nadia in Vence in the south of France, where she had bought a house with her sister Nahed. It was easier to get to than Sifnos, by far, and we had begun going there from time to time. I never had any real interest in it other than as a lovely place to visit once in a while and a way to spend time with her, but on these visits we had started looking for La Bastide du Roi, my great-grandparents' house in nearby Antibes. My father never talked about it and was no help at all, but Tim and I kept looking. And after a few false starts, one year I had the bright idea of going to the Antibes police, who told me that there was in fact a *rue* Brechneff that led to the Antibes golf course, Le Golfe du Roi, and from there it should be easy to find the house. I knew of the golf course, as my stepgrandfather had spoken of it; it had been part of my great-grandparents' property, and he himself had bought it from them as an investment, and incidentally to help them, and later sold it as a golf course.

We found the road and then, a bit farther on, a set of gates we assumed led up to the house. I got out and spoke into a little speaker phone in the wall, explaining that my name was Brechneff, and this voice said, "But I know all about the Brechneffs. Come up." And the gates swung open and we drove up this zigzagging treelined drive to what had to be one of the loveliest houses either of us had ever seen—a long, high, narrow, hip-roofed brick house with a huge tank or pool in front surrounded by ancient pines. We met the person who lived there and walked through the house and the gardens to a terrace with a view of a truncated *allée* of trees that had once led all the way to the sea. It was like a dream for me, this house I had heard about as a child but had never seen, never quite believed in. This beautiful house had been the Brechneff's home, my family's home, and suddenly I had a Tara, a Brideshead, a home, a past, not a particularly happy one, perhaps, but a past.

—

I kept going to Sifnos of course. But there were times when I got there and, at least at first, wasn't always so sure quite why I had left Tim and come all this way to a place that it seemed I hardly knew and hardly knew me anymore. More and more of the old people I had known were gone, and I wasn't as interested in making friends with the newcomers or the younger generation. Maybe I was simply getting a bit jaded, but the young islanders seemed . . . different. And they were different; Sifnos was different.

For one thing, the island had become the preferred summer resort of Konstantinos Simitis, the then prime minister, which gave it perhaps a little too much cachet for my liking. Actually, Margaret Papandreou, the American ex-wife of Andreas Papandreou, the former prime minister, and a great friend of the Keeleys, had been coming there for many years without creating much of a fuss, but now everyone was starstruck by Simitis's presence there and began competing for his attention and for invitations. Rich Athenians started building everywhere on the island, and there were now regular high-speed boats that brought more and more people, even weekenders from the capital, an unimaginable notion a few years before.

tou Vounou

Because of Simitis being on Sifnos—there was almost always an upside to these changes and developments—the island got new cell phone antennas, and we ended up having the best reception in the Aegean. And I secretly loved the high-speed boats—they made life so much easier—but the crowds did make one shy away. Exambela remained a safe zone of familiarity and privacy, and I still had my painting, though I was beginning to find that work called to me there less urgently. After all those years of coming to Sifnos, I had to crank myself up more than before to paint. Most times when I arrived now, there would be a couple of days of calling Tim to ask why I was here and he was there and of complaining how lonely I was and wondering why I had come at all. But then I would take a walk, see something, a sky, a sunset, a fall of light on the water, and I would begin painting again.

Still, something had shifted. Somewhere, somehow, I knew it wasn't the same. Or I wasn't. And after all these years, I began to wonder if I wasn't just going on going on.

The Hadjiminas almost saved the day, for a time totally renewing my pleasure in Sifnos, and Greece itself. They were a glamorous young couple from Athens who had taken my old architect friend Koressi's grandmother's house on the hill above Chrissopighi on a ten-year lease. I had always thought it one of the most wonderful houses on the island. Though the hill was slowly but surely being covered by houses and villas, the tiny Koressi house still stood alone, halfway up the hill directly above the church, looking straight out at the sea and sky beyond. Inside, the house was just a few small, simple rooms, hung with wonderful old sepia photographs of the Koressi family arriving for the summer on donkeys they rode up from Kamares.

I met Claire first. She was a painter, and my friend Koressi thought she should meet another painter on the island and he sent her to me. I fell for her on the spot. How could I not? Suddenly one day, there was this tall, slim, beautiful, smiling dark-haired girl coming up the path toward my house, speaking in this wonderful voice—the first Greek woman I fell for who didn't have a deep smoker's voice—and this marvelous accent I had always loved. And we became fast friends immediately.

Soon after, I met her husband, a strikingly handsome man with thick, slicked-back dark hair and pretty darn slicked-back clothes, a very elegant and, it turned out, very successful businessman. In Athens, when I stayed with them, he often seemed to be always and everywhere—from the breakfast table to dinner in the best restaurants—on too damn many cell phones at once, but on Sifnos he was quite relaxed, smiling, friendly, charming.

Claire and I had our own special bond. We were innocently nuts about each other, and we were like two children who could play together endlessly, completely forgetting or ignoring what was going on around them. But I also had a bond with her husband, a rather curious one. First of all, his name was Christian. Unusual, but I had been there before with Christian in Switzerland. He was, though, exactly ten years younger than I to the day, having been born on the third of September in 1960. Even more astonishing, almost unimaginable really, was the fact that we had been born in the same hospital in the same town, Watsa (where? you may well ask), a mining town in the former Belgian Congo—the absolute back of the back of the beyond.

When I was born, my father was working there as a doctor in a small government-owned hospital. Though he had studied medicine in Switzerland, not being Swiss, he was not allowed to practice there, so he had found this job and carted my mother and older brother off to the Congo, and I was born soon thereafter. They loved it, we all loved it, but we had to leave by the time I was three. It appeared that the Belgian government doled out this post to young doctors in a sort of rotation, and suddenly my father's time was up. A tragedy, it seemed to them at the time, but very lucky as it turned out: soon after that, many of the white people in my parents' village were killed in one of the Congo's many bloody blowups. Christian's parents had been living in the Congo for some time, and he was born in that same little hospital. This coincidence, this link, was so startling as to bond us to this day.

The Hadjiminas were a breath of fresh air for me, my new best friends. And a new kind of friend for me altogether on the island. They were not just people I found there; they were truly my kind of people—people I might have known and been friends with anywhere. Whenever I went to Sifnos, I always looked forward to their being there, Claire especially—she was there more often than Christian. She lived directly on the route to and from my rock for swimming and my favorite restaurant for lunch. But I was as likely to stop and have lunch with her, the two of us sitting on old Mrs. Koressi's dazzling little terrace above the sea. We talked and talked; we were both painters, I a painter for years, she relatively new at it, struggling with it, but talented and determined, and we could talk about our work for hours. We really made the island for each other.

About the same time, I had started to have an actual life in Athens, not just my rather louche stopovers, but working visits. I had begun staying there, days, weeks at a time, working on producing a catalog for a major show I was to have at Kreonides, a gallery just off Kolonaki Square. As a result, I had begun to meet Athenians and, something new for me, to make an effort to meet the Athenians on the island, partly in hopes of building some kind of client base in Athens, but also because I suddenly discovered it was fun.

Claire and Christian became very much part of all that. I always stayed with them in their beautiful terraced apartment in Kolonaki and then, as Christian became more and more successful, in the amazing nineteenth-century villa they had bought and were doing over in Thission. It was a marvelous, grand, imposing place with a dazzling view of the Acropolis, but perhaps a mistake, somehow catapulting them into a life, a world, and a set of responsibilities that were not such a happy fit with their young personalities. But they came to my shows there and bought my pictures, they and their friends too, and we were as much part of one another's lives in Athens as we were on Sifnos.

They transformed Athens and Sifnos for me, brought the island back to life for me, made me look forward to going there again. And I think, looking back, that they, in turn, may have been at their best and happiest there as a couple. They truly loved the island, going so far as to renew their wedding vows in "their" church down the hill at Chrissopighi. After a while, though, it seemed that Claire grew bored with the house; it was too small for her and her two children, she said, too small for them and all the nannies and staff she wanted. Of course the children loved it there, running half wild on that flower-covered hill above the sea. The house wasn't really too small for them. It and the island, I think, had become too small and poky for the life they wanted. Bigger houses, bigger islands, bigger worlds beckoned. And to my dismay and total regret, suddenly my best friends were gone. The lease was up, and they left. For Mykonos.

And it was a real blow for me. I mean, they didn't die like Popi or Jeanne, but it had never occurred to me that they might leave, that they were not permanent fixtures on Sifnos. They were younger than I, they were Greek, they loved Sifnos, how could they just leave? In some part of my mind, nothing was ever supposed to change there. Nobody was supposed to die or leave Neverland. Especially not them. They were the first people there who were part of my life, not just part of the island's *tableau vivant*, a little play, with me as the perpetual juvenile lead living in my Greek village. These were my peers, part of a possible adult life on the island. And they were gone.

Though they are divorced now, they are still friends of mine, both of them. I still see them, but those fun years are gone, left behind for them and lost for me.

—

Kreonides was one of the oldest and biggest galleries in Athens. The only other comparable gallery was Zoumboulakis. Both were just off the square in Kolonaki, as always the most fashionable part of town. I had met a backer, Phoibus, a partner in the gallery. Taken with my pictures, and with me, he had introduced me to his friend, the owner, Iannis Kreonides. The gallery was organized really as a gallery for Greek painters; my old acquaintance from Kastro, Panayiotis Tetsis, whom I hadn't dared speak to all those years before, showed there. I slipped through because of painting Sifnos landscapes and having a house there, and they scheduled a retrospective of my Sifnos work.

Obviously, the chance of this exhibition turned me on totally; if, as I said, my urge to paint there had begun to wane a bit, the idea of this show revived it, and once again I began churning out pictures. It wasn't all that surprising, really. Sifnos had always had a charged atmosphere for me, sexual and elemental, that set me working, lit me up, and brought me to myself. I had been painting the island there and even in New York for years now. I didn't have to be there; I carried it with me, the shapes, the colors, and above all the light. It was as if I could close my eyes and still draw it. This place was literally in my mind's eye—more, it was in my very hand.

I painted the island, clear or fogbound, in the blazing light of day or the ink black of night. I could paint the contours of the mountains by heart, the patterns and rhythms of the endless walls and paths as they climbed and descended the hills, echoing their shapes or defining and sculpting them. I painted the olive groves, the trees gnarled and twisted, their branches sometimes like open fans, at other times all leaning together away from the wind, and the thousands of wildflowers growing around their feet and tangled roots.

In the eighties, there was a terrible fire near Chrissopighi, everyone on the island rushing out to help try to extinguish the flames that flew over the tinder-dry landscape. The fire devoured terrace after terrace, the crops, the bushes, even the olive trees, which, as the fire reached them, burst into flames, exploding one after another into the sky. Somehow the fire was finally put out, but from it came my Burning Tree Paintings, a series of gouaches and oils— rows of olive trees burning with not just yellow and red flames but flames of every imaginable color, as if the fire were drawing in and sucking up every thing and every color on the island.

This series, in truth, was also driven by the tag end of a serious love affair I had with a young painter in New York. It was over by then, or a bit tamped down at least, and I was still with Tim, had never left him; but as usual, wanting it every which way, I couldn't stop thinking about this young man. He was to die of AIDS, and not so very much later I started a series of Fallen Angel Paintings, huge nudes that an art critic compared to the Tree Paintings, asserting that the nudes "radiated the same heat as the olive trees . . . and are ablaze with some erotic power." He said, "One might wonder whether some event in the artist's life might explain his sudden interest in the human body." One might indeed.

Somewhere in those years a Swiss friend of mine gave me a huge collection of old, dry pastels that she had inherited. They were made in Danzig before the Second World War—quite a provenance. I had never used pastels before and had always thought of them as sweet and decorative—unless you were talking about Degas and a few others—pretty, just as the word says, pastel colors. But I started fooling with them, climbing up onto my roof terrace at dawn or dusk and "painting" the amazing colors of sunrise and sunset over the Aegean.

Little did I know that that little box of pastels was going to lead to a huge series of plein air drawings of sunrises and sunsets all over the world. But more immediately they led to another series of pictures from Sifnos, my Halfway to Heaven pictures, long, vertical works based on views from my studio window and rooftop, views of the mountains across the way, the paths and steps climbing up out of the trees at the foot of the mountains, up and up toward the dazzling white monasteries of Agios Andreas and Profitis Elias. I called them flags, a little like the Buddhist prayer flags Tim and I saw on our trips to Asia, long flaps of color affixed to poles along one side.

Looking back, my passion for painting Sifnos had, as I said, begun to flag, but this Kreonides show was a huge shot in the arm. I mean, Muses are all very well, but there is no better muse than a show date, and I worked and worked and worked. The first show was quite a success, a big crowd and good sales, and they asked me to do another four years later. Very pleased and excited now that I seemed to have a gallery in Athens where I could show regularly, as well as in Switzerland and New York, I threw myself into even more pictures, another whole set. But by the time I got back to Athens for my second show, I knew there was something going on, something wrong. There was a new director, and my friend Phoibus, the partner, was "unavailable," in the hospital with very bad hepatitis, they said.

I had the show, which was also a success, but everyone seemed distracted, unfocused. And indeed, within a month the gallery was closed "temporarily," for "tax reasons," they said. But it never

Profitis Elias

reopened, and in fact, I was lucky to get my money and my pictures out. And to make matters worse, Phoibus, my friend, had been arrested for embezzlement. It had nothing to do with the gallery, but it left an unhappy taste in my mouth. Poor man, I've completely lost track of him.

It was sad to witness the collapse of this distinguished gallery, not my first or last time, but it also threw a cloud over my Greek life. I knew this was probably the end of the nascent professional life in Athens I had so looked forward to. It wasn't as if there were galleries lined up to pick up the slack, and I knew I didn't have the energy to go out and try to find another gallery on my own. And with no outlet there anymore, it seemed harder to crank up the creative juices and paint more pictures of Sifnos.

Having a dealer in Athens had given a whole new life to my painting on the island, but without the gallery, my urge to paint there, all my usual endless energy, just sort of whooshed out of me. I stopped painting on Sifnos in 2000, and my last major drawings there were completed in 2002. As it happens, they were probably the best drawings I ever did there, quite figurative, drawn on large sheets of paper from the roof terrace. I had finally totally absorbed the landscape, and my hand flew over the huge sheets of paper. But it turned out that these drawings were my swan song, a farewell to thirty years of painting on the island.

At first I thought I was just taking a break, fair enough after all those many years and all the work I had put into those two Athens shows. I assumed that I would come back to it, to painting and drawing this island I loved. And it took a couple of years of coming to the island and not going near my paints, not even going near that corner of my studio, for the penny to drop, for me to begin to realize that the unthinkable had happened: I was done, done painting there. The island still touched me, I knew, but it no longer had its arm down my throat, deep inside me, gripping my heart. What had seemed an endless visual and emotional resource, a seemingly bottomless well for looking and seeing and feeling, had dried up.

In 2001, Greece joined the eurozone. And nothing has ever been the same there. By the late eighties Athens in particular had begun to grow by leaps and bounds, and by the nineties it was almost unrecognizable, a vast, sprawling city with major traffic and pollution problems. Even though it was by the sea, there was something about the bowl in which the city was built that kept the air from clearing, and there were days when sunny Athens would be covered by a yellow-gray cloud that lay over the city like a bruise.

With the coming of the euro, though, the new currency, the change went into overdrive. Suddenly the quaint little drachma, whose value for years had packed about as much punch as the Egyptian pound, was gone, and the country exploded. Almost overnight, it seemed, money was everywhere, as well as all the accoutrements of modern Europe. The streets of Athens and Thessaloníki were filled with SUVs, Mercedes, and BMWs, and art galleries and fancy restaurants began to open everywhere. The climax of this reentry onto the world stage was, of course, the Olympics in 2004, an event designed to show that Greece was now a world player. As if by magic, Athens became a city of broad highways, parks, tramways, even subways, a totally modern city. It nearly killed them, and may yet—the money spent on the Olympics qualifies as a major part of the recent collapse of the Greek economy—but they did it, and the euphoria that went with having their own Olympic Games back in Greece was almost palpable.

While the signs of change were most visible in the major cities, they were starting to appear on the islands as well, even on Sifnos. Some of it I didn't mind. The high-speed boats, as I have said, I secretly loved. I missed the old bread man and the men selling fish in the square, but I loved Katerina's new supermarket with all its choices and delicacies. I hated that everyone could rent cars, which increased the traffic on the island, but it made all the difference when you had guests: they could rent their own cars and go places on their own. And I loved my own car once I had one. And while I missed that feeling of being far, far away and wonderfully cut off, I wondered, honestly, how I had lived all those years without my daily *Herald Tribune* with my morning coffee.

One of the things that did affect me negatively, and immediately, in Athens and on the island, was that, with the arrival of the euro, prices went through the roof. What had been one of the least expensive places in Europe was suddenly very expensive indeed. Though still nothing like Paris or London, the price of dinner or a hotel room in Athens, now, overnight, was on a par with most other cities of Europe. Even on Sifnos, *to logarismo* for stuffed tomatoes and meatballs at the still funky, neon-lit Hotel Sofia was a shock when it came in euros, particularly having known not just what it cost twenty years before but literally the day before. There is no question that I could never have afforded to go to Greece the way I did all those years, and could certainly never have bought a house there as a struggling twenty-six-year-old painter, if the euro had been in place.

The summers were the most jarring; the off-islanders and all their cars clogged the tiny island roads in high season. With the coming of the euro, car dealerships opened all over Greece, and the Greeks really went a little bit crazy buying the damn things. There were no restrictions on the island the way there are on, say, Capri, and in July and August the pristine beaches became parking lots, and since the mainland Greeks particularly hate to walk even ten feet, they tended to drive their huge SUVs right up to the entrances of the tavernas. I could avoid all the cars by staying in Exambela, but I couldn't avoid them in Chrissopighi, where I had gone regularly for lunch for more than thirty years.

One day, a young Greek drove his BMW SUV over the beach to the taverna and parked right in front of my table, blocking everyone's view of the sea and the monastery. A huge cloud of dust swept over the restaurant terrace as he ground to a stop in the sand and got out, his shining, glaring car clicking away as it cooled. I politely sug-

gested that he park his car in the parking lot at the side of the taverna. He answered with some anti–American remark, and I went in
to the owner, whom I had known since he was maybe twelve years
old, and told him his guests would move to the taverna next door if
he did not keep his view clear of cars. The young man was made to
move, and he drove off with a screech of tires and another cloud of
dust over everyone's food. Mind you, I was perfectly aware that it
was "his" country, but he certainly wasn't giving much thought to
caring about it.

Otherwise, compared with most of Greece, changes on the
island were fairly subtle, more petit mal than grand mal. It wasn't as
though everybody had gone crazy and paved the island with parking
lots. I mean the island wasn't "ruined," you know, in that way that
people talk. But it *was* different. In the village, when you walked
through the streets in the evening, the little *kafenion* was empty. No
one was outside the houses, chatting, smoking, greeting evening
strollers. The light coming through the shuttered windows was the
dull flicker of televisions, the only sound laugh tracks or the clatter
of keys on a laptop.

Indeed, the village paths themselves were different, tricked and
fiddled with so as to be passable for the huge BMW motorcycles
that now sat outside the farmers' doors, taking the place of tethered
donkeys waiting to go to the fields. The walls and terraces were being
neglected, the dovecotes not whitewashed, the little towers at the
corners tilting and crumbling. Interestingly, during those days there
was a major campaign on the island to rebuild all the walls and restore
some of the monasteries, but the reason was of course simply tourism. It was tourism that long ago, after the Colonels, helped save
Greece, helped bring it back. But tourism is often like a cure that is
worse than the disease, nearly ruining whatever it touches, more
often than not destroying the very object of its interest and affection.

No, it was not earthshaking, the change on the island. But the
island was different. Some delicate thread of tradition, of context, or
connection between the islanders and the past was breaking or

already broken. And the change, this shifting underfoot, had done something to them, the islanders. The arrival of the twentieth century, and now the twenty-first, had happened so suddenly, so abruptly, that the breaking of that thread was like cutting a lifeline, leaving them, for the time being at least, without any of their familiar certitudes, untethered, at sea.

—

For all my complaining about the Greeks and their cars, I wasn't actually so pure; I had made my own little contribution to Sifnos's nascent automobile culture. Quite early on, in fact. Back in the eighties there was a moment when I had begun thinking I should get a car. Tim and I were older and finding it less wonderful to walk everywhere every day, and I was beginning to have trouble with the blazing Greek sun and my skin, and I hated having to cover up and wear a hat every time I went anywhere. In summer the buses back and forth to the beach were packed and slow. And hot. And I thought with a car we could really explore the far reaches of the island more easily, go and draw new places if we wanted, and eat in restaurants that were starting to open all over the island, far out of the villages and not so crowded.

By then I had lived through quite a few generations of Sifniots, and I had known Apostolos from the time he was a young boy selling tickets on his cousin's bus, the first bus from Apollonia to Platy Ghialos. By the mid-eighties he was a handsome, rosy-cheeked bus driver himself. Many of the girls on the island took the bus just to flirt with him, or so I would tease him. I knew that another cousin, still another bus driver, took care of an English friend's car, a Deux Chevaux, the car of choice on the island in those pre-euro days. And I approached Apostolos, who loved cars and knew all about them, to be my partner in a similar enterprise.

At that time, cars in Greece were all imported and still had heavy duties and taxes on them, which pushed the price way up, so almost no one on Sifnos had a car, certainly not just for pleasure. I would buy whatever car he advised me to buy in Athens, I said, and he would deal with all the paperwork and insurance and servicing. I would have the car whenever I was there, along with the little sweetener for me that he would meet me at the boat when I arrived and take me there when I left. And in return, he would have a car at his disposal about ten months of the year for almost no money other than for repairs and servicing, most of which he could do himself.

He loved the idea and immediately set about researching cars. I was coming back that spring from New York, and we made a date to meet in Athens, where he told me he had found two secondhand Deux Chevaux during the winter for me to choose between. One was quite cheap, a traditional dull gray Deux Chevaux, and somehow not much of a car, we thought. The other was slightly more expensive, a better car, but a horrible, screaming green color. I took a couple of drives in both cars and decided that the green one really was better. And although I thought the color appalling, I figured I could get used to it. I had gotten used to my screaming blue tiles, after all, and I would just suck it up and get used to this. Appropriating, well, stealing, a name from a friend's very green car on Patmos, I dubbed the homely thing Froggy. It looked like one and jumped like one when you drove it.

Deux Chevaux are strange and hilarious cars. The weird gearshift sticking straight out of the wannabe dashboard, the canvas sling chairs for seats, the loosey-goosey suspension, and the goggle-eyed headlights make it a comical sight as it bounces cheerfully along the road. Parked, they are even stranger and funnier, the wheels tilting weirdly, the car appearing exhausted, leaning against the wall. But back then on Sifnos, any car was Big Stuff, and we created quite a stir driving down the ferry ramp in Kamares, everyone smiling, waving, patting our new car.

I had truly arrived.

I even got to like the color, the only drawback being that it was so unique, everyone always knew where I was. But I loved having it, driving everywhere with the top open, racing (sort of) over the island roads, zipping off to buy supplies or have one more swim at Chrissopighi or drive to Nikos's restaurant in Cheronisos for dinner. Froggy created tremendous freedom for me, and just picking up guests in this green bomb was a showstopper.

When I went back to New York, Apostolos would take the car as agreed. Of course, not quite as agreed, as Apostolos allowed his wife and his children to learn to drive with Froggy, and my dear little car took quite a beating during the winters. Froggy also went on holiday to Crete and traveled all over the mountainous Greek mainland; it was not exactly my idea, my view of our deal, but what could I do to stop it. "We need new tires, *Christaki mou*. We need a new suspension. A new roof." We did indeed. And I loved him and his family, and I loved the luxury of having my own car meet me at the ferry. And so I would pay up. The little nuisances and expenses were worth it. And Apostolos did take good care of the car; he loved it even more than I did.

Still, over the years, I was aware that it was getting a little worn-out. One day, as I was driving back from the beach with my two grown nephews, it became pretty clear that we simply weren't going to make it up the hill, and we had to get out and push. And from time to time the car would just gasp and stop, and I would have to call Apostolos to come and work his magic, which he did—in much the way old Aristides used to when healing my little lemon tree—stroking Froggy and speaking to it, and giving it a little pat when he was done.

One night, after about eight years, I got a phone call in New York from Apostolos: there had been an accident, no one was hurt, and it wasn't his fault, but the car was badly damaged. Froggy had been happily parked as always along the road below Apostolos's house when a drunken driver smashed into it in the early hours of the morning. The man had tried to leave the island with the first ferry, but Apostolos had caught him just as he was about to get on the boat. His car not only had a huge scrape on the side, but it was smeared with hideous bright-green paint, a dead giveaway. That color had paid off at last.

The police were called, the man confessed, papers were exchanged, and we thought that would be it and the car would be repaired soon. But few things in Greece are ever so simple. In fact Froggy was in the shop in Athens for two years! The culprit didn't want to pay, nor did his insurance company, and it turned into an endless battle with lawyers and bureaucrats all piling on before it was settled and we could drive Froggy back to Sifnos. Looking like new, we thought. But it wasn't like new and indeed was never the same. On top of everything else, that comical suspension had been badly damaged, and after a while I got scared and simply stopped driving it; it just wasn't safe anymore driving on the island's steep, winding roads.

"We must get a new car, *Christaki mou*." But "we" weren't going to, I wasn't going to, and though I knew Apostolos was seriously disappointed, I just couldn't go through all that rigmarole again. Besides, by then it was easy to rent cars for the short stretches of time I had come to spend on the island.

—

All those years passing, at times I had begun to feel like a bit of a relic. Like some cranky, grumpy old-timer. And I would find myself talking to visitors about how things had been "before." Of course people who came for the first time probably loved it just as much as I had when I first got there.

And people did still come. More than ever. Some "we" liked, some we didn't. Among my favorite newcomers was Natasha, a Russian-born lady, somewhat older than I, who lived with her opera-loving Swiss banker husband in Geneva during the winter months but came, mostly on her own, to Sifnos for several months every summer. To my great joy, she rented the same house that Claire and Christian had rented all those years on the hill above Chrissopighi, the old Koressi house. Quite heavy, warm, and welcoming, Natasha was a brilliant cook whose greatest joy was preparing food for a houseful of lunch or dinner guests, and I went there often and with pleasure, meeting all kinds of people, many of them also new-comers.

Naturally, there were plenty of people arriving one wasn't so sure about. Instead of just being a tourist destination, the island was becoming more of a resort, with more and more different kinds of people finding their way there and staying, buying or building houses. Diagonally across the street from me, for example, was a couple who had just recently moved in. He was Greek, from Athens, a relative of the old lady who had owned the house for many years. She herself had rarely come there, and he never, as far as I knew, and it had always been empty. But he was an acquaintance of the prime minister, and they started coming to Sifnos at about the same time.

He was a rather mysterious man, and the gossip was that he was probably some sort of arms dealer. I do not know, but he was married to a very nice woman who was a former Swedish bra model, a pretty marvelous notion, I thought. What was not so marvelous was the booming music flowing all day from the house. Opera, fortu-nately, like the music I played all the time, but really loud, deafen-ing. I played my music loud too, but not quite that loud. And I was there first, I thought. But it made me worry that someone could move into Old Aphrodite's house next door and play recordings of Yanni, the Greek recording star, all day. And then where would I be?

Aphrodite had died a couple of years before, her heirs had put the house on the market, and I was very worried about it. It was one thing to have Old Aphrodite, the Evil Eye chaser-awayer and her trickle of old gentleman clients next door; it was quite another to start over with someone new. Our houses and terraces literally bled into each other. Whoever lived there would be living in my lap, or just plain on top of me. What would I do if the newcomers had children? And actually lived there all the time? I thought of buying it myself, of course. Tim and I would buy it, I imagined, and run the houses together, making a proper guest suite and a big studio for him. It might even goad him into starting to come again and staying.

I did in fact go to see the heirs, to find out how much they wanted for it, and perhaps to make an offer, but they were asking a preposterous sum, the moon, I thought, for such a minute house jammed back there at the end of a dead-end path under the looming walls of the ruined Prisani villa. I felt the house was absurdly small and only made sense if it were attached to mine, and in fact, in spite of my obvious chauvinism, I was basically right. I made an offer, they refused it, I went up a bit but not much, and they came down, but not much, and pretty soon we reached an impasse. I was convinced they would never get what they were asking, but they were clearly prepared to wait, if only for me to cave in. I was sure they thought I would come around, simply to protect myself, but I wasn't going to budge either. Even though it would have made a nice addition to the house, it was an insane amount of money. And I suspect I already sensed that I wasn't sure I wanted any more financial or emotional commitments on Sifnos.

Nevertheless, I was in a panic about who might buy the house. If I wasn't careful, I could find myself living between Mad Aphrodite below me, the opera-loving bra model across the street, and, literally in my courtyard, a family with four children, a full library of video games, and a BMW motorcycle. Or worse.

One glorious morning, as I went down to fix breakfast, I found a middle-aged couple climbing around on Old Aphrodite's terrace and, incidentally, mine, measuring walls and doors and windows. I introduced myself. Louella and Bruce were British, both artists, they had these strange accents I could not figure out, and they didn't seem overly friendly. I went into the kitchen, ostensibly to make my coffee, but I could hear them making plans for a totally illegal roof terrace, as well as how they could use my terraces when I was not there. Right away I didn't like them, but I tried to be as nice as possible, and we had dinner together that night. Happily for me, they seemed dubious about Aphrodite's small, hemmed-in house, and I immediately offered to ask around for other houses for them.

A day or two later I heard of a house in Artemona and made a date to take them there. On the way to meet them, I passed the house of Nikos, the grandson of old Popi, the young man holding the rabbit by the ears in his mother's kitchen years before, grown now and married and living in a house near Artemona. When I stopped to chat, he whispered to me in that secretive Greek way that they wanted to sell the house, and if I knew anyone who might want to buy it, to tell them. He didn't want to use Spiridulla (the real estate agent I would eventually employ) because, his voice dropping even lower, he did not trust her.

Well, I thought, if ever there was a wonderful coincidence. And I told him I was on my way to meet some people who might want the house. While we were talking, I noticed a beautiful old ceramic pot there in the courtyard. "Do you like it?" asked Nikos, seeing my eye linger on it. "Yes. I would love to have it," I said. I had quite a collection of old jars and pots by then. "Would you sell it? Can I buy it?" He threw up his eyebrows and his chin with a *tst*, for don't talk nonsense. He talked about the years he had known me, about his grandmother, my neighbor and friend, his mother, Simone, and said the pot was a gift from him to me. I insisted, but so did he. Very grateful, I told him I would come back later with my nephew and pick it up.

As it happened, Louella and Bruce weren't much interested in the house in Artemona, so I told them about Nikos's house, and they accompanied me back immediately. As they spoke little Greek, I translated for them, and to my delight and relief, they were very interested in this house, and I spent much of the afternoon with them, explaining what they should do and would have to do to buy it. On leaving, I reminded Nikos that I would come back later for my pot. "What pot?" Louella rasped with her horrible accent. And fool that I am, I explained about the pot Nikos had promised me as a present.

That evening, Tobias, my nephew, and I went up to Nikos's and found him and his wife very excited, very grateful: Louella and Bruce had come back and made an offer, and Nikos had accepted it. Smiling, he handed me a folded piece of paper, a note from Louella, he said, who had told him to be sure to give it to me. No doubt he thought it was a thank-you note of some kind from people he assumed were my friends. It was not.

"Christian," it unceremoniously read. "We have decided to buy this house. Do not remove the pot. It belongs to this property and to us. Louella."

When he saw my face darken as I read this snarky, imperious note, Nikos's smile vanished; he was no doubt fearing that there was something wrong with the sale. But when I told him what the note said, he was very upset for me. I had seen the pot first and he had given it to me. It was I, he said, who had found them the house after all, and in Greece, one always gives a gift of thanks in such a situation. I should just take the pot, he said, Tobias chiming in in agreement. But I just didn't have the strength to fight with Louella and Bruce. Certainly not over a pot.

At least I knew they would not be my neighbors. Mission accomplished.

I guess, until Louella and Bruce, I had always thought that anyone who found his or her way to Sifnos and wanted to stay there was someone special, a breed apart, and that we shared a bond and were destined to be friends. No longer.

As it happened, a year or so later a very nice Athenian architect and his wife bought Aphrodite's house, and they came only for Easter and August, when I was never there.

—

Well, that's not quite true. Sometimes I was there for Easter, once about two years later, in fact. But it wasn't a very happy visit. I was there alone and was having lunch by myself at the taverna by the beach when a large group of Greeks and Greek-Americans I knew, some of them well, all of whom had houses on the island, came in together for Easter lunch. They all said hello, but I was struck? amazed? and hurt, actually, by the fact that they didn't ask me to join them, but left me eating alone two tables away. It wasn't that I felt they didn't like me, exactly, but it seemed evident that I clearly was not one of them, part of their world. Wow, I thought. I guess somebody is telling me something.

And a pang went through me. How I missed Claire and Christian.

—

The morning of September 11, 2001, I was in Tim's apartment in New York reading the *New York Times* weather forecast, worrying about a possible rainstorm on the thirteenth, the day of my—till then—most important one-man New York show at the Salander O'Reilly Gallery, then on Seventy-ninth Street.

Then the first plane hit the North Tower of the World Trade Center.

We heard it on the radio. No one knew what had happened, some plane had hit the tower, a freak accident, it said. We turned on the television just in time to watch, openmouthed, the second plane, a huge passenger jet, not some little lost private plane, come screaming in behind the already burning North Tower and crash into the South Tower. Not an accident at all. Neither of them.

For two days, time stood still. No one really knew what had happened or what might happen next. Then slowly the city picked itself up and went back to at least some form of living. Broadway theaters and restaurants reopened, and my gallery decided to go ahead with my opening. It was, to say the least, a memorable opening, but not a very auspicious one. Quite a few people came, desperate by then to leave their apartments and the horrors and tragedies they had been watching all day every day on television, above all the endlessly repeated image of the towers crashing down. Most everyone was still in shock, some in tears. Nobody felt that life would ever be the same. And in truth, with the passage of time, more and more time, it actually seems that it never has been the same, and never will be.

—

"I need someone or something to hug," I said to Tim. "A beautiful twenty-five-year-old boy or a puppy. Take your pick." Making it sort of a joke. That's how I tell it, anyway, that after 9/11, I needed something to hug. And I did. It wasn't just about that day, of course. I suspect I had been feeling somewhat jaded and detached about my relationship with Tim for some time. We had been together a long, long time by then and had had a variety of ups and downs, and Tim probably wouldn't have minded a twenty-five-year-old himself. But he decided on getting us a puppy and soon found a breeder with a litter of Scottish terriers, our breed of choice. We bought one, and to my surprise, I fell totally, goofily in love with this little dog we named Nairobi.

I went to Sifnos alone the following spring. It was a relatively easy, uneventful trip, no problems with planes or boats, nothing. Apostolos picked me up with his taxi. Froggy was long gone, but he still had his taxi and his bus line. Driving up to Exambela, we talked about this and that and finally about 9/11. I casually mentioned that I had gotten a dog, jokingly saying that after that horrible day, I had decided I needed a dog.

"Christo, you don't need a dog, you need a wife," he said, shifting gears as we climbed up the winding road.

I sat smiling, or rather with a smile still on my face, fixed there. It was such a silly little remark. But it was like a slap. Not a hard one, but hard enough to bring someone to his senses. Me. Suddenly everything out the car window looked different, the familiar road, the fields, all looked different, strange, unfamiliar, foreign. And in a flash I realized that I had no place here, that I was living in someone else's world. And I wasn't sure I wanted to do it anymore.

Apostolos had been my friend for many years. I and my parents had shared Easter meals with him and his wife. I had watched his children grow up, and I felt very close to them all. These were the sweet friends who surprised me in Athens, having come all the way by boat from Sifnos, all dressed up in their best clothes and beaming shyly as they arrived for my opening at the Kreonides Gallery. And I was full of love for them, and they, in their way, I knew, for me. But I realized that in Apostolos's world, my family of Tim, my partner of twenty-five years, and my funny little dog did not exist. It wasn't so much that it was pathetic or immoral or disgusting but that for him, it just had no meaning. It wasn't real or even possible. It didn't exist.

And I didn't really exist. That was the astonishing revelation for me: that for him, for them, I, the real me, didn't exist. And that to some extent it was my own doing. Apostolos was speaking to Christo; and Christo, I realized for the first time, was a kind of fictional character that I and these people had invented. When I was young there, on Sifnos, at least part of me yearned to be part of their culture, their world. I loved and envied their clarity and simplicity, their certitude. Like most gay people, or people who are in the process of discovering that they are gay, I had a strange kind of early, preflight nostalgia for the straight world that I was on the verge of leaving. To me, messily—and I mean messily—muddling around in my overheated and confused sexuality, the straight world seemed so clear and . . . straight.

Together we had created Christo, pieced him together, and so as not to rock the boat of island life or get into confrontations there, I had played along and become this suddenly, to me, strange figure. He was me, of course, but a cleaned-up version, the islanders' *kalo pedi*, their good child, the boy who kept coming back. And I had loved them calling me that, loved being Christo, this simpler, calmer, less driven and sexually harried person. And when I was on the island, I moved into him, inhabited him, just like my little house. And it came to me that they all knew Christo, but not me, not really.

I knew that I was not the good boy, and never had been. And now I was a fifty-two-year-old man who, here on Sifnos, was still living out a version of himself tailored years before—even if only by the sin of omission—to fit, or at least not offend, a culture that could not or would not accept that the real me existed. My Lord, I thought, my parents have known I was homosexual since I was a boy. Everyone, everywhere knows. Except here. Or if they knew, they certainly were not about to deal with it. I mean, I thought, it isn't as though I had actually been lying. After all, I hadn't been on the island with a woman since Joanna, twenty-five years before, and Tim had been coming there for all those years in between. But it clearly wasn't getting through.

I realized that I had no idea of how the islanders saw me. Years before, in fact, Stephanos, my contractor whom I loved and who I knew loved me, stopped me in the street one night near his house. I don't know what provoked it, whether it was simple friendship, dismay at the presence of Tim every year on the island, or indeed that he, remarkably handsome man that he was, had had some kind of past of his own, some relationship with someone. I had certainly never understood either of his marriages, his first to a very glum woman, or, when she died, his second wife, though she actually took very good care of him. But that evening he begged me, pleaded with me to marry, said that I absolutely had to get married, that it was the only way to live.

I suppose I jollied him along about it. And may have been jollying everybody along for years. I had finally stopped going to weddings on the island because as a "bachelor," I was the target of so many toasts and jokes. "To your own wedding," they would say, smiling. "When are you getting married?" *"Tou chronou?"* "Next year, maybe?" For years now, I had smiled, laughed with them, hahaha, but never quite cleared the air on this issue. But how could I? How could I make them see that I was never getting married the way they meant? How could I make them understand that I had been married for years, but to a man? It wasn't a confrontation I had ever wanted there. But now I realized I had been painting myself into a corner; my island maxim of no confrontations had somehow turned on me, locked me into a role I couldn't escape.

Now I was stuck in Christo, a persona I couldn't grow into or grow out of. I realized that it wasn't anything the islanders had done to me. Apostolos wasn't trying to insult or hurt me; like the rest of them, he was just being himself, and was concerned about me. It was Christo who was the problem—Christo, who had somehow gotten away from me, literally become someone else. And I understood that I was tired of trying to be him, that maybe I had been tired of it for some time. And that I was coming to an end of it.

It also occurred to me that it had something to do with the house, with owning a house there. When you own a house, it is impossible to just pass through, the way one can in a hotel or a rental. Buying a house is a kind of marriage, after all. When you have a house, all those phrases like settling down, putting down roots start flying around. And you lose what Tim always calls your "amateur standing," your ability to shed a skin and move on. In buying my house, the house I loved, I had somehow bought into the village, that world; I had given up my freedom to be myself. As in a marriage, in buying the house, I was allowing myself to be clothed in other people's assumptions about me, or what I imagined their assumptions to be. The house was not the root cause, but it created a powerful stage, a powerful setting for me and my little play about Christo and his life in Greece.

All of this swam in my head as Apostolos dropped me off that afternoon and I lugged my bags through the sleeping village, only a cat scooting long and low out of my way or an old farm dog half woken from his sleep in the afternoon heat, wagging his tail as I passed. Here and there I heard a quiet voice talking, the scrape of a chair, or a bit of music from a radio. I got to my house, and Chrysoula was there waiting for me. Exhausted, I begged her to come back the next day for her money. She showed me the food she had put in the fridge and left. And as I settled into my house, my wonderful house, the whole experience with Apostolos began to slip away.

I was home, surrounded by the familiar late-afternoon smells and sounds of my village. And Apostolos and my little one-sided confrontation, for I had said nothing to him, seemed not so very important anymore. But I knew. It took me a while to get my head around it, around what Apostolos had told me about myself, my house, and my life there on Sifnos, and it took another couple of years to put the house on the market, but I knew. That afternoon, I knew it was over. I suppose I really knew anyway and had known for some time. But like a romance, a love affair that is over, it takes time for the penny to drop, it takes time for it to actually end.

For the moment, I put it aside. I would think about it tomorrow, some other day. I called Tim to tell him I had arrived safely, and I asked about the dog, but I told him nothing about my conversation with Apostolos. I lay down for a while in my wonderful upstairs room, the blinds down against the sun and heat, the long white cloth—hung across the French doors to keep the flies out—moving gently in the nearly still afternoon air. Then I got up, had a shower and a dressing drink, and went to have dinner with my friend Natasha.

5

A great friend of Tim's and mine died recently at the age of ninety-seven. A marvelous, larger-than-life character, she had been married five times. I will always remember when I turned fifty and, half joking, half serious, was complaining at dinner about how my life was over, how it was all downhill from there. The friend, then almost ninety and a widow for eight or ten years, piped up from down the table. "Darling," she said, "when I turned fifty, all I had to show for my life was a difficult daughter and two failed marriages. I had lost my looks, I was sure, and my youth. It was all over. Little did I know"—she smiled—"I would be married three more times."

We all have so many lives, or the potential for so many lives. So many beginnings, so many endings. So many possibilities coming at us during our lives, should we choose to be aware of them. And most of them, these routes and unexpected destinations, like the best paintings, no doubt, are the ones that surprise us.

I had never imagined owning a house in Greece, and of course, once I had it, I never imagined letting it go.

—

The house was sold in 2007, the same year as Tim's and my civil union. Because yes, we finally had a civil union. It took thirty years,

Christo's house

and I suspect it would have taken thirty years even if it had been legal way back then at the beginning.

Our civil union not only tied us closer together but tied me closer to my life in America. In reality, my home, my life had been in America for some time now. I still loved Sifnos, I suppose, but now more the way one goes on loving a person one is no longer really in love with. The French, naturally, have a largely untranslatable way of saying of a lover *je l'aime bien*, the way you love a dog being what they really mean. I loved it, still, my island, but some connection was gone, had fallen away like a piece of a spaceship dropping away during liftoff. I kept on going there, but to my surprise, I realized more and more that *spiti apo Christo* no longer meant so much to me. And I didn't quite know why I was going there anymore.

It might have been different if I had still been painting there. I am always fine if I am painting, working. Painting keeps me honest, keeps me sane, keeps me myself. But when I am not working, I get so I do not know quite who I am or what I am doing or why. If I had been painting, it is even possible that I would not have noticed all the things that were changing on the island or cared so much about them. If I had been painting, they wouldn't have reached me, gotten to me. If I had been painting, it is possible that my little confrontation with Apostolos would have just been water off a duck's back. But as I was not working, it began to seem that the only reason I was going all that way for two weeks at a time—I almost never stayed longer now—was to check on the house and pay bills.

I would make this endless trip from New York and call Tim again and again there at home with the dog (damn him). I would have repairs done and pay bills and go out for dinner and drink too much. I was on a holiday I didn't want or really need, and I would just read and take endless naps, or sit around worrying about whether Mad Aphrodite was poisoning my jasmine or about who was going to buy the house next door. As I said to Tim, talking to him in Connecticut, "All I do anymore is fluff pillows. And I have a lot of pillows."

There was something else as well, though, something more disturbing to me. I couldn't quite put my finger on it, but I knew somehow that not working, I was at risk. I knew that if I was not painting, not having some direction or focus, something was going to happen, that someday something was going to happen that would really screw everything up. I wasn't quite sure what I meant by that, but I knew how it would happen. I was always horny. Even when I am painting, I am horny. But not painting, I am apt to be horny and careless, and I knew someday I would get into trouble.

I was very aware, for example, of all these handsome Albanians on the island, and one night when I was at Lakis's having a drink before heading home, there was this man, this beautiful young man, dark-haired, dark-eyed, and sexy, hanging around outside, across the square there under the pines. I was older now, of course, but I was still tall and blond, and I knew he had noticed me, and I certainly noticed him. And I knew he was cruising me, hustling me. I remember suspecting at that moment that my life as I had known it on Sifnos might well be over. That someday or other I would succumb. I knew it. I would do something that was at least . . . careless. I knew that like Tennessee Williams's Mrs. Stone in her Roman Spring, I would throw down my keys. Not purposefully to be destroyed or killed, like her, but just because it was there, it was happening, because he was incredibly sexy, and why not. And I knew if that happened, everything would tip right over.

So in the end, it was easy. Surprisingly easy. One day it was just over. It wasn't any particular one of these things, my quibbles or quarrels; it wasn't as if I had a "beef," really. One day I realized a period of my life had come to an end. And I decided to put the house on the market. I just woke up one morning and went down and listed the house.

Back then, in 2005, there was no actual real estate office on the island. Sofia's son Francesco was still probably the most in the know, and Thesaurus, the big tourist office, often seemed to know of houses for sale or rent. But then, almost from one day to the next, there appeared a sign that went up just outside of Apollonia on the Kamares road: ISLAND REAL ESTATE, it said. It was run by one Spiridulla, a woman from Athens who had married a Sifniot and gone into business. An omen, I thought. Serendipity, I thought, the office opening like that, at that moment.

I should have known better.

An overweight chain-smoker, she was an unlovely creature. I had known about her for some time, and even before she opened her office, I knew she had a bad reputation. Young Nikos that day with Louella and Bruce had said she was unreliable. And nobody much liked her. She lived right next door to Natasha there above Chrissopighi, and they hated each other. She had apparently had two strokes or heart attacks, and as Natasha, a hugely nice person, said of her with palpable distaste, "*Elle a eu deux crises cardiaques. On attend la prochaine.*" But as I said, I wasn't planning to have dinner with her, and I assumed she would be the sharpest, hungriest agent I would find on the island. So I went in and spoke to her, she assured me that my "charming" house would sell within three months, and I signed a contract with her.

And I stuck with her and all her nonsense for the next two years. I suppose I thought I had no choice. How else would I list the house? I wondered. Who would keep the keys and show it, who had the contacts to handle all the bureaucratic and legal problems that might arise? But unhappily, she failed on all counts. From day one, to my amazement, there seemed to be no interest; there were no bites, no nibbles, nothing. No wonder, since, as far as I knew, she almost never showed the house. She hated climbing the paths and steps in Exambela and liked to show potential clients her own houses, part of a development in Vathi.

When Anthony, the man who ultimately bought the house, went to her, he told me she never even mentioned my house. And when a possible client appeared, a young Greek I knew who lived in London, she was impossible, he said, insisting that he sign a whole series of documents before she would show him any house, and he fled. Worse, or better in the end, the following winter her e-mail address was disconnected and the website with all the information about my house, such as it was, disappeared.

Tim was pushing for me to get rid of her. "Shades of Leila," he would say to me, referring to a dealer of mine who was constantly moving her offices—in her case, one step ahead of the law—and whom I had stood by and believed for far too long. When I arrived on Sifnos that year, Spiridulla's office was also gone, although when I saw her in the village, she assured me that she had been showing my house and almost had a client. She didn't need the office, she said, she was working via the Internet only now and was creating a new website for the house at that very moment. By now, almost two years on, I believed none of it. Island gossip had it that she was having legal troubles, had maybe even lost her real estate license, and I wanted as little to do with her as possible.

I went on the Internet myself, found a real estate website, listed the house, and was immediately flooded with responses. One of them from the same Anthony, the Englishman who had been to Sifnos that time before and had gone to Spiridulla. Amazingly, he made an offer immediately, sight unseen, and then, on another trip to Sifnos, when he was shown the house by my niece Francesca, who was staying there, he made yet another offer, which I accepted.

It was wonderful! After almost two years! But suddenly I was thrown back into the tobacco-y—I was sure carcinogenic—embrace of the impossible Spiridulla. Having dealt with her before, Anthony wanted nothing to do with her, but by then I was back in New York and she had all the legal documents about the house. At the time I signed with her, I had given her everything—deeds, architects' drawings, the original surveyors' papers, and the estimates I had had done for tax purposes, all the paperwork for the house, ninety-five percent of it in Greek. I had asked her then that it all be checked over by lawyers, which she promised me she would do, and later assured me that she had done.

Then one day, just when Anthony and I were about to close and

I was visiting my brother in Tuscany, I got a faint, broken-up phone message from Spiridulla's cell phone: there was a problem, she said, coughing richly, a big problem with my courtyard. I didn't own it, she said, coughing some more. What? Didn't own it? My God, my courtyard, what was my house without my courtyard? My lemon tree, the only stairs to my bedroom, even the bathroom. In a total panic I called her back, but I still couldn't understand what the problem was, what it meant, and how it could have happened. What was I to do?

Finally I worked out that the woman wasn't talking about my courtyard in back with the lemon tree, but about the sliver of walled space along the path outside the kitchen door, a piece of terrace there that ran like an elongated, glorified front step the length of the house. I certainly didn't want to lose it, but still, it was a huge relief. It was a tiny strip of terrace, and worst-case scenario, we could at least get some kind of variance, some kind of permission.

When I got to Athens and saw my lawyer, I learned that in the nineties, when all Sifnos deeds had been transferred to a computer system, my deed was incorrectly recorded through some kind of oversight and part of my property was left out, treated as part of the path. It became perfectly clear that Spiridulla had never had my papers checked properly. Of course she was not responsible for the original problem, which had been my fault because I never had the new property papers checked either, but according to my lawyer, if she had done it when I asked her, we might still have been within the grace period during which you could challenge the new documentation. Now, thanks to her, here I was in the middle of the sale, with a buyer waiting to close the deal, and part of the property was in dispute—a seller's nightmare.

Mercifully, Anthony didn't seem to mind and was ready to go through with the purchase anyway. He said it wasn't a life-threatening problem, and we would work it out eventually. A dream buyer, Anthony was never anything but a delight to deal with. And although, as it turned out, there would be endless delays over this and large legal fees, Anthony and I had already gone through with the closing.

During all this I had not heard a word from Spiridulla. Indeed, after her phone call I never heard from her again. She had handed back all the documents long before and, it seemed, largely vanished, and I hoped to never speak to her again. And when I came to Sifnos in the fall of 2008 to meet Anthony and go over some final details about some pictures and furniture—he wanted to buy the house with everything in it, and we were dealing with all that—the last person on my mind was that disagreeable woman.

But one morning, there she was in the post office, and she accosted me about the house. Fool me, I told her the house had been sold the year before, and she announced that she wanted her percentage. I told her that she deserved nothing, that she had had nothing to do with the sale of the house, and that her carelessness had cost both Anthony and me much more than her fee. And I stalked out of the post office. Running after me, she hurled her body at me and—wheezing, screaming, and yelling—began kicking me. An infelicitous sight, to put it mildly, her hair wild and loose, her chubby legs flailing at me. And it hurt besides. I looked around for an escape route, saw a bus about to leave for somewhere, I didn't know or care where, and jumped on board.

All in all, too much to go on about, but an unhappy footnote to my Sifnos life. In the end I offered her a flat fee, a generous gesture, I thought, as she hadn't sold the house. She never claimed the fee, either from me or from my lawyer, but while I hated the experience and was mortally embarrassed by the image of me being kicked to death by this woman, there on the square, it's too good not to record it. A nightmare at the time, it makes me smile now.

—

It was so strange. By the end, I had so little feeling about selling the house. No second thoughts, no regrets, no lingering sadness. It seemed at times almost a relief. And I didn't get the feeling that my beloved Sifniots cared much either. I knew Mad Aphrodite would not miss me. But then maybe she would, I thought. She would have no one to obsess about, alone there in her shuttered house.

But I was startled when, on almost my last day on the island, I passed by the little shop in Exambela, stopping to buy some last item or other, and told the shopkeeper, whom I had known for thirty years, that the house had been sold and I was leaving. She looked up, handed me my change, and said, "Bye-bye, Christo." And that was that.

Perhaps she knew, maybe all Sifniots knew, that at some point *xenoi* leave the island.

—

I am finally leaving, taking the night boat from Kamares, and it is late, of course, the boat and the hour. I am taking the night boat because, although Anthony wanted to keep almost everything in the house, furniture and paintings, books and even CDs, I still have a few things I want to take and have come back to the island to get them, a couple of pictures I can't part with, among them a nighttime oil of Kastro and the walking stick carved by my father, and I can't take it all on the high-speed boat.

Anthony and his children stayed there this last summer, and they love the house. They call it, rather touchingly I think, the Painter's House.

Last night I gave a little cocktail party on my terrace, then we went for dinner in Kastro. Afterward, Paul, a friend I met through Natasha a week ago, suggested that I not spend my last night in the house all by myself, but come to him, and I accepted. He wasn't asking me to stay in the guest room; he doesn't have one. A stylish gesture, I suppose, on his part, perhaps not so stylish on mine, but it was actually a good idea. I had not been looking forward to returning to the house alone. I was afraid, with some reason, that I would get all weepy and maudlin, especially as I had had a lot to drink at dinner.

I slept late and then went for one last lunch at Chrissopighi. I don't think of it as a last lunch. As I say to everyone I see, I am not selling Sifnos, just the house. I am sure I will come again. I will be back, I say. I am just not sure when.

After dinner, waiting for the boat, I wander around Kamares. For all that has happened in the last thirty-five years, Kamares is still a tiny harbor and, though different, is also much the same. At least it seems comfortingly that way tonight. The crowd waiting endlessly, as always, for the boat is clustered together on the mole, leaning against the sloping wall there or sitting, half asleep, on their luggage, which is scattered everywhere. The harbor police in their sharp white uniforms and caps self-importantly "keep order." Where there was one old Volga taxi, there are now several Mercedes, and where there was one old lady offering rooms to let, there are now several people standing about waiting for the boat and the arrival of new tourists. Not that there will be many tonight; it is early October and the brief high season is long over. I see the Exambela exhibitionist there, older now, but still wandering around goonily. And there is Andonis the once handsome Kamares hunk, the island Lothario, waiting to pick up yet another blond German or British tourist and show her all over the island on his motorcycle. And there is Apostolos, who gives me a big wave, standing by his bus.

I wave back at him, reminded that ironically, he is the only person who has told me how sorry he is that I have sold the house. I had run into him in Apollonia a couple of days before, and he seemed genuinely upset that I was leaving. Well, that I was selling—people were always leaving, and for the islanders, selling a house was different. I told him I wasn't leaving forever, that I would be back. But for him, selling the house was cutting a cord, somehow final, and even if I were to come back, it would never be the same. And how could it be.

Bored waiting, I stroll back along the main street, still the only street, with its tavernas, mostly closed for the night, faint music playing from one of the bars, even though there are only a couple of people left there, a very sleepy mini–St.-Tropez indeed. On my left, the harbor is filled with boats, not so many fishing boats, almost none really, one brightly lit cruise ship, an unusual sight and far too big for the harbor, its lights spilling across the water, yachts and sailboats all over the place around it, but all neatly facing the same way, as moored boats do. I go on past the end of town to the beach, empty now, as people are seriously discouraged by the police from sleeping there these days.

And I remember Chuck and me, the Rhodesian newlyweds, and the two long-legged Australian beauties on the beach. And all at once I decide to go for a swim. I slip out of my clothes and walk naked into the glittering water. The water is dead still and amazingly clear, even here in the harbor. I swim a bit, and sure enough, I am suddenly surrounded by phosphorescence, every move I make creating millions of little flashes of light. And suddenly I am there with Chuck, the two of us waving our arms around in the water, creating these sweeps and avalanches of light around us. Both of us shouting "Wow, wow" in the silent, sleepy harbor. And then,

Poulati

suddenly I remember now, Chuck laughing and saying "Look! Look!" and he is peeing under the water, creating this amazing volcanic explosion of light. And just as young, certainly just as juvenile, I join him, the two of us hooting and laughing.

"Wow! Wow! Wow!"

I roll onto my back, where I can no longer see the ships and their lights or hear the disco music from the bars, and float there with my head back in the water. Looking up now, I can see the stars, lost before in the glow of the harbor lights. And I can see, rising up on either side of me, the huge black mountains against the sky, embracing the little harbor. And me, I think.

"Wow! Wow! Wow!" Two boys peeing in the sea. How young we were.

All those years. Who could have imagined?

ACKNOWLEDGMENTS

Without my coauthor and partner, Tim Lovejoy, this book would not exist. I cannot thank him enough for a creative collaboration that increased my insight and maintained my voice.

Thank you, Elisabeth Sifton, for supporting this book from its earliest stages and for being our great editor. Thanks too to Alexander Star, Christopher Richards, Mareike Grover, Rodrigo Corral, Jonathan D. Lippincott, Gregory Wazowicz, Jeff Seroy, and the rest of the staff at FSG for seeing this book into the world.

I am grateful to my photographer friends Michel Zumbrunn, who provided the image of me painting in my studio in Sifnos that appears on the frontispiece and back jacket, as well as "Georgos, my neighbor" on page 80 and "Christo's house" on page 142; E. V. Weissman, who provided "My kitchen" on page 220, "Christo's house" on page 274, and "Poulati" on page 283; and Jacques Burkhardt for his portrait on the book's back flap.

Michael Selleck, André Bishop, Chuck Sims, Martha Hallett, Rosemarie Mahoney, Georgios Troullos, Carola Lott, Leon Byan, and my agent, Gillon Aitken, deserve thanks for reading and believing in *The Greek House*.

Most of all, our infinite gratitude goes to Jonathan Galassi for all his encouragement, guidance, trust, and enthusiasm. Thank you.